The Guaymas Chronicles

THE GUAYMAS CHRONICLES

La Mandadera

DAVID E. STUART

University of New Mexico Press
Albuquerque

Library of Congress
Cataloging-in-Publication Data

Stuart, David E.
The Guaymas chronicles : la mandadera /
David E. Stuart.— 1st ed.
p. cm.
ISBN 0-8263-3188-2 (Cloth : alk. paper)
1. Guaymas (Sonora, Mexico)
—Description and travel.
2. Poor—Mexico—Guaymas (Sonora)
—Social conditions.
3. Guaymas (Sonora, Mexico)
—Social conditions.
4. Stuart, David E.—Journeys
—Mexico—Guaymas (Sonora)
I. Title.
F1391.G985 S88 2003
972'.17—dc21
2003002334

Printed by Sheridan Books, Inc.
Set in Janson 11/14.5
Design and composition by Robyn Mundy
Maps by Carol Cooperrider
Author photograph on p. 394 by
Cynthia Stuart
All photographs courtesy of the author
unless otherwise identified

1 2 3 4 5 6 7 8 9

JOHN DENSMORE STUART January 9, 1945–January 3, 2002

This book is dedicated to the memory
of my beloved twin brother, who was
killed a few days before our fifty-
seventh birthday. He so loved my
stories of Mexico. I miss him terribly.

contents

maps & illustrations

VIII

acknowledgments

First let me thank Gail Wimberly of Tularosa, New Mexico, who, in 1984, transcribed my lengthy taped narrative of this period in Guaymas. Second, my deep appreciation goes to Danita Gomez, who typed four drafts of the current manuscript.

I am also grateful to Eric Ehrmann, author, for his review and comments on my narrative—a style of writing I have not heretofore attempted. Kijrstin Bauer, a charming friend, herself a writer, also read my drafts and made many suggestions on just how to tell Lupita's story, as did Marilyn D'Ottavio, Ann Hendry, and Kathy Linn (Albuquerque) and editor Jane Kepp (Santa Fe). Luther Wilson, Director of the University of New Mexico Press and publisher of several of my other works, also read drafts and provided support, as did his predecessor, Elizabeth Hadas. Designer Robyn Mundy and mapmaker Carol Cooperrider made the book both appealing and far more intelligible. Copyeditor David Margolin

ix

provided rich, knowledgeable textual advice and corrected many errors. Thanks, David!

Thanks also to my wife, Cynthia, who listened to scores of draft passages and made suggestions. She met many of the people who appear in this book and had her own take on how best to tell portions of their story. Marta Aurora Monteverde of Guaymas, eldest daughter of Mercedes (chapter 1), provided hard-to-obtain maps (obtained from Sr. Mauro Estéban Barrón Robles), as well as advice. *¡Gracias, mija!*

I also owe a very direct debt of gratitude to Tony Hillerman. In the eighties, though already a professor, I took an under-graduate writing class from him at UNM and actually worked up the courage to submit, as assignments, the first snippets of what eventually became this book. He not only tolerated these snippets, but also encouraged me one day to "write the book." I will never write with the clean, spare description and easy grace that are hallmarks of the Hillerman style, but you now hold the fruits of that encouragement in your own hands.

More thanks go to the folks at the Flying Star (formerly Double Rainbow) coffee shop on Route 66 (Central Avenue) near the University of New Mexico campus. I wrote about 80 percent of this volume while sitting in the front window every evening and most weekend afternoons for nearly a year. The "kids" there treat me well—BJ, Katie, Jesse, Cedar, Lizz, Sarah, Karin, John, Jouelle, Juliann, Nancy, Heather, Elena, Truett, Kindra, Kenny, Kerry, Kevin, Diane, Andrea, Edel, Mazen, Khalil, and all the rest.

To the people of Guaymas who shared their lives with me, I extend my sincerest gratitude. They remain the finest group of people I have ever met. I am also indebted to Dr. Jorge Cueto and his lovely wife, who took care of me in Mexico City when I first arrived from Ecuador.

Finally profound thanks to my mom, Avis Stuart, who first taught me the meaning of love as a child, then fought, and sacrificed, for my chance to start a new life in Mexico during the mid-1960s. That new life eventually led me north from Mexico City to Guaymas, its shrimp fleet, its people, and little Lupita—who never failed to amaze me.

xi

author's note

 This volume is a memoir of life in the port of Guaymas, Mexico, during the late 1960s and early 1970s. Based largely on hand-written journals and tapes made at the time, in 1984 I used the originals and memory (with all its flaws) to create a full, taped narrative. This was transcribed into a huge typescript of seven hundred thousand words by Gail Wimberly, of Tularosa, New Mexico. Subsequently the original journals and tapes disappeared from the garage of our little house in Albuquerque while the place was rented. But Gail's transcription survived.

This volume is nonfiction, but I have "novelized" the story in significant ways. To protect identities, some names have been altered and others omitted, while some dates, events, places, and people are described in a way that will make it very hard for anyone to pry into the details of individual lives. I make no apology for these changes—there are no villains in this book, save one, an unknown "sailor," who appears in chapter 14.

I have translated "quotes" from Spanish into my idea of equivalent English. I was never fluent and have lost much of my former facility with Spanish, so relied heavily on my earlier translations. My original journal notes were often more cryptic than the "finished" quotes I have fleshed out here. Every conversation in the book was originally in Spanish, unless I have said "in English" in the text, or was talking directly to an American, such as "Mr. Smith." The language of this text (both mine and others') reflects both the late 1960s and early 1970s and Mexico at that time; a world not yet "politically correct" and, alas, a world now gone.

Finally I was not "on-the-clock" as an anthropologist when I wrote the original journals. I was a twenty-five-year-old guy who went home to see his girlfriend and whose life became unexpectedly entwined with a number of warm, interesting people. Sometimes you just get lucky.

David E. Stuart
Flying Star Coffee House
Central Avenue / Route 66
Albuquerque, May 6, 2002

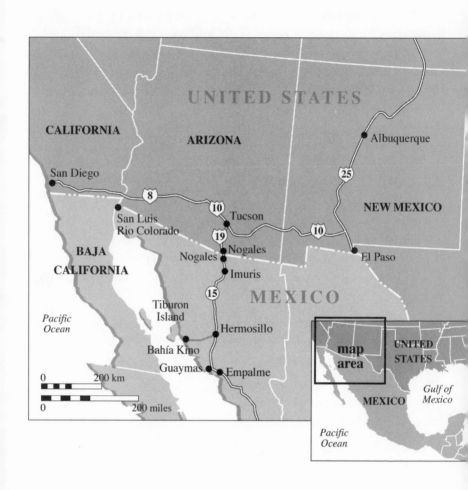

one

RETURN TO SONORA

It was a Wednesday in May. I had been riding along the rim of the Rircay River gorge in southern Ecuador, enjoying a spectacular view of the lower Andes. For months dense, gray clouds had risen daily from the coast to smother the entire landscape in a dark, bone-chilling fog. Finally the sky had cleared. I could see for miles. As I leaned forward in the saddle, the snow-capped peak of Chimborazo glinted in the sun, more than a hundred miles to the north.

Nearly a thousand feet below, the river roared through its narrow canyon and I smelled sun-warmed eucalyptus for the first time. That morning I had even managed to buy two eggs from a farmhouse to top my plate of rice. It was the first good day I'd had in Ecuador. It didn't last long.

As I reined in the mare to reach for a smoke, I heard a hollow "whunk." It sounded as if someone had thumped a watermelon. The mare jumped straight up, then rolled. Everything went into slow motion. I tried to catch the falling pack of smokes, but they spiraled slowly, slowly into the gorge as the horse rolled over me and disappeared. I never heard a sound nor felt a thing.

Now they were telling me it was Thursday and I was in a clinic in Cuenca. And everything hurt. Shit! I still couldn't find my smokes. What were they doing to me anyway?

The young doctor pulled hard on my arms and drove his knee deep into my back. He needed the leverage. I retched and broke into a cold sweat. It was unavoidable. To get my shoulders back into their sockets, he first had to stretch the supporting muscles, now horribly constricted. It had taken more than a day to reach the clinic. No anesthesia. Typical Ecuador.

As he pulled harder, the pain intensified. Nearby another patient screamed convulsively. That is when I panicked. Jesus! Why didn't anyone go to stop the screaming? My pulse raced, I fainted, and it got quiet.

Later someone lifted my chin, a cold towel pressing my forehead. Aah! The pain had eased and it was still quiet. I felt better. "¿*Hecho?* Done?" I asked, bathed in sweat. "I am sorry, señor. The procedure will take time. Try to think about something else. Something nice!" Then he pulled even harder.

I focused on Mexico—trying to picture the beach and palm trees, now four thousand air miles away. He increased the pressure. Oddly the pain was making me sleepy. The bastard down the hall had started screaming again, but I ignored him this time and drifted off into a delirious dreamland . . .

For a moment I saw my fiancée, Iliana, standing under a palm by the little seaside restaurant where she waitressed. She smiled. I reached out to touch her, but she was gone . . . replaced by several friends at my favorite hotel bar in Guaymas. Someone reached over and poured from a bottle. Overjoyed, I lifted my glass.

At last, an ice-cold beer! It tasted fabulous. Bohemia— my favorite—and Mexico's best. They sure didn't have anything like it in Ecuador. As I sat on my customary stool and surveyed the bar, I was surprised that absolutely nothing had changed. A palm tree swayed gently in the courtyard.

My friend, Negro Jacinto, was playing dice with several of the regulars, while the bartender watched. Marta, a drop-dead knockout wearing a short black skirt and gray-striped blouse, was walking toward the door. Jesus! She had simply amazing legs and wore a mouth-watering scent loaded with vanilla. I watched her calf-muscles ripple as she walked.

I was still savoring the vanilla and enjoying her legs when the doctor shook me awake. "¿*Listo* (ready) *señor?*" It took me a minute to realize I was still at the clinic in Ecuador.

Disappointed, I nodded "yes." An orderly steadied me. The doctor grunted and, with a tremendous pull, jerked my shoulders up, then back into place. The pain was unbelievable. Exhausted, my head fell forward, forcing me to watch the protruding collarbone slowly disappear into place under my left jaw with a sickening pop. It was quiet for a while.

In the distance someone complimented me, "*el meester,*" for not screaming again. Apparently I had been the shrieking bastard down the hall. I would have been embarrassed, but fainted instead.

Another cool towel awoke me. They were already well along at building the cast. Thank God! The distinct smell of hot plaster and wet gauze reminded me momentarily of the hospital emergency room where I had once worked the night shift. I remembered nothing else until I awakened in bed, three other patients watching me intently, and silently, from their cots.

It was mealtime. A young nurse shoved several pillows under my head, pulled up a chair and started spooning hot chicken soup into my mouth. I reached for the spoon and realized the cast had immobilized my arms. The soup tasted wonderful. Over her shoulder I had a lovely view of Cuenca's oldest church.

4

After she left I took another look at the tiled dome of the church, then worked up the courage to survey the damage. I was a mess! There was no way I could continue my doctoral fieldwork on haciendas in rugged southern Ecuador trussed up like a Christmas goose. My research station was perched on the side of a mountain seventy miles from the nearest pavement, no running water, no electricity, no supermarket, no phones. Hell, there were so few facilities even the Peace Corps didn't operate there.

Several anthropologists—one American, the other local —came to visit later and questioned me about the accident. They had each gotten somewhat different stories from the provincial gossip mill. I wasn't much help. I told them that the last thing I could remember was that I had been riding a horse along the rim of the Rircay River gorge.

The Ecuadorian anthropologist didn't like that—it didn't match the story he'd gotten from one of the locals. Typical academic—never let a fact get in the way of your pet theory. Disgusted, I realized I had wasted months of hard work.

Another anthropologist I knew had once described Ecuador to me as "like living in a Russian novel, only worse." I now understood him fully. It had been both a physically and emotionally bruising experience for me. In the district where I worked, babies died regularly for lack of a dollar's worth of penicillin, and the big landowners treated "their" peasants like cattle. Like the livestock, they went with the land when it changed hands.

Graduate school simply doesn't prepare you for this stuff. To survive I had begun to detach emotionally from the worst of it. I also had a hard time accurately reading the ordinary "people signals" around me and had dubbed this and the detachment the "Ecuador Effect."

5

The "Ecuador Effect" was rather like being submerged in a swimming pool while someone shouted instructions at you from above—everything came through garbled, distant, and detached. No matter how hard you tried, you simply could not accurately decipher the messages. Ugh!

Now I needed a place to recuperate and reconnect to the world around me. Mexico was my logical destination. I had a return ticket to Mexico City, a lovely young fiancée in the state of Sonora, and longed to see the beach and palms I had conjured up while they rearranged my upper body. Mexico was bright, warm, happy. It was time to go. The sooner, the better.

No one had warned me that escaping a Russian novel was as complicated as living in one. It took time. More than two weeks had already passed before my bus from Mexico City approached Guaymas on a brilliant morning in mid-May. Proof of my deliverance first materialized through its side window in the form of beach, palms, and rolling surf only 250 yards from old Route 15.

Next we skirted the village of Empalme, where my fiancée and her family lived—but express buses didn't stop there. After crossing the bridge that spans the wide Mátape River estuary, old Route 15 climbs a steep, craggy hill overlooking Guaymas. The view was breathtaking.

Tucked neatly below immense sandstone bluffs that confine the town to the sea, jagged cactus-studded mountains jut up in every direction. A vivid blue morning sky dipped to the horizon far below, where it met the Sea of Cortés's darker blue-green waters, like turquoise set against malachite.

From this vantage point I could look right down into the old town, see the plaza and its white-washed cathedral, neat rows of prosperous merchants' houses, the stone warehouses where Guaymas's famous blue shrimp are packed, and the little cut-away, half-moon-shaped *embarcadero* where the great Guaymas shrimping fleet spent half the year at berth. After all of the cold, hunger, squalor, misery, suspicion of outsiders, and colorless leaden skies in Ecuador, I realized that I had never before seen anything more beautiful nor more hopeful.

Fifteen minutes later my taxi turned into the dusty, narrow lane in Empalme where my fiancée, Iliana, lived. Huge mango trees shaded the family house behind its white picket fence.

I asked the driver to tap the horn. The first one to run out of the house was her little sister, Lisa, then about nine. She was adorable. Looking back on it, I suppose I always loved her as much as, perhaps more than, Iliana. A sweet kid, she was skinny, gangly, had big brown eyes and displayed lots of warmth.

Lisa hugged me around the waist, babbling in Spanish that she had told folks in Empalme over and over that I would return for Iliana, just as I had promised. Even though nearly all the neighbors had warned her repeatedly that *gringos* never come back for their women, she had nurtured an unshakable faith that I would return. I had proved her right. She didn't even notice the cast at first. In those days Lisa was one of the few who called me "Davíd." I was simply known to most as Güero, "whitey."

Moments later Iliana came to the door. She was twenty, petite, about four feet eleven, with striking Indian features. Her dark olive complexion, big eyes enhanced by black eye-liner, long jet-black hair, and well-defined jaw line combined to give her a compact, regal quality.

When I first met her I had been instantly attracted to her serene, happy demeanor. I had been raised in a tense, competitive environment, so found her outlook completely intoxicating. Our early dates had been old-fashioned—formal courting, often escorted; slow dancing; and smoldering, unconsummated sexuality. One part of her was warm and accessible. The other was formal, veiled, mystical. The combination is very Mexican.

I stood at the door and smiled, hoping for a warm, responsive Iliana to fold me into her arms. It didn't happen. Perhaps the cast, lopsided left shoulder, and thirty-pound weight loss in Ecuador had shocked her. Perhaps my mere presence was a shock. She had expected me in the fall. As I looked at her I couldn't tell. The Ecuador Effect?

Iliana was too reserved to come hug me, squeeze me, scream, or make a scene in front of the ever-curious neighbors. Instead she merely touched my arm gently and motioned me inside. Several minutes later her little brother went out and retrieved my gear, placing it on the concrete porch hidden under the latticework "roof" that fronted the house.

I had yearned for more of a welcome from her, but Lisa was ecstatic. That took the edge off my disappointment. It was she who first commented on the cast and weight loss: "What *did* they do to you in South America, Davíd?" she cried, burying her face in my belly. I loved her even more for it, encircling her sobbing frame with my good arm. She felt good, warm like a puppy.

Iliana smiled at us, touched my arm again, lingering this time, and asked softly, "*¿Un café con leche, quieres?*" (do you want coffee and steamed milk?) It was a favorite, and I hadn't had one in six months. Grinning, I nodded, "yes." She motioned me to a chair, and I rested, eyes closed, while she prepared it. I had made it home.

I expected to stay only a few hours, then go to the Hotel Rubi, over in Guaymas—it was the Rubi's bar I had hallucinated about in the Ecuadorian clinic. Given Iliana's muted welcome, I had reconsidered and decided to leave right after coffee. But when she returned with the coffee, she invited me to stay. She said the women had talked it over and thought I should sleep on the front porch and let them "fatten me up." I was surprised. Delighted. Perhaps I had simply misread her at the door—the Ecuador Effect.

The house Iliana lived in was unusual in that it was made of whitewashed wood clapboard and would not have looked out of place in a small town in the Midwest. It had been built in the late 1930s to house railroad workers. But like many dwellings in Mexico, it was small and sheltered a typical extended family. Iliana, her little sister, mom, and little brother, Kique, formed one axis. Her childless aunt and uncle formed another.

Iliana's uncle was an engineer on the Pacífico Railroad and worked the long route from Empalme (railroad junction, in Spanish) to Guadalajara. Sometimes he would be gone for a week to ten days at a time. He was a quiet man, pudgy and pleasant. His wife was barren, gaunt, tense, and high-strung.

Iliana had once told me secretly that her uncle had another family, a wife and children, at the other end of the line in Guadalajara, even though her high-strung aunt was his legal wife. She considered this "natural," since her aunt could not bear children.

Considering that I knew of the uncle's second family, it was odd that I never knew many quite ordinary things. I never knew, for instance, exactly who held title to the house, though I presumed it to be her uncle. I never even knew her uncle's first name. I simply referred to him as señor D., and his wife, señora. The same with Iliana's mom; I never knew her given name.

Iliana also had both an older brother and sister, neither regularly at home. The older brother, Jesús, was a nice-looking guy, then in his mid-twenties, who came and went.

Iliana's older sister had a child. Drop-dead gorgeous, she had light skin, red hair, bore no family resemblance at all to Iliana, and worked at a boutique in downtown Guaymas. I had no clue where she actually lived. Iliana implied that "sis" was having an affair with a prominent businessman, who helped pay her expenses. I asked what her mom thought of that. Iliana didn't think that her mom knew. More secrets. In other words, it was a rather ordinary Mexican household.

The house itself was decaying in spots from dry rot. But it had warmth and charm to it. Through a front screened porch, one entered a long, narrow living room that ran straight through the house to the kitchen at the rear. At the rear of the living room a cast-concrete sink sat on a pedestal. There were no cupboards; pots and pans hung neatly from hooks on a long board nailed over the sink. The kitchen wandered into the dining area, which was a narrow, screened-in porch with a table, two benches, and a chair. A two-burner propane stove sat near the sink, but most cooking was done on a brick barbecue out back, under the dense mangos.

The living-room furniture was plain—two or three straight-backed chairs, several nice locally made rocking chairs painted white, and a high sideboard tucked under one of the living-room windows. An old-fashioned table radio sat on top.

At midday I'd sit in the front room, rock in the chair, and take in a serial radio show whose main character was called El Tuerto, "the one-eyed man." We'd listen to it almost every day. It always ended with the reminder that "in the land of the blind, the one-eyed man is king." It was reminiscent of the Green Hornet series on American radio.

On the opposite wall a Victorian glass-front china closet and a large wardrobe served as cabinets and closet. To the left were two small bedrooms. The front bedroom was the private domain of Iliana's uncle and aunt. The rear bedroom was occupied by Iliana, her mom, and her little sister. All three slept in one bed and shared another clothespress, or *ropero*.

Folded burlap cots, beds for Iliana's two brothers, were stored in one corner of the living room. One of these became mine for the next few days. There was also a baby crib near that corner. The women of the household cared for the older sister's baby daughter, but she came to visit her child several times a week.

When I arrived Iliana's uncle was in Guadalajara. Had I not been in such pathetic shape, they surely would not have invited me to stay and sleep on the front porch. It wasn't a common thing to suggest. But I accepted—a house with running water, electricity, and toilet was a huge step up from Ecuador. The mango and lime trees in the shady yard were gorgeous and fragrant. Besides I had only about $500 to last me until fall.

The women of the house were very solicitous. Iliana's mom, Iliana, or her little sister brought me café con leche each morning when I arose and my burlap cot was stowed in the corner of the living room.

Every day after morning coffee and sweet rolls, the household bustled with activity—mopping the concrete floors, dusting furniture, laundering, ironing, feeding the baby, and starting the beans for the early afternoon meal.

My dirty clothes were washed every two days, kept immaculate, mended as needed, and pressed. By stateside expectations it was a very modest home, but it was cleaned daily to a standard virtually unknown in suburban America.

My favorite time of the day was the *comida*, the main meal, around 2 P.M., when the family, including stray neighbor kids, would gather round the picnic table in the backyard underneath the mangos. The locally made plank table was covered with a checkered plastic cloth. Two ordinary benches and assorted boxy, handmade chairs were brought out to accommodate the family.

Except in winter most of the cooking was done right there under a tin-roofed *ramada*, or lean-to, next to the barbecue fueled by locally produced charcoal. Pots of beans were usually boiling by noon every day. An impressive, blackened griddle, originally the bottom of an oil drum, was used to cook the large, paper-thin Sonoran-style flour tortillas patted out by hand every day. The food was very simple but fabulous.

At comida, beans flavored with cilantro, onion, and garlic were served with tortillas, chopped onion, tomatoes, green chiles, and shrimp or bits of meat. Most of us fashioned these fixings into delicious hand-rolled burritos. The hot paper-thin flour tortillas made by Iliana's mom were second to none.

Occasionally she would take a large dollop of mashed, refried beans, punch a hole in the center with a spoon, then drop a fried egg into it. Served with fresh sliced tomatoes and a homemade tortilla to dip in the egg yolk, it was fit for a king.

Local fruits and vegetables were cheap and plentiful—oranges, mangos, papayas, young corn, tomatoes, green beans, cantaloupes, and melons. Vendors frequently worked Empalme's narrow lanes, offering fresh fruits and vegetables from both hand- and horse-drawn carts.

Little Lisa always called me when she heard them passing. I'd hand her a five- or ten-peso note and she'd take off, squealing, to chase down the vendor. She loved to smell the stem of each cantaloupe, pick the sweetest, then make the transaction.

Occasionally I set out with her to contribute more generously to the food supply. I'd buy meat, fish, or shrimp now and again, as "fair pay" for my board and the care given me. Once I bought several cartons of local mango ice cream and brought them home. That drew an enjoyable flood of neighborhood kids.

There was a small refrigerator in one corner of the living room that operated indifferently. It wasn't safe to keep meat there for any length of time, but the baby's formula and sodas were at least cool.

I slept on the screened front porch the first ten days in Empalme. At night I could smell the limes, hear the crickets, enjoy the soft breeze, and actually feel the trains passing nearby. I thought I was in Paradise. True, Iliana wasn't nearly as communicative as she had been at Christmas, but I chalked that up to shock over my condition and her recovery from a scorpion sting to her foot.

13

Still recuperating myself, I often stretched out on my cot in late evening, even as the others lingered on the porch to chat. I liked closing my eyes and listening to the soft vowel sounds of Spanish conversation—so much gentler and more relaxing than the hard-edged English I grew up with.

Much to Lisa's delight, she quickly discovered that I had a devilish problem getting my Red Wing boots off with one good arm and a cast that kept me from bending freely. She could not have been happier had it been Christmas. She became my official boot remover each evening. For ten centavos—the price of a "penny" candy—she'd also scratch my back under the cast. If I'd had any sense, I'd have waited ten years and married Lisa. But I was male and twenty-five; having good sense was far too much to expect of me.

For the moment I clung to the illusion that all was well. Empalme was lively, colorful, and its citizens so cordial, that it was an utterly amazing contrast to Ecuador. In Ecuador everyone was suspicious of strangers. Getting spit on by passing male bicyclists was a frequent occupational hazard in the provincial capitals and market towns. Getting stoned by an angry mob was an occasional problem out in the mountain villages. True, very few front porches in Empalme sported a convalescing gringo—and folks were curious—but pleasantly, and politely so.

Hardened and desensitized by isolated, suspicious Ecuador, I really did not fully react to how reserved Iliana was until I had been there four or five days. That's when I first felt genuine gut-level unease. Iliana and I had so much that we needed to talk about: each other, a marriage, our cultural differences.

I was in no rush to get on with a wedding ceremony, though. Originally I had expected to be in Ecuador till fall, finish my doctorate at the University of New Mexico before returning to Mexico, then marry. But Iliana simply didn't talk enough, and I was really beginning to suffer. The warm, happy side of her had simply vanished.

When I tried to engage her, she protested again that the recent scorpion sting had left her out of sorts and in pain. In fact one of the saddest things for me after the first several days was that I simply could not get her out of the house to walk the lanes with me, as we had done the year before when I came to court her.

We had never had an affair. Heck, we had rarely gone out unchaperoned, but we had talked and danced and touched like any other couple. At the same time, I noticed that her mom was overly solicitous and too anxious to discuss our wedding and set a date. That something was awry really began to penetrate. My emotions were beginning to reawaken as the Ecuador Effect wore off. But still off-balance emotionally, I largely dismissed the warning signs.

As a consequence I spent a lot of time with Lisa. She compensated for Iliana's reserve and went everywhere with me. I'd walk in the afternoon and again in the evenings—good distances—trying to get my strength back. Animated, cheerful, and endearing, she followed me endlessly, as if she were my own shadow.

If I played checkers with her, she was happy. If I took her for a walk, she was happy. If I stopped to sit at a soda stand and smoke a cigarette, she was happy. Her happiness was healing me. I enjoyed the sense of warmth and closeness that she gave me; it was a very fragile time in my life, and I really needed the affection. That was when I first decided I absolutely needed to have a daughter of my own someday.

At the time I thought I'd marry Iliana in a few months or a year, then stay in Empalme. Perhaps we could move up a block or two into one of the other little railroad houses near the main street, start a family. I imagined that I might be able to make a living there by running an underground English school for local kids who wanted work in the tourist industry. I could not legally obtain working papers, and Mexico had not granted citizenship to a single American since the 1940s, but no one in Empalme would run to the authorities and say anything.

If a "school" didn't work, I had a bit of capital, $700 or $800, including the travelers checks I carried and a few hundred dollars in my account in Albuquerque. With that money

15

I could have started a tiny business, like a cigarette stand, even purchased a half-share in a taxi license. So in spite of Iliana's unexpected reserve, I continued to accept her explanation that she felt out of sorts because of the scorpion sting.

About ten days after my arrival, Iliana's uncle returned from Guadalajara. I had gained back several pounds, reoxygenated my body, and become a bit stronger. But Mamá was beginning to press me more frequently about the date and time of the wedding. My gut sent me danger signals every time she did that. And with the uncle's return came a new level of tension in the house. It had nothing to do with me and everything to do with his high-strung wife. Nonetheless, I decided to move on to Bacochibampo Bay, my old stomping grounds just north of Guaymas.

In those days many American tourists flocked to two well-known hotels on the bay, the Miramar and the Playa de Cortés, built by the Southern Pacific Railway as an elegant spa. The hotels were located at the south end of the long, sandy beach that was dotted by seaside houses constructed after World War II. The setting was spectacular. At either end of the beach rose jagged mountains that jutted right out into the Sea of Cortés.

One narrow, paved street, Bacochibampo Avenue, provided access to the seaside colony. At the far north end of the avenue, a little trailer camp had been established next to the small mangrove-rimmed estuary at the mouth of El Tular Creek. Fronting the beach across from the trailer camp was a bathhouse, a bar, a large glassed-in ballroom, a row of palm-thatched shelters, and a small restaurant. Frequented by local Mexican families, this rambling spa was called Playas Primaverales, or "Springtime Beach."

Before I left for Ecuador, I had lived on this beach, sleeping under a palm-thatched shelter, or *palapa*, on the sand in front of the bar and ballroom. I had first met Iliana in the little restaurant next door, where she worked as a waitress.

During winter storms I would tip the barmen and move my sleeping bag inside the pavilion, which had glassed walls facing the sea. Cleopatra García was the general manager. The head bartender's name was Manuel. They both had thought me crazy when I departed their lovely seaside haven for South America. They were right—it had been madness.

So in late May the wandering anthropologist, cast and all, returned to Playas Primaverales on Bacochibampo Bay to stash the same sleeping bag and gear that had gone to Ecuador behind the long mahogany bar at one end of the dance floor.

Like the prodigal son of biblical fame, I was received with open arms, followed quickly by a clinical appraisal of the damage done during my hegira. It was nearly June—hot but not brutal. Before returning I had gone to the Guaymas jail with Iliana to purchase an inmate-crafted hammock made of nylon fishnet. I hung it under a thatched hut out front.

That first night at Primaverales was magical—an immense, lemon-yellow moon hung behind jet-black mountains that cascaded into the glistening sea. As the surf whispered, flying fish rocketed ashore, their beating "wings" shimmering, luminous in the moonlight. On the far horizon faint streaks of pearly iridescence rose like delicate tendrils reaching out to caress the night sky. My hammock swung gently in the ocean breeze, matching the rhythm of the surf.

Over the next few days I took frequent walks along the beach. I ate rice and beans in the little restaurant at midday, then visited Iliana each afternoon, taking one bus into

Guaymas, then another to Empalme. When I left Iliana's house at night, I would return to Primaverales by taxi, as it would be too late for buses. The long taxi rides quickly became too expensive.

One evening, frustrated with Iliana's reserve, I left early and took a bus back to Guaymas. Restless, I walked along the main street enjoying the bustle of the crowd, until I passed an excellent little restaurant where I had eaten several times before going to Ecuador. Called the Colmenar, it was nestled three doors inside a bright brick and tile passageway near the city's largest taxi stand.

I stepped into the passage and took a table out front, where the evening breeze and lively aspect of street life were too tempting to pass up. A pleasant young waitress came out with the menu. Feeling extravagant I ordered a small *bistec* (flank steak) and a café con leche. The coffee arrived first. I lit a smoke, relaxed, and absorbed the scene.

The young clerk standing in the door to the Kodak shop thirty feet away was very cute. The little shoeshine boy she was chasing from the shop was not. Scruffy, dirty, and dejected, he sat down on the streetside step to the passageway and watched the food arrive at my table.

Still in the cast, I hadn't thought about how I was going to cut my meat—you simply don't have this problem with basic beans and rice. The waitress watched me struggle, then came out offering to cut up the steak. Grinning to hide my embarrassment, I accepted and introduced myself. As she carved she told me her name was Mercedes. Nice smile. Freckles. Twinkly eyes. All right!

Fifteen minutes later she took my plate away and returned with another big smile and a second mug of coffee.

I liked this place! Meanwhile the shoeshine boy had deftly sidled up to the table, looking pathetic.

"Pathetic" was natural for him, as he was crippled and disconcertingly lopsided. He asked to shine my Red Wings, since I couldn't. He had a point. And my boots were a mess.

I asked how much. Ten pesos (eighty cents). *"¡Demasiado!"* (Too much!) I declared. *"Cinco"* (Five), he gurgled. *"¡Hecho!"* He crouched on his wooden box and went to work. Jesus! The kid was good at this. First he cleaned the oil-tanned leather with saddle soap, then covered the battle scars and gave the boots a soft glow.

Impressed, I told him I didn't realize he could get the oiled leather to glow. He assured me he could make it brilliant, "like a diamond," for just fifty pesos. I told him "next time" and gave him ten pesos anyway.

Pleased, he told me his name was Juanito (Johnny), then limped off with his box to show the ten-peso note to an equally dirty little girl who had been watching us from the end of the passage. His sister, I assumed.

I finished my coffee and thought about my situation. I was getting stronger and it was time to get the cast removed. I decided to go back to Albuquerque, collect my favorite books and personal effects and retrieve the gray 1962 Rambler that I brought to New Mexico from West Virginia when I first enrolled in graduate school. The Rambler might work as a taxi.

Iliana's uncle got me a pass on the Pacific Line's night train from Empalme to Nogales, Sonora. The evening of my departure, Iliana and I sat under the stars in her front yard. It should have been warm, poignant, and intimate, but we simply could not communicate. I pressed to find out what was wrong, but got nowhere. Locally the silence implied secrets. What frustration! About 11 P.M. we walked down to the station in Empalme, and I boarded the midnight train to the border. Only little Lisa cried as I waved goodbye.

20

two

IN LIMBO

I arrived in Nogales at dawn, crossed to the American side, and hopped a bus to Tucson. Once there I took a city bus to the hospital, walked into the emergency room, and asked if someone could remove my cast. An intern on his orthopedics rotation came out, shoved me behind an x-ray machine, then got out the vibrating saw. As he cut me out of my plaster prison, he asked, far too casually, where I had been treated. "Ecuador," I replied.

Relieved that he wasn't about to rat out one of his own colleagues, he told me that I really ought to have the clavicle rebroken and the left shoulder reset. I shrugged. Then he asked why, given the damaged muscles, had they merely reset the breaks, rather than do reconstructive surgery. I replied offhandedly, "They had no anesthetic."

He was still staring, open-mouthed, and trying to process that as a candy striper helped me put on my shirt, easing the freed arm into the left sleeve before arranging the canvas sling. For the first time in more than a month, my left arm was actually in a sleeve. Cool! I flashed my Blue Cross card at the desk and left, elated. Everything is so easy in the States.

Back at the bus depot I ate my first American food. It was truly disappointing—greasy, with no flavor. Worse yet it had no real smell to it. In fact absolutely nothing around me smelled distinctive. Culture shock!

Philip Bock, one of my professors at New Mexico, had actually coined the phrase and written the book titled "Culture Shock," introducing the concept forever into the English lexicon. Until that day at the bus station, I frankly thought he was full of shit. But as I sat there gnawing on mystery meat and picking at flaccid, greasy fries, I experienced a flash of genuine respect for his concept. Epiphanies come at the strangest times and in the strangest places.

The next bus took me to Las Cruces, where I waited for another to Albuquerque.

The bus pulled into Albuquerque about 5:00 A.M. the next morning. It was just beginning to streak dawn over the Sandia Mountains, which dominate the city's eastern skyline. Though it had been just seven months, it seemed like a lifetime since I had left. Once at the bus station, I didn't want to spend the money for stateside taxi fares. So I swung a small duffel over my stronger, right shoulder and walked uphill from the bus terminal near the railway yards.

My route took me up Central Avenue, old Route 66, to the Anthropology Department at the University of New Mexico. I had been a graduate assistant there before I left for Mexico, then Ecuador, and still had my keys to the building.

There was no other sensible place for me to go at 6 o'clock that morning. So I dug out a long-unused key and let myself into the Anthropology Department through the side door nearest Alumni Chapel. I walked down the polished flagstone hallway past the cases of Basketmaker mummies, went into the men's room, got out my shaving gear, stripped out of my clothes, and took a stand-up bath. I shaved with the hot tap water there, then used my dirty T-shirt as a warm compress on the battered left shoulder. That felt wonderful.

Relieved, I stuffed my dirty clothes into a plastic bag that went back into the duffel, then put on a clean outfit. Done, I went down the hallway to a dark corner of the main corridor, threw my duffel on the floor for a pillow, and took a nap. Universities are great places for learning. They also make great hotels—nice bathrooms, hot water, and plenty of places to spend the night if one isn't too obvious about it.

I awakened about 8:30 A.M. to sounds of activity in the department office. The secretaries had come and had opened for business. I got up, retucked my shirt, and started down the hall. Professor Frank Hibben was coming my way—on his way to a summer class, I supposed. He stopped and, quite friendly, asked how I'd been. I had worked for him for nearly two years as his assistant when I first came to graduate school.

Frank was rich, Republican, and a big-game hunter. I always got on well with him, but most of the faculty hated his guts. Envy, perhaps. It might have been his money, his attitude, or his politics. But I assumed it was primarily because he always had huge classes filled with hundreds of enthusiastic students.

Most of the other faculty had to settle for smaller classes with several dozen bored undergraduates. As I walked toward the office, I thought about money, politics, academics, America, and tasteless food. Before I reached it, I had decided to ditch an academic career and live in Mexico.

I had been promised another graduate assistantship for the coming year. But at that moment, academics simply seemed too much like Ecuador—mean, competitive, detached. No thanks!

Once in the office, I asked to use the telephone and called a classmate, Kenneth Ames, who had stored my old gray Rambler in his driveway. I retrieved the car, got it serviced, and closed my bank account, withdrawing pocket money and a $200 cashier's check.

I returned to Ken's place on Girard Boulevard and collected a footlocker of essentials: clothing, books, notepads, blank field journals, a tape recorder, and odds and ends. The trunk had been too heavy for me to take to Ecuador. Next I bought a table fan; it was going to be a hot summer in Guaymas. Then I stocked up on toiletries, packed my good clothes, and got ready for the trip back to Mexico.

Before leaving I determined to find a nice gift for Iliana, something special. I hoped that might make a difference in her attitude toward me. I remember looking through the *Albuquerque Journal* and spotting an ad for a litter of mixed-breed husky puppies. Iliana loved animals, and the family dog had disappeared while I was in Ecuador. I bought a cuddly little male husky pup. I fixed him a cardboard box for the backseat, bought dog food, a little dish, and a gallon of water—ready to head south the next morning.

Just one night in the States and it was time to go back to Mexico. My own reactions disturbed me. I had liked Albuquerque. I had enjoyed graduate school—great professors and fabulous classmates. I should have been sad, and if not sad, at least poignant. Instead I was excited.

Mexico was bright and lively. Socially, it was one immense network of human relationships that radiated outward from millions who cherished the concept of *corazón* (heart). Mexico was a huge, complicated community that, along the way, had decided to call itself a nation. In contrast the States comprised, first and foremost, the world's most powerful nation. Socially, its heartbeat depended on money, power, and things—not people. I was drawn to Mexico's human connection.

The next morning Puppy howled, frightened, as I drove out of Albuquerque on old Route 85 south. Poor little guy. I stopped in Los Lunas and bought him canned milk, a cheap fluffy towel, and an old-fashioned wind-up clock. The milk, heat, and tick-tock put him to sleep. Later in the day I put him on my lap, under the steering wheel.

Fourteen hours later, just after midnight, I crossed over to Mexico at Nogales. There are no formalities leaving the United States. You simply drive out of one world and into another.

About two hundred yards into Mexico, one must stop at their immigration station, *Migración*. I pulled over, parked, and went inside to get a new six-month tourist card. Several *Federales* came out with me to check the car. They opened the trunk, nosed around, and saw the little gray-masked puppy.

Though Puppy was legal, they saw an opportunity to get a bribe, a *mordida*, from me. I gave them fifty pesos (four dollars), chatted them up in Spanish, and explained that Puppy was a gift for my *prometida*, my fiancée, in Guaymas, where I was soon to be married. They warmed up, asked only the obligatory questions, and sent me on my way with a wave.

Nogales behind us, Puppy and I headed south. Two army checkpoints, the first at kilometer 21, another in Imuris, then it was clear sailing. I should have stopped to rest, but I was too eager to get back to Guaymas. Besides, it had turned into a nice night. The heat of the desert had faded, the stars were out, and everything smelled normal again—diesel exhaust from the buses, dry desert creosote bush, and the odor of livestock.

As the Rambler hummed through the night, things looked right, smelled right, felt right, and I began to feel at home, like I belonged. In the States I'd always been the kid who was "different," who didn't think like the crowd. At that point nearly all of my life had been spent as an outsider. Guaymas and Empalme were the only places on this earth that I had ever just lived in. They made perfect sense to me.

Elsewhere I simply watched what went on around me, detached and curious. As these thoughts ran through my head, Puppy began to cry. I stopped at an all-night restaurant, gave him his milk, changed his soiled newspapers, and got myself a real meal of food I could both smell and taste. Then back on the road.

Mexican highways sound different than American ones. The trucks and second-class buses were almost all diesels with tall exhaust stacks. At night their drivers would open the throttle and roll like hell, the big diesels screaming as they went. The trucks had such stiff suspensions, to handle the rough roads, that their headlights had a distinctive vibrating bob and jiggle as they roared down the highway toward you.

In the desert night I could hear their diesel stacks miles away. I drove the old Rambler with my front window all the

26

way down, radio off, listening to the sounds of transport in the night. The little husky howled at several trucks, in primitive recognition of their kindred sound. Oncoming buses passed me going north toward Nogales, Mexicali, and San Luis Río Colorado, south of Yuma.

Just as dawn was breaking, I reached the village of San José de Guaymas. Two minutes later I spotted the right turn from Route 15 down to the Playa de Cortés and the entrance to Bacochibampo Bay. Five minutes more and I pulled into the dusty car park behind the pavilion at Primaverales.

Once parked, I got out, stretched, and watered the dog. My friend Manuel, who was just stirring for the morning chores, was glad to see me and willing to keep an eye on the dog. I tipped him, then sacked out till noon in the back room behind the bar, where employees usually slept. When I got up, I went to the little restaurant next door, where I had first met Iliana.

After a quick meal of beans, tomatoes, and Spanish rice, I got cleaned up in the men's toilet at the far end of the ballroom. No hot water, of course. Puppy was fine. He had already enjoyed his first fish dinner when I went to retrieve him from Manuel. Several of the kids who hung around Primaverales had cleaned up my car, washing and polishing everything. Another went next door to the restaurant to find ribbon for me. I wanted to put a bow on Puppy before delivering him. I've always suspected that some apron strings were sacrificed for the project. I tipped them, then drove to Empalme, passing Guaymas before crossing the high bridge over the Mátape estuary and continuing down the unpaved main avenue. Turning left, I pulled up to Iliana's house, nestled beneath the mangos.

Lisa, true to form, was first to reach the gate. I carried the little husky, now howling and protesting, inside. Iliana was waiting for me. She was truly pleased over the puppy—and very surprised. Lisa was barely able to contain herself, since no one in Guaymas had ever seen anything like this dog except in photos. In those days there was probably no other husky in the entire state of Sonora. Lisa's bragging rights in the neighborhood were destined to be immense.

I explained that the husky was an Eskimo dog. Iliana was thrilled, and I was very relieved. As she petted Puppy she seemed much more like her former self, and I hoped her gentle happiness would return. After hearing me call him Puppy, she promptly named the dog Poppys, which in border Spanglish means "puppy," much like *guayina* is "wagon," as in a station wagon.

Puppy was a smash hit. Huskies are instinctively crazy about kids, so Lisa and Kique were as happy as Iliana was. I thought our relationship would now blossom anew. How wrong I was.

Iliana and I did go for a walk that afternoon. She talked a bit more, and Lisa didn't tag along. Progress! We walked past the local chapel. Finally, Iliana herself spoke of marriage, wanting to pin down the date. But I wasn't yet ready to set a date, because I first wanted to talk to her about intimate things, beliefs and hopes, children. Those things were important to me.

As we walked along, I brought up the subject of having a family. That notion created a very startling reaction. Frankly, she panicked, looking dazed, so I quickly dropped the subject. Even though I changed the topic, she insisted on returning immediately to the house. That was the first time I noticed how much weight she had gained since I went to Ecuador.

After Iliana retreated to her room, I took Lisa for a walk. An hour or so later we returned, and I convinced Iliana to have dinner with me at a little open-air restaurant on Empalme's main street. I didn't raise any delicate issues, so it was cordial. We sat outside in the shade at a little metal Carta Blanca table. These metal tables advertising one brand of beer or another were ubiquitous throughout Mexico. I'd have loved to own a piece of the factory that produced them.

Dinner, as at nearly every casual streetside Mexican restaurant, was good and cheap. We had small filets of pan-fried fish, rice, beans, tomatoes, corn tortillas, and sodas. Limes and fresh salsa were served on the side. The tab was about $3.50. This dinner gave us our first time alone since before Ecuador. I hoped she'd talk and laugh, but she didn't.

At one point I told her, "*¡Mira!* (Look!) You were so happy and *simpática* (outgoing) when I left for Ecuador that I need to understand your current reserve." Silence. In desperation, I pleaded, "Iliana, I need to know how you feel about things!" Answer, *"No sé"* (I don't know). "But you still wish to marry?" *"Sí,"* she answered.

I could simply find no way around the wall she had erected. All I could get from her was a date to go out to the beach. Totally frustrated, I was already beginning to detach mentally and leave Empalme behind me. It was almost as if she was the one suffering the "Ecuador Effect."

So I settled for the date to drive her and Lisa to Cochorit Beach the next afternoon. This magnificent beach a mile or so south of Empalme, though virtually unknown to American tourists, was the place that gave me my first view of sand and palms from the bus window on the morning I returned from Ecuador.

That date was a disaster. I had wanted to go swimming with Iliana, but she wouldn't even get out of the car. Lisa discreetly left us alone in the car for a few minutes, but Iliana wouldn't even let me cuddle her. Pissed off, I called Lisa, bundled her into the Rambler again, turned the car around, and headed back to Empalme. It was tense, and just midafternoon. Even Lisa was bummed out. The silence was total agony.

As we bounced along the sandy dirt road from Cochorit toward Empalme, there were many local people walking along the roadside on their return from day picnics. Poor families, carrying their ubiquitous plastic-net shopping bags, had gone to the beach for the day to swim, eat oranges and tortillas, and share bottles of Orange Crush. This was the local version of a cheap family outing.

To relieve the tension I stopped, offering rides. We quickly filled the car with folks from along the road, jamming them into the Rambler. Two miles later I stopped again, got out, opened the trunk, and a group of four or five hot, tired kids jumped into the trunk, lid up. Before we reached Empalme and began dropping people off, the Rambler held fourteen, including those in the trunk. This wasn't even unusual. Autos sagging under the weight of a dozen people were an everyday sight in small-town Mexico.

Jammed in with everyone else, Lisa was happy again. I returned to Primaverales after dropping her and Iliana at their house. Iliana went in first. Lisa commented that her sister was being *muy mula* (very stubborn, mulish) with me. I said nothing but grinned. Then, having dumped on her big sister, she ran back into the house like a bat out of hell.

I drove to downtown Guaymas, parked, and treated myself to another meal at the Colmenar. Soup and coffee. Mercedes, still all smiles, remembered my name. Halfway through the coffee, Juanito appeared again with his shoeshine box and put a bit more glow on the Red Wings. The little girl watched him from a distance.

"*¿Tu hermana?*" (Your sister?) "No. *Mi patrona. Me cuida en la calle.*" (No, my protector. She watches out for me in the street.) Ten minutes and ten pesos later, the pair disappeared. I said goodbye to Mercedes and drove back to the beach. Bored at Primaverales, I drove to the hotel Miramar at the other end of the beach.

I killed some time there talking to a friend of mine, José Jacinto, who was a waiter in the dinnerclub. I had first met him in the spring of '69, while hanging out at Primaverales.

He had become a good friend. Locally, nearly everyone knew him simply as Negro. He had been in the Hotel Rubi's bar when Marta walked in one afternoon the year before, part of my Ecuadorian clinic hallucination.

About nine I drove back to Primaverales and had a beer before hanging my hammock for the night.

The next day I went to see Iliana in Empalme. It was late afternoon. Lisa came out to talk, as did Iliana's mom. I went inside, but Iliana was in her bedroom and simply would not come out. Disgusted, I went out back and ate some beans with Lisa. About dusk, just as I was ready to leave, Iliana came out of her room. She had been putting on weight, and in a stroke I knew why. Pregnant! My look of surprise must have been obvious—she looked back, gasped.

I asked her, "*¿Estás embarazada?*" (Are you pregnant?) She ran into her room and slammed the door. Lisa started

31

bawling, and insisted that Iliana loved me. I yelled at Lisa. "But I'm not the father. I've never slept with your sister!"

Then I yelled in at Iliana, "At least come out here and talk to me." After a bit she came out, and I asked her again if she was pregnant. She told me that she was. Lord, that really hurt. I had hoped it wasn't true. But I knew that it was. I didn't know why I hadn't realized it before. Denial, I guess.

That night I was angry, and hurt. I look back on it now and I realize that she was in pain, too. She was in so much anguish that she couldn't really cry. She was just petrified. My own emotions were a confusing mix of anger, sorrow, compassion, and hurt pride. I wanted her to tell me about it. But she clammed up and I got shaking mad. Since there was nothing to say, I stomped out to the old Rambler, slammed the door, popped it into gear, threw dirt down the lane, and drove back to Guaymas. Lisa stood at the gate, sobbing.

That night I didn't go to Primaverales. Instead I went downtown to the Hotel Rubi, the venerable commercial hotel on the waterfront next to the shrimp-packing plant. I rented a nice upstairs room on the balcony. I felt angry, foolish, and hurt, all at once. I did not want to see anyone at Primaverales.

Later I went downstairs to the hotel's south bar. I had been in it a number of times the year before, but had never been a "regular." The bar was refreshingly cool. A big wood-paneled place, its glassed doors opened to a patio at the rear. It had buff tile floors, ceiling-fans, and a huge mahogany bar.

When I entered, an old round-top Wurlitzer jukebox was playing a *cumbia*, "La Chiva Española." How poetically ironic! A *chiva* is a chick who cheats on her man. I was still shaking, so I took a stool and ordered a shot of tequila with a beer.

The bartender introduced himself as "Jesse." He told me in English to let him know if I needed anything. I answered in Spanish. He was a good-looking Mexican, well-built, with slightly reddish hair and light skin. An imposing guy, his hair was styled in the best James Dean ducktail I'd ever seen.

I'd noticed him in the bar the year before but hadn't really known him. The others there simply called him Canelo (Cinnamon). I ordered another shot of tequila, nursing the same beer chaser.

After the booze took effect, I quit shaking and noticed two attractive local girls at a nearby table. In those days it was still quite uncommon for a single Mexican woman to be drinking in a man's bar. Jesse saw me checking them out and said, "Oh, you like the girls?" I said, "Yeah, the one with the blue bow, she's very pretty." She was slender. Nice figure and an appealing face.

He said, "I'll introduce you." I asked if she was a hooker. He said, "yes," and told me she was a friend. We talked for a few minutes. So I went back to my room. A few minutes later she came tapping softly at the door. I let her in, closed the door, and pulled the curtains.

She had brought a couple of beers up with her. I asked her her name—Eva. After a few minutes she took off her dress. Good looking. She grabbed my belt, unzipped my pants, got onto the bed with me and gave me a good, plain, professional fucking. Not love, not compassion, no tender caresses. Just plain, clinical sex that actually made me feel much worse.

Afterward, while dressing, she asked, "Why are you hurt so? You are angry, too. You are hurt and you are angry. What has happened?" I asked her how she knew. She replied simply,

"I know men." Then I told her, "All my dreams have turned to shit, to *mierda*, and I don't know what to do now." "Tell me," she replied.

I gave her the rough outline of the story. She looked at me intently while she swigged her beer, then said, "So you are the one from Primaverales that the *taxistas* (taxi drivers) talk about." I nodded and she went on, "I'll be honest with you. Mostly with me it is business, but occasionally I also meet a man that I like. So your dreams have turned to shit, have they? Very well, then you are like us, like all of us here. You are one of us, and we will look after you." Then she left.

I rested on the bed a few minutes, consumed by a sense of unreality and curious at what she had said. It seemed stunningly direct in a world where most messages are oblique. But Mexican hookers, you know, they didn't play by the rules and they didn't have to. They were outcasts from polite society. And one of the great rewards of their profession, for all they put up with, was the freedom to say and do things that other women in Mexico simply could not.

Our conversation had certainly been an odd way to end a hundred-peso assignation. At first I thought her assertion, "we will look after you; you are like one of us," was just a way to deflect my far too revealing and direct tale of "woman trouble." Later I discovered she was telling me the truth. In some fundamental respects I was one of them and would be looked after. I walked out of the door a few minutes later, banging it behind me.

Once downstairs, I walked back through the lobby and had my first encounter with a fat, disgusting son of a bitch named Ramón. A night clerk, he sprawled on the couch, his feet up, and demanded forty pesos. I asked "For what?"

Pudgy hand extended to receive his cash, he insisted, "For the other guest in your room!" Leering nastily, he reminded me that it was against the law to have lady "guests" in one's room in Guaymas. Sure it was. The only place the girls were allowed to openly ply their trade was in the Zona de Tolerancia. I didn't need trouble so gave him the forty pesos and returned to the bar.

Eva had gone, so I ordered another beer. Jesse confided in English, "She say you treat her nice. She like you." I asked where he learned English. He said, "Oh, I worked on the other side, you know, *'el otro lado.'*" I asked, "Did you like it over there?" He said, "No, not so much. They treat me like a Mexican, you know. Your *paisanos* (countrymen) are some-times difficult with foreigners." Embarrassed, I acknowl-edged the reality, "Yeah, I know." He smiled, "Drink your beer. A friend of yours is coming." I said, "Oh really, who?" He said, "Oh, wait; you see."

I drank my Superior, feeling screwy and weird. I'd paid for a quick lay with Eva out of anger at Iliana. I was not proud of myself—not then, not now. It was a mean thing to do. It was mean to Iliana, mean to me, and mean to Eva. In those days I didn't realize that meanness could ever be constructive, but it was; it cleared the way for a new era in my life.

Minutes later, Negro Jacinto walked in the door. He'd just gotten off his shift at the Miramar. Delighted, I greeted him, "Negro, what are you doing here?" He said, "But Davíd, surely you understand. We're all barmen, *cantineros*. We are a very small community here. I want to talk to you." So we sat and I finished my beer with Negro. He asked, "What has gone on?" I told him I had gone back to Empalme and . . .

I told him, "She's pregnant, Negro. My *prometida* is

pregnant and I'm not the father." "Did you beat her?" he asked. I said, "No, I didn't lay a hand on her. I yelled a little." "Will she talk to you?" I said, "No." "Who is the father?" he asked. "I don't know," I whined, then hung my head. Having someone else screw your woman is a huge disgrace in Mexico.

It was Negro's turn to talk. He said, "I must tell you that I heard rumors. Along the beach, you know, there were rumors." I asked him what he knew. He answered, "Well, I know nothing, but the rumors—she had a friend, you know, Mexican." I asked if people had been talking about it. He nodded "yes," then said, "I don't think this baby will look like you. It is something to think about." He paused, looking at me. "You are still thinking of marrying her, perhaps?"

I said, "I don't know. I feel like a fool." He paused, then said, "We are all fools. We are born fools, we live fools, we die fools." He told me that what separates the good from the bad is how gracefully we behave as fools.

I thanked him for talking to me and went upstairs. I wanted to be alone. It was a moonlit night. I rocked on the hotel's upstairs balcony all night long, looking out over the harbor while watching the moon slowly descend behind the rim of mountains to the north that separate Bacochibampo Bay from Guaymas. I still didn't know what to do. . . .

The next day I settled on an early afternoon bowl of soup and coffee at the Colmenar. Like magic, Juanito appeared again. Installment three on the Red Wings both brought out the full shine and new information. Juanito told me his patrona's name was Lupita. She had asked him to find out if I was the one from Primaverales the taximen knew as Güero.

I handed him the ten pesos and nodded. He shuffled back to her and must have told her she was right, for she looked at me and nodded in return. When they disappeared, I slipped back into my funk.

I still couldn't face Iliana, so that second night was as tough as the first. I gravitated to the Rubi bar, drinking tequila and beer, which got me shit-faced. Most of the night I again spent rocking on the balcony. Finally I went to bed early in the morning and slept late.

I awoke to someone banging at my door. It was the pleasant-faced woman who ran the day desk. I had a phone call, so pulled on my Wranglers and went out to take it at the old-fashioned phone on the front desk. It was Iliana. She wanted to talk.

Apparently she had gone to a public phone to call me from Empalme. Obviously the whole world knew where I was and what I was up to. Lovely. But we did need to talk. On my way out I got an iced Orange Crush to tame my cottonmouth and drove the Rambler to Empalme. Once there, I eased into the alley that ran along Iliana's backyard fence. Discretion, you know.

37

I needn't have bothered. About then a neighbor boy darted out, extended index fingers sticking up from his head, mimicking horns. In Mexico this meant that someone had been tapping my woman, and it sure wasn't me. The little fart was announcing to the town that I had officially become a *cabrón*.

Had I been working-class Mexican, this would have been the appropriate time to either whip out a knife and cut off one of the kid's offending fingers or to beat the shit out of Iliana in order to save a tiny scrap of my honor. But I wasn't Mexican. Feeling like a complete fool, I merely sat in the scorching-hot car rehearsing an opening line. Pathetic!

Mercifully, it wasn't necessary.

Iliana materialized at the back fence and started the conversation. She had decided to stay with a girlfriend in the town of San Luis Río Colorado, near the border, until she had her baby. She begged me to wait for her and told me how much she cared for me. Her plan was to leave before her uncle returned from Guadalajara and her older brother got wise and beat her. She was deathly afraid of him. Judging by the kid next door, she would have to work fast.

That's when I asked her precisely when she intended to leave. She answered, "Tomorrow." I asked her to tell me more about her plans. She shook her head, then pleaded again, "Please, wait for me until September."

I told her I was hurt, confused, and angry. She responded, "Then go away." So I got back in the car, but she came running over to the window, "Will you come see me tomorrow?" Petulant, I said, "Perhaps; perhaps not." She begged, "Please. At least take me to the bus station tomorrow."

Finally her voice sounded like the authentic Iliana I had once known. Angry or not, it hurt to witness her anguish, so I agreed. As I pulled away, I flipped a really good finger to the kid next door. No language problem at all—he understood me perfectly.

The next afternoon I went for her around one. She was waiting on the porch, her two possessions a little, old-fashioned cardboard suitcase and her embroidered pillow. I walked onto the shaded concrete porch where I had recuperated during my first days in Empalme and reached for her suitcase. It already seemed long ago since I had slept there—like a dreamy, indistinct childhood memory. I asked, "Have you money?" Looking away, she said, "No, I have only my ticket and eighty or ninety pesos, but my girlfriend says that she has money."

My God, the poor thing was going to go off and have her baby with the equivalent of just eight dollars in her pocket! I offered her money. She told me she didn't want it, that she didn't deserve my money. I told her I didn't want anything bad to happen to her, reached into my jacket pocket, and pulled out my traveler's checks. I peeled off several hundreds, signed them, wrote her name in, and explained how they were cashed.

It hurt her pride to take my money, but she needed it, so she took it. She looked ghastly, dazed and heartbroken. By then I truly felt sorry for her. At the same time, I was deeply relieved that she had decided to go and have her baby in San Luis.

Iliana didn't want Lisa with us. The kid just stared at us from the front room, silent as a ghost. But when I put Iliana in the car and slammed the door ready to pull away, she wailed. It was so primitive that Poppys wailed in response. There were no winners in this tragedy.

Iliana didn't want to leave from the bus station in Empalme, because people would see her, so we drove into Guaymas and waited for the bus to San Luis. There wasn't much to say. Iliana got on her bus and took a window seat. Her head right above me, she opened the window and looked down at me, silent tears running down her cheeks. She wanted assurances. Again I promised her that I would wait for her and asked how long she expected me to wait. She answered, "The fifteenth of September?"

After a pause I said, "Okay. I promise you nothing more than I will still be here in Guaymas on the fifteenth of

39

September. That is all I promise you." She said, "That is all I ask; that is enough." Then she stuck her pillow out the window. "Take it, I want you to have it. Please sleep with my pillow. It has always been with me, and I embroidered it for us." I took the pillow, feeling foolish.

I walked out of the bus station, pillow under my arm, crossed the road, and waited for the San Luis bus to pull out. As it passed, I got one last glimpse of Iliana, her anguished face pressed to the glass. Our relationship was over.

I drank my way through most of the next week until I had a massive hangover and only about fifty dollars to my name. That's when I checked out of the Rubi and returned to Primaverales.

40

three

PLAYAS PRIMAVERALES

In the past, Primaverales had always been more than just a place. It was a state of mind. My secret haven—powerful, mystical, and exquisitely beautiful. The rhythmic call of its surf soothed me. It was there that I had met Iliana in '69 as easily and as naturally as breathing, and it was there that I returned when I lost her.

Losing Iliana and Lisa had been a blunt trauma to my soul. Yet I believed my depression and growing detachment would go away in a few days at the most. Broke, chastened, unattached, and hopeful, I stowed my gear then pulled the blue hammock from the Rambler's trunk and hung it under my favorite *palapa*.

After reclaiming my territory, I ambled over to the little restaurant next door. Rice, beans, and a tortilla at six pesos (48 cents) A miniature cup of black coffee came with it. For an extra two pesos you could upgrade to *café con leche*.

As I ate I thought about Iliana. She had been the first to

serve me a meal there. I had upgraded to café con leche that day. She smiled serenely as she set the steaming mug on my table. Then asked softly, "*¿Azucar, joven?*" (Sugar, young man?) A rush of warmth had shot through me and I looked up at her, startled at my reaction.

Why hadn't it worked out? Why wasn't it my baby? What's wrong with me? I had gotten past my anger with Iliana and was now blaming myself for everything—an old habit. "Get over it, Dave!" I told myself as I sat there, miserable. "She's gone! Let it go." I took a deep breath. To compensate for my loneliness, I concentrated on my physical surroundings.

From where I sat I could see the full, compact sweep of Bacochibampo Bay. To the south a ridge of rugged saguaro-studded mountains formed the bay's southern arc. The Playa de Cortés and Miramar hotels had been built on a low rise, where the southern end of the sand met the rocky hills that separated the red-light district from the beach.

Due west, several sandstone islands jutted up, partially protecting the mouth of the bay. Thousands of pelicans nested there, their guano whitewashing the surrounding rock. It looked as if each island wore a white Panama hat over freckled, sun-reddened skin. The freckles were sea lions sunning themselves at the waterline.

To the north, across the stream that fed the estuary, lay a mountainous rock-laden peninsula called Las Tinajas, named for the ancient storage jars found in its caves. The peninsula separated Bacochibampo from the nascent yacht basin at San Carlos. At the time there were only half a dozen vacation houses on the waterfront of Las Tinajas. About three dozen more homes were strung out along Bacochibampo

Avenue and constituted the Miramar Colony. Walled, gated, architect-designed, and servant-operated, these private compounds housed local elites like don Florencio Zaragosa, owner of several markets. The Miramar Colony "neighbors" rarely frequented Primaverales.

The main beach, mangrove estuary, and cattail thickets on the inland side of Miramar (Sea View) had all been created during the last ten to twelve thousand years by ancient shell collectors. Among their descendants were Sonora's Seri Indians, a vanishing race of a few hundred souls. Their huge piles of whelk, conch, and clamshells had slowly built the beach. Then the tidal pool behind it became a prime environment for the mangroves that sheltered fish and shrimp.

My engagement may have gone up in flames, but I was perched on top of one of the most beautiful archeological sites on the planet. I would feel better soon, I told myself.

43

The next day was a Sunday, which cheered me a little, because I had always loved Sundays at Primaverales. There were people everywhere—kids, dogs, whole families. A typical Mexican working-class family usually included mom and pop and four or five kids. In many families there were children of varying skin and hair tones, and these differences often gave rise to rivalry among siblings. One saw everything from red hair, fair skin, and freckled kids, to dark-complected children with straight black hair. Features ran from "European" to classic "American Indian." As a nation, Mexico claims to be color-blind, but on the street they call dark-skinned folks *negro* or *negra*, belying the idea that no one notices.

Playas Primaverales catered to the modest-income set. Sunday was the day because, contrary to U.S. stereotypes, the average Mexican worked a six-day week—often in ten- to twelve-hour shifts. Those who didn't pull long shifts generally had second jobs. Young accountant or schoolteacher by day, taximan by night, was a common pattern.

Early arrival on the beach allowed a fortunate few to stake out the palm-thatched palapas and narrow, shaded area under the densest stand of palm trees. I paid fifty pesos a week for the privilege of hanging my hammock and using the bathroom, but was expected to vacate the palapa when a holiday family claimed it.

That first Sunday it was claimed about 9 A.M. as I swung idly, facing the reality that I was dry, roasting, and tormented by sand flies already too numerous for further sleep. Dad was about forty, heavyset, and wore the standard cheap, black trousers. Cuffs rolled high, shoes and socks removed, his outfit was topped off by a Hawaiian-style straw hat and a pink, fraying, polyester shirt. He had a pleasant, jolly demeanor. He shook hands and asked me politely if the bartender was correct, that my palapa might become available.

I assured him that it was his for the asking and began to unhook my hammock. I wished him a pleasant time, shook hands as I departed, and carried my night gear to the trunk of the Rambler. In the bar area, I bought an Orange Crush and surreptitiously watched his family.

They dug into their colorful, woven nylon shopping bag, typical of the ones in which people of that class in Mexico almost always carried their belongings: bags that were reused till the handles fell off. They spread out an old army blanket on the sand. Many local men had served in the military, either in the United States' Korean campaign or in Mexico, or both. It was one avenue of upward mobility for poor folks.

Once spread, the blanket was anchored by two blue-and-white net bags, containing the day's supply of food and kids' toys, among them an inexpensive paper checkerboard. Most folks, like this family, did not buy genuine checker sets. Rather they used "red" and "black" bottle caps from sodas.

My palapa family was only thirty feet from me, the kids giggling and flipping coins to see who would play Dad the first game of checkers. One son won first go. As they took up the game, Mom ordered the others to get two cold sodas from a barman working the beach. Kids always shared sodas, not without squawking and screaming, of course. So Manuel and the others in establishments like Primaverales always sent out two or three straws, *popotes*, with one soda when kids would come to purchase them.

Feeling hungry, I bought tacos from the Primaverales "taco lady." She was heavyset, playful, late thirties, and had one bad eye. Behind her back some called her "La Tuerta" (the one-eyed woman). She was there every weekend with her daughter, then seventeen. Sunday was taco day at Primaverales and the taco vendors all carried their big metal buckets of speckled blue enamel, hawking to the crowd. The "taco lady" had started selling tacos there with her mother, some twenty-five years before, and was readying her own daughter to take her place.

My palapa family had brought their own food in a three-tiered metal set of bowls that clamped together with a big wire handle. These were as typical of the working families as their net bags. One of the stacked pots held the corn tortillas; the second held tamales; and the third, stewed *frijoles* (beans). A separate pail held rice, cooked with peas and carrots. There were dozens of families just like this one scattered along the beach.

At one point my palapa family caught me eyeing their lunch pail. Dad, pointing with open palm to the pail, motioned to me in invitation. Thirty feet away, I smiled and responded with Mexico's gesture of "thank you, but no," which is done by tilting your head slightly in respect as you jerk your hand up to eye level, back of hand toward your benefactor.

One had to be careful with such invitations. Had I nodded "yes," his family would have fed me, even if there was not enough to go around. The generosity of average folks in Guaymas, as in most of Mexico, was mind-boggling.

Watching the palapa family actually made me lonelier, so I turned my attention to a group of young folks nearby. Someone had brought a portable radio. Others nearby asked them to turn it up. So "Mexico." In the States it would be, "Oh, please turn off the radio." At Primaverales it was usually, "Please turn up the radio!" They played local favorites—lively rancheras, cumbias, and standards like "La Llorona," as common at Primaverales in 1970 as were the Beatles on stateside beaches.

People walked up and down the beach, hunted seashells, or napped, their kids screaming and running in every direction. Near the pavilion, young women rented bathing suits. In those days individuals of modest means didn't own such a thing, but for a small fee they could be rented from the concrete dressing stalls. Young men who owned dark boxer underwear often used them as bathing suits, saving the five-peso (forty-cent) rental fee. Little kids of both genders up to about age ten usually splashed around in their underpants. Nobody cared and no one criticized.

In striking contrast to stateside beaches, many adult couples necked and petted, albeit modestly, while their kids napped on the blankets with them. Babies slept on dad's tummy. Girlfriends held each other's hands while they walked, giggling. Adult men wrapped their arms around best buddies, as they sat in the sand and passed a cigarette back and forth between them. The human contact was intense, laughter was common, and generosity ruled. This aspect of Mexican society usually made me very comfortable. But that day it only made me feel detached and withdrawn.

Things looked up temporarily when I saw Marta on the beach, coming from the direction of the Miramar. She was the girl I had hallucinated about in the Ecuadorian clinic and I recognized her instantly because she was wearing the same distinctive, gray-striped blouse that she had worn the year before when she came for a drink at the Hotel Rubi. Dark and slender, this time she had a little boy with her.

"*Buenas tardes* (good afternoon)," she called out in her throaty voice.

"I remember seeing you at the Hotel Rubi," I told her.

"I remember," she said, smiling, "but it's been quite a while."

I told her that I had been in Ecuador and was only recently returned. I wanted to talk more, but she said "*Adios*" and walked on. I watched her go, checking out her sexy legs, and caught her glancing back over her shoulder.

As the afternoon wore on, more single men showed up to drink beer. Then the pavilion itself began to fill up. Several big floor-model fans inside kept the heat from becoming too excruciating. Families with young children drifted off, and the younger teenagers went home by the city bus, which pulled up in front of the pavilion about once every half hour.

Meanwhile those same buses unloaded twenty-year-old guys and their girlfriends in droves. So the night crowd changed. A local band showed up about seven in the evening to play for several hours. The dancing was very lively, music playing and strands of colored lights hanging from the bandstand.

The big dances took place in Primaverales's main pavilion, which was at least two hundred feet long and eighty feet wide. The long side, all glassed, faced the sea. The main room accommodated somewhere between fifty and a hundred tables, easily seating two to four hundred partygoers. On the south end was the men's toilet. A huge, high-walled concrete room, there was nearly always a sea breeze flowing though the large, unglazed window in the south wall. A long, tiled urinal ran for about twenty-five feet along one wall. A row of showers graced the northeast corner.

The seaside wall of the men's room had three toilets with no seats and four old-fashioned porcelain pedestal sinks with single cold-water spigots. Above each one, shaving mirrors were screwed to the wall. Every weekend the men's room was jammed from morning till night with guys shaving, showering, even getting haircuts from friends. In a country where bathroom facilities in working-class homes were stretched to maximum use by large families, facilities like those at Primaverales were heavily used for primping.

By nine thirty or ten on Sunday evening things had pretty well broken up. It was back to work Monday for nearly everyone. A few couples hung on as the crowd thinned, sitting at the inside tables, strolling the beach, or petting in dark

48

corners. The Primaverales crew began the cleanup, sweeping, mopping, and stacking the tables and chairs.

On Sunday night, at the change of weekly shifts, it was traditional for the workers to play the jukebox and enjoy a round of beer on the house. The change of *turno*, or shift, was no small event in Guaymas's resorts and hotels. Typically Manuel and the others would work seven days to two weeks straight, arriving early on a Monday morning and leaving one or two weeks afterward, on a Sunday night. While on their turno, the staff ate, slept, and remained on the premises for the full shift. In other words, when you were on duty, you were ON DUTY.

After everyone else had gone, Manuel and his crew drank their free beer and ate leftover tacos. While cumbias played on the jukebox, the guys would run around dancing with the mops, laughing, twirling handkerchiefs, and wiggling their asses. It was liberating. Later we danced with the taco ladies and women from the restaurant. Since there weren't enough women to go around, we took turns, then danced as pairs of guys, laughing and enjoying an hour or so of tomfoolery. But by eleven o'clock it was over.

49

Like an evening ebb tide, the families, mariachi bands, and gaiety all floated away quietly. Night had already swallowed the last hints of a brilliant sunset and Guaymas prepared for another long, hard workweek.

I was sad to see Sunday night end. The crew left, and I hung my hammock again, dreading the solitude. Monday mornings were a letdown, a drag.

That Monday morning I went back to sleep after the first bustle of activity—a fresh crew raking the sand and collecting trash from in front of the pavilion.

The second time I awoke, about ten, it was to the sounds of English being spoken. A rusty Volkswagen bus full of American hippie kids had wandered in from the States. One girl came over, saying she understood that I was an American.

She was about twenty, a child of the sixties. Blonde, she was cute and pleasant, but looked remarkably washed-out compared to the local girls. She wanted to know all about the area. I gave her a quick verbal tour. But, when her group went to eat in the little restaurant next door, I didn't join them.

By the early seventies I was badly out of social sync with my stateside generation. Their idea of a good time was to sit on the floor in a darkened room and smoke pot, while staring blankly at a lava lamp. An occasional "Oh, wow!" or "Far out!" kept the proceedings lively. Not my thing! Instead I took a walk along the beach toward the fancy hotels south of Playas Primaverales.

50

A half-mile walk brought me to the south end of the colony, announced by Bacochibampo Avenue's abrupt left sweep away from the water. Beyond lay a no-man's-land between the colony and the hotels. This open, sandy area, about two hundred yards across, accommodated a large corral where they kept docile little ponies for hire, so vacationers could ride up and down the beach. The ponies were only brought out on weekends. That Monday morning they were already herding them into a big truck as I walked by.

On the other side of the corral there was nothing but an empty parcel of land, bordered by a dune on the bayside. Working-class families, too poor even for Primaverales, often partied there long into the night. Beyond was the Hotel Miramar's high stone wall with iron grillwork along the top.

Although the wall of the Hotel Miramar stopped short

of the sand and could easily be circumvented to get into the hotel grounds, the poorer, working-class Mexicans didn't cross that barrier. No signs or rent-a-cops were needed. The hotel was simply off-limits. Working-class people didn't belong there, couldn't afford anything that was sold there, and except for those that worked there, weren't found there.

But I was not among the excluded, so that Monday morning I walked along the sand to the front of the Miramar restaurant. I wanted to talk to Negro Jacinto, but he wasn't around. I was still depressed and smarting over the mess with Iliana. The Primaverales "magic" hadn't yet kicked in.

After lunch I worked my way back up the beach, slowed by July's staggering heat. When I reached Primaverales, a small crowd of locals had gathered around a large handmade skiff piloted by five Seri men. They had pulled into the estuary and tied up at the footbridge near the restaurant. Most folks at Primaverales had never seen a genuine Seri Indian up close. The Seri were legendary, elusive, and feared. This group had come down the coast "to trade"! A once-in-a-lifetime opportunity for most in the crowd. And for me.

The crew were all full bloods, descendants of Sonora's ancient coastal inhabitants. Few in numbers, these seafarers and desert foragers ranged along the Sonoran coast from Puerto Libertad in the north to Punta Baja, south of Kino Bay, about seventy miles north of Guaymas. Their largest settlement was at Desemboque, about 150 miles up the coast.

By 1970 they rarely came down to Guaymas, even though their ancestors had likely created the beach where we stood. They had aboriginal fishing rights to hunt the Sea of Cortés's huge, threatened sea turtles, locally called *cahuamas*. They took them on the open water, using specialized handmade harpoons. Ever the anthropologist, I went over to inspect their boat.

They were in the process of unloading a giant sea turtle, just purchased by the restaurant. It had been harpooned with a hand-forged tip designed to catch in the shell, but not penetrate deeply. The harpoon hole had been plugged with moss, leaving this two-hundred-pound giant cahuama very much alive.

It took four men to carry it into the restaurant's cooled storeroom. There it was flipped on its back, its immense flappers slowly undulating, to be covered with moss and wet seawater-soaked burlap. They piled blocks of ice over it, to put it in a torpor, and the proprietor immediately took out a newspaper ad. The Saturday to come was going to feature stewed cahuama, an unbelievable delicacy.

While they carried the turtle, I traded two packs of my precious American Pall Malls, a twenty-peso note, and small Buck pocket knife to the headman for several gorgeous items they had skillfully carved from rock-hard desert ironwood. The headman wore a Panama hat over his colored headband. Dark-skinned and lean, with ropy muscles, these long-haired fellows were as tough as the ironwood they traded.

Later, as the Seris pulled the skiff away, I felt sad. The Seri people had given both the Mexican army and Mexico's professional Indian hunters the finger so many times that they had finally earned respect, if not awe, among Spanish-speaking Sonorans. They had paid an enormous price in blood for that freedom. But by the early seventies, it was finally theirs. All six hundred of them.

I walked to the front of the pavilion and waited on the beach, watching their boat pass the rocky islands that stood sentinel duty out in the bay. The sea lions splashed and barked in salute as the skiff passed their rookery. As the Seri headed back to their one small, remaining coastal toehold of existence, north of Kino Bay, I felt I was witnessing the passing of two ancient ways of life—those of the Seris and of the once-numerous green sea turtles they had hunted for thousands of years.

After a week, uncomfortable and unhappy, it seemed as if the old Primaverales magic had vanished. Worse yet, intense summer heat gripped the beach, and I woke up each morning completely dehydrated and bathed in sweat. I was shaky, had no appetite, and wasn't gaining back the weight lost in Ecuador.

I had only the equivalent of thirty dollars left and was buying one meal of beans and rice a day. My two-hundred-dollar cashier's check from Albuquerque was still waiting to clear at the Banco de Comercio. I resented the delays, especially since I had spent days hunting down the head of the tourist bureau to countersign the check. Too poor to eat at the Colmenar and get a shoeshine, I stayed on at Primaverales, anticipating the big cahuama feed on Saturday night.

One evening I walked back to the trailer camp by the mangrove lagoon and talked to an American fellow named Edward Meyers, who I had first met the year before at Christmas, just before I left for Ecuador. He was living in his truck—an honest-to-God converted refrigerated grocery truck. Inside were a sleeper couch, table, folding chairs, propane cookstove, and a small gasoline generator to run the lights, toaster, and radio. Some cases of food, luggage, and fishing gear were stuffed haphazardly into the corners.

Edward was in his late forties, with the start of a beer gut, tired puffy eyes, and unkempt gray hair. In fact everything about him seemed disheveled and gray—his work pants, his open-collared shirts, even the bags under his eyes, which perfectly matched the ash that fell from his cigarette. In a country where both the landscape and its people came in rich shades of brown and umber, Edward stood out like a sore thumb.

He was a loner and depressed. His wife had died quickly of liver cancer the year before and his kids were gone, making families of their own. He owned a string of laundromats in the Los Angeles area, operated by an efficient manager. Nobody needed him. So he had drifted south in his truck, bringing his grief and loneliness with him.

He once had been a nice-looking man but was now on the decline, depressed and hitting the rum and Coca-Cola too hard in the solitude of his truck.

54

As we talked, he confided that he really wanted to get married again. He had it in his head that somehow or another he wanted to find a local woman who might be interested in marrying him. He spoke just a bit of broken Spanish, but he understood more than he could speak. As we sipped rum and Cokes in the evening heat, I asked him how he thought he'd find a woman by drinking in the back of his truck every day.

He answered plaintively, "Well you know the local people, and you know the town. Could you find me a wife?" I wasn't expecting this. For a moment we were both so quiet that we could hear mullet splashing in the mangroves, sixty feet away.

Finally I said, "Oh gee, I don't know. I'm no matchmaker or anything like that!" He said, "Well, I'd pay you." I said, "Oh yeah, come on. I don't know about that sort of thing."

So we dropped the subject. It made me nervous. Hell, I was as alone as he was, and his desperation made me uneasy.

Later Manuel came over from the bar at Primaverales with some ice, and we made fresh rum and Cokes, ate some smoked mullet and olives, got mellow, and talked. The conversation turned to "loneliness." Manuel got lonely on his long turnos, missing his family. Surprisingly, it cheered Edward up. The poor bastard needed to talk it out. Actually, I felt better, too. I was glad Manuel wasn't due to go home. He, like Negro Jacinto, had always been kind to me. He had a great sense of humor, and at Primaverales played the role of Zorba the Greek—making life enjoyable. Heck, he even looked like Anthony Quinn.

I drifted away when it had cooled down enough to sleep, Edward and Manuel still soaking up rum. As I swung in my hammock, I thought about Manuel, Negro, Jesse, the taco lady, and Mateo, the taximan. All had their roles in Mexico. Those roles were theirs. They took pride in them and derived a strong sense of identity from them.

55

One of the great revelations of my life was that by stateside standards these people had nothing. In the States, we would probably judge them to be "nobodies."

But the taco lady wasn't nobody; she was somebody. And when you had eaten one of her tacos, you knew it had been made with pride. I came from a world where many ordinary folks were nearly invisible. Guaymas was already beginning to teach me special respect for those who had mastered the ordinary.

The following Sunday, still in a funk, I packed my gear and looked for a cheap place to stay in town. I told myself that it had gotten too hot for me on the beach, but the truth was that each day when I went into the little restaurant where I'd met Iliana, the overwhelming sense of my failure returned. She should have been there, touching me gently, and smiling her secret smile when she brought my coffee. If only I hadn't gone to Ecuador!

It was time to go. Primaverales was no longer my magical haven. It had become just another place, haunted by the past.

four

TWO HOTELS

I drove the mile and a half into town and down the seawall and on to Guaymas's main street, Avenida Serdán. About six or seven blocks short of the Rubi and across the street from the restaurant called the Copa de Leche, stood an imposing two-story, white colonial-style building. I had passed it often while walking "uptown" from the Hotel Rubi.

Later I heard that it had been the *cuartel*, or barracks, used to house Maximilian's troops during the 1860s, when Guaymas was controlled by pirates and the emperor was making his bid to bring the Hapsburg Empire to Mexico. Subsequently it had housed federal troops during the last, but bloodiest, Yaqui Indian uprising in the late 1920s.

Now it had become a sailor's boardinghouse, a *pensión* of the cheapest variety, called the Casa Blanca. To describe the property as "well-used" would be a monumental understatement.

Architecturally, the Casa Blanca was gorgeous. Its facade was dominated by rows of huge, arched French windows with elaborate lintels and by small balconies on the second floor. Downstairs the wide, arched doorway was perfectly centered. At one end of the facade, an immense arched carriageway opened to the interior at street level, where cavalry and carriages had once come and gone.

The courtyard, half a city block square, had apparently once functioned as both a carriage yard and a corral. More recently, its back walls had had rooms built against it, probably servant's rooms, but the right side wall had no additions. To the left stood the cuartel itself.

Nearly every time I passed, one of its pair of huge wooden doors was opened partway and guarded by the oddest couple I had ever seen. The man was a sleek, effeminate mulatto with short-cropped hair and one gold earring. He sat in the doorway for hours on end, perched on a folding wooden chair, watching the world go by. I never once saw him wear anything other than black pants and a dirty white undershirt.

His partner always stood in the doorway, arms folded. She was a fat black woman with shocking red hair and matching lips painted on. She always wore the same bright pink muumuu with big, white amoeba-shaped prints all over it. Her ensemble was finished off with long, dangly golden earrings and pink rubber flip-flops. Personal hygiene was not a priority for either.

But I was down to about twenty-five dollars, so I stopped there anyway. I drove the Rambler to the courtyard door and asked "How much for a room by the night?"

Undershirt answered in a wispy falsetto, "Ten pesos." That's eighty cents. So I said, "Jeez, I don't know, that seems like a lot of money," and started back to the car. She butted in, offering a room on the waterfront at fifty pesos, four dollars, for a week. Her voice was a husky bark—clearly she should have worn his black pants and T-shirt; he her muumuu.

I accepted with some misgivings, paid for the week, and was led through the courtyard to an open stone stairway that rose up from the huge courtyard to the second story. At the top was another arched doorway to a wide, wooden-floored hall. There were no lights, no electricity, and no running water up there. Hence the price cut. I got a room overlooking the water, facing southwest.

The room itself was large, at least eighteen feet square, and nearly bare. One tall, antique French door with a fan-shaped transom, the glass long gone, opened onto a narrow wooden balcony that overlooked the harbor and the street below. I was warned not to step onto the balcony—it had dry rot and was unsafe.

All that actually separated the window opening from the outside world was wooden grillwork of one-by-two board construction. This rough latticework was, in turn, partly covered by a cheap piece of "curtain" suspended from a wire. The floors were of wide, deeply worn oak planks. In several places you could actually see the light from downstairs through the cracks.

The ceiling was about fourteen feet high, and chunks of cracked stucco hung down. The walls were also of cracked white plaster, now quite yellowed. Just like the window, the "door" was another open wooden lattice, "secured" by only a common hook and eye. There was no electric light in the room.

The only furnishings were a dented brass bed frame covered by a thin, broken-down mattress, stained and mended sheets, and a small sweat-soaked pillow. A large, homemade double-tiered table stood next to the bed. On it were a pitcher and washbasin, a metal chamber pot, and a ceramic candle-holder. That was it. No closet, no hangers. I asked for a chest of drawers. They brought me two orange crates.

There were perhaps fifteen rooms along the hallway facing the harbor. Near the head of the outside stairway were the only bathroom facilities. They consisted of a small, open room where a thin layer of concrete, reinforced with chicken wire, had been poured over the original plank floor. In the room's center an open skylight, its glass also long since broken out, lit up the large drainpipe set in the center of the floor. This was the toilet. One simply stood or squatted in the middle of the room and peed or pooped into the drain-pipe.

The resident population of flies was impressive. Once a day an odd semidwarf who did chores came in with a bucket of water and a scraper to shove whatever was on the edges of that drainpipe down it, then he "flushed" it with the bucket of water.

After arranging some of my belongings, I went down and walked to the Rambler to check the trunk. Enrique Velarde happened by on his way to work at the Rubi, and said, "*¡Por Dios!* I didn't see you coming out of the Casa Blanca, did I?"

I answered, "Yes! I need a cheap place to stay. My money's almost gone and I can't get the cash, *efectivo*, from my cashier's check." I told him I was about to put my Rambler inside the courtyard.

He said, "That's a dangerous place. You shouldn't be stay-ing there at all." I shot back, "*¡Mierda!* I already paid for a week." He looked shocked. "Well, at least don't put your car there and don't leave anything valuable in your room. You're crazy. I'm not kidding you—this is a weird place."

Enrique was such a straight shooter that I took him seriously. So I said, "Well, what the hell am I supposed to do? I'm nearly broke." He said, "Look, at least bring your car up to the Hotel Rubi. We'll park by the door of the public bar, across from the stone *bodegas*, warehouses. Canelo and I will ask the shoeshine boys to watch it. I'll tell the patrón, Hector Morales, that the car is there. Lock your valuables in the trunk. Tomorrow we'll work something out to store your belongings, but don't put the car in here." I said, "Okay." So I drove on down to the Hotel Rubi and parked the car around the side.

On my way back to the Casa Blanca I got a couple of hot dogs from the cart next to the Chapúltepec Pavilion; next I bought two candles, matches, and a pack of cheap Delicado cigarettes from a small shop next to the pavilion. Then, because I remembered there was no electricity at the pensión, I wandered back to the Rambler to retrieve my flashlight.

Even though I had avoided the afternoon sun, I still felt queasy and pasty. God, it was hot! The afternoons in town were 40–41 degrees centigrade, 104–106 degrees Fahrenheit! Of course the late afternoon sun would be pouring into the huge window of my new room, so I walked up to the Colmenar restaurant and ordered a bowl of soup, the cheapest thing on the menu.

I hadn't seen Mercedes for a while. Pleasant, young and sociable, she cheered me up. I shot the breeze with her, dreading my return to the Casa Blanca, but had to decline a shine from little Juanito, who shuffled off, disappointed.

It was after dark when I worked up the courage to return, hoping that it had cooled down inside. I walked past the odd couple at their post by the main door and went upstairs. No luck. The upstairs hall was stifling and stank. Enrique was right, the whole scene was strange. Spooky.

Guided by my flashlight, I went in, "locked" my door grate, lit a candle, and put several bottles of 7-Up on the table where I could see them. I thought the lukewarm 7-Up would settle my stomach in the night. I opened the curtains facing the street for light and air, then went to bed. God, it was hot! I lay there drenched in sweat. The whole place smelled of sweat and urine. Not a breath of air stirred from the harbor. What a Sunday night!

Worse than the physical misery, I was lonely. And it was precisely the kind of gut-wrenching loneliness I had come to Mexico to escape. I had wanted it to work out with Iliana. Why couldn't it have been my baby inside her? And why couldn't I even make myself go back to Empalme and see Lisa? For three weeks I'd mostly been watching the world around me again— not actually living in it. What the hell was the matter with me, anyway? I fell asleep still grasping for answers.

Later in the night, I half-awakened to the sounds of an ugly brawl up the hallway. A male voice shouted, "*¡pinche joto!*" (fucking queer!) at someone. Joto answered, threatening to cut off his tormentor's *monda* (sailor's slang for penis). Idiots! Probably drunken sailors from a freighter moored out in the outer harbor. Wooden cage doors slammed. People came and went all through the night. Occasionally the light from a flashlight or a candle would flicker past my grate.

It was a surrealistic experience. The hot night was punctuated again and again by cursing, screaming, and the sounds of pushing and shoving out in the hall. I was frightened, but too worn out to get up. So I just hugged the bed, sipped warm

7-Up and figured, what the hell. The hallway conflicts weren't my immediate problem, so I tried to drift off to sleep.

I woke up for good early in the morning, still bathed in sweat, dehydrated, throat parched, and shaky. Soon I realized that I was actually shivering cold, so must have some kind of fever. I got out of bed to take off my clothes—in those days I slept mostly in pants and T-shirt.

I wanted to find water someplace to take a sponge bath and clean up. As I stripped off my soggy clothes I discovered I had been eaten alive by bedbugs! You can always tell when it's bedbugs; I had huge welts all around the waistband and legs of my jockey shorts and along the T-shirt's seam lines under my arms.

Bedbugs always go for meat close to the seams. If you've got an elastic band on, or a seam, or a pair of socks, they'll go for the edge of the socks, the band of the underwear, or the band in your pajamas.

I was covered with huge, raw bedbug welts and felt like shit. Dizzy, I managed to get out of bed and stagger to the window. I shouted down at Undershirt, the doorman, sitting below on the sidewalk. I told him I needed a big bottle of purified water for the room, since I wasn't feeling well.

Instead the dwarf brought me up a big pitcher of water and filled my washbasin. It probably came from a tap someplace downstairs in the courtyard. At least I hoped it was city water. So I gave myself a sponge bath, put alcohol from my medicine kit on the worst of the bedbug welts, and drank a couple of quarts of the clean-tasting water the dwarf brought in a big crock on his second trip to my room.

I paid a few pesos for the services, then went back to bed. I felt like hell, but in spite of the heat, fell into a fevered sleep that lasted all through that day and right through most of the evening. Later that second night I grabbed my flashlight, got up, and went across the hall to pee. It hurt, and my urine was tinged with blood. I thought, "Oh shit, what's the matter with me?" Still feverish, I staggered back to bed and slept fitfully, bathed in sweat.

My God, it was stifling! The running feet, bumps, shouts, and intermittent flashes of light out in the hall kept waking me. I seized several of those opportunities to flip on my flashlight and nail the bedbugs going at the band of my underpants by slapping them with a wet bar of soap I kept on the bedside table. I'd catch a bunch of them on the sticky bar, then snap off the flashlight and roll over again.

Late in the night someone who'd been drinking barfed all over the hallway, right outside my door. I could hear the puke splattering against the wall by my grate. God, it was awful, and I retched for a long while before falling asleep, exhausted.

Next morning I got up, inspected the dark specks of foul-smelling bedbug carnage on the cake of soap, smiled to myself, managed to get dressed, then went downstairs and out. I walked only a few doors before nearly fainting. After resting, I made it to a nearby restaurant, the Copa de Leche, which had air conditioning, and sat there dazed, drinking a cold soda.

Though shaking badly, I tried to think what to do. I asked the waitress if there was a clinic, a doctor nearby, since I was feeling sick. She told me that Clínica Sánchez was good and nearby—in the narrow street just behind the Pasaje Marví, where the Colmenar Restaurant was located.

I was in a daze, feeling bad and frightened. When I had

awakened that morning there was not only blood in my underpants, there was pus. Again I thought, "Lord, what have I got? Have I got gonorrhea?" So I left the restaurant, walked up the street to the Pasaje Marví, and passing the Colmenar, walked through it until I exited at the rear. There I ran smack into the clinic.

It was a clean, private clinic. Dr. Sánchez came out fairly quickly. They took some smears of discharge from my penis. Embarrassing! I was having a lot of pain in my back. I asked him if I had gonorrhea. He said it was possible, but he thought it more likely that I had a kidney infection. My temperature was running about 103°. So he gave me antibiotics and told me to come back in twenty-four hours. They expected to culture the slides and make a diagnosis by then.

I took the medicine, walked slowly back to the Casa Blanca, and went to bed again, feeling like shit. I was up and down a half dozen times again that night. I had to pee blood a couple of times. I was depressed, I was frightened, I was nearly broke.

I thought, "Damn! Coming here had been as dumb as sleeping on the beach in the summer heat. This is a low point in my life. This place is beyond awful." Guys would piss in the hallways and soak those big wooden flooring planks, and as the day wore on and the building heated up, it smelled powerfully of piss and puke and diarrhea. I really didn't know what the hell I was doing there. All this to escape the relentless sun out on the beach.

The next day I went back, but was even weaker. It took me a long time to walk the eight blocks up to the clinic. They had done the smears. It was not gonorrhea, but a raging kidney infection. It could have been from anything and

65

everything, including not drinking enough water. Dr. Sánchez hit me with penicillin, the super stuff imported from Germany.

I bent over the table as he shot my ass full of that stuff. Wow! I nearly fainted. The sweat just came right out on me as I reacted to the antibiotic. They helped me onto a cot. I must have been there an hour or more before I recovered enough to pay him and dress to leave.

Sánchez was the only doctor in town listed as "recommended" by the American Medical Association. Americans were usually directed to him. His bill for the shot and treatment took most of the money I had left.

On the way back to Casa Blanca I picked up another bottle of water. I undressed, treated the bug bites with ointment Sánchez had given me, and went back to bed. By late that night the fever had broken. I woke up soaked in sweat, but was beginning to feel better.

66

The next morning I went to the Colmenar, ordered a café con leche, and sadly pictured little Lisa bringing me coffee. Then I bought a cheap bowl of soup and felt better as the flush of heat and energy from the food worked through me like a double shot of tequila. The walk back to the Casa Blanca was suddenly easy.

Thursday. Time to visit the Hotel Rubi and see if my money had come. I had just closed the grate to my room when Enrique Velarde came up the stairs. He clapped me on the shoulder, said he heard I'd been sick and had gone to Sánchez's clinic.

He told me that the Hotel Rubi's staff were distressed, that the patrón himself, señor Morales, didn't want me staying at Casa Blanca. It wasn't an appropriate place, and I was enough of a friend of the house that I should come back and stay at the Rubi. I said, "Enrique, I am broke. Has my money come in?" He said, "No, no money has come."

But he insisted, "Look, the patrón is going to give you credit. He is going to give you a monthly rate on a room. You must come back to the Rubi. I've come to take you back with me. I've got a taxi outside. We're going to the Hotel Rubi. That's all there is to it. *¡Ya está hecho!* (It is done!)" Man, was I grateful. I was never so glad to get out of a place in my life. If there was a hell on earth, the Casa Blanca was its front door.

Enrique helped me gather my gear and carried the spare bottle of water. He took me downstairs to the taxi. The driver was Mateo, from the Sitio Rubi (taxi stand). It was old home week.

Enrique ushered me into the lobby. The patrón himself met us at the front desk. A short, abrupt man, he had only spoken to me briefly before—*"buenas tardes,"* a nod, and no more. Now he was giving me, "Davíd, *está en su casa* (This is your home). Let us pick you a room." The people at the desk were nice. The sweet-faced lady seemed genuinely glad to see me. Several American hotel guests gawked. I must have looked like shit.

I had spent money at the Rubi. I'd talked to virtually everyone who worked there. I'd invested time, courtesy, and small favors, because people there were warm and likable. Folks like these had drawn me back to Mexico. I admired the human dimension there. Now I realize they had understood that.

Then my luck had turned bad. I was broke, sick, hungry, sexually disgraced. Had I been in the States, it could easily have become a free fall into oblivion. But in Mexico suffering, pain, sorrow, and sacrifice are sacraments of the human condition.

The mangled shoulder, Iliana, the beach, and Casa Blanca had all humanized me in local eyes. In the States, these misfortunes would have had the opposite effect. I didn't yet understand all this as I stood shakily at the Rubi's front desk that day. I was simply overwhelmed with gratitude.

They took me right through the back of the lobby to the hotel's original gallery of rooms, which opened onto a long, narrow glass-roofed courtyard, two stories tall. Well-tended banana plants and bougainvillea grew in profusion, set off by red tile walks on either side. There were no air-conditioned rooms on the ground floor, but I had a fan. They offered me the last room on the left, at the very rear of the narrow, leafy conservatory.

It formed the cooler north end of the hotel. Señor Morales didn't escort me to the room himself, but Enrique and the deskman took me back, indicating that this was the room the patrón had picked. Since there was no air conditioning, this whole room block was only lightly used in the summer.

Being on an outside corner of the hotel, there was the bustle of street life around room 21, and it had two sets of windows, one to the northwest and one to the north. The west window meant no morning sun; the north window meant cool shade. The north window faced the street behind the Hotel Rubi and yielded a lovely view of several massive colonial-style houses.

In fact, everything about it was lovely. It had a double bed with headboard, a writing table and chair, a nightstand and lamp. The room was about fourteen feet square, with its own bathroom. The floors of the whole suite were red tile. The bathroom walls and shower were tiled floor to ceiling in a colonial white-and-blue pattern. The atmosphere was bright and cheerful. I was completely overwhelmed by the smell of clean sheets and fresh towels. Thus began a new phase of my life in Guaymas.

I tried to set up a few of my things. Mateo and Enrique helped. But the exertion got to me quickly. They noticed almost immediately that I was still weak and shaky. Someone's sister was a nurse, so they sent for her to come and check me out.

Meanwhile Mateo had another fare, so Enrique and a couple of the bellhops brought in the heavy stuff from the trunk of my Rambler, which sat parked at the other side of the hotel. My dad's olive drab WWII army footlocker was packed with my anthropology books, equipment, and some spare clothing. Seeing the trunk reminded me that he had been dead almost exactly three years.

It also reminded me that I had not seen my twin brother, John, since the funeral. In 1965 he had visited me in Mexico City. He spent Christmas, and we celebrated our twenty-first birthday together in Veracruz. He was a genius at higher math, but languages were not his forte.

No matter how many times I corrected him, he started every conversation with *"No bablo español,"* pronouncing the "h" with a huge grin. It didn't matter—he was bubbly and simpático, so he somehow managed to communicate the basics.

We rented the ballroom of the Hotel Emporio, right on the waterfront, and threw a dance to celebrate our coming of age. The revelry was joyfully outrageous! I smiled as they put Dad's trunk under the far window that faced the shrimp packing plant, set my electric fan on it, then left me to my new digs.

About an hour later, the nurse arrived. She took my temperature and checked my bites. More ointment got applied to the bedbug welts. She called for a week's supply of antibiotics to kill the kidney infection completely, then got a hotel maid to collect all the clothes that had entered the Casa Blanca. I was sent into the shower and stripped of everything that might have become infested with bedbugs, then scrubbed. The maid put everything in a big canvas sack and sent it out to be boiled.

As I dressed in untainted spares from the footlocker, soup and rolls arrived. To this day I don't know who got the soup or where it came from, but I ate this huge bowl of chicken soup with cilantro and a roll, then was ordered back to bed. I hadn't been taken care of like this since leaving home at eighteen. So "home" became room 21 at the Hotel Rubi. I would live there until I left Guaymas.

I awakened that evening feeling a lot better, so dressed and went down to the Rubi's public bar. Enrique and Jesse were both there. People were nice, even solicitous. Jesse gave me a couple of tacos and several Orange Crushes on the house. For the first time in nearly a month, I had eaten twice in one day.

About five that next morning I woke up convinced that I was having a heart attack. Never before had I experienced such pain in my chest and shoulder. I couldn't breathe. I couldn't move my arm. It was as if there was a sack of rocks on my chest. I was terrified. There was no telephone in my room, so I struggled to get to the doorway and hollered *¡Ayúdeme!* as loud as I could.

A deskman heard me and came. I told him I needed a doctor, so he called Dr. Sánchez from the desk. Thank God it wasn't fat Ramón on duty, the jerk who had nailed me for the extra forty pesos when Eva visited my upstairs room a month earlier.

I staggered back and lay in bed, waiting. No Sánchez! I thought I was dying. I felt guilty, afraid my death would be one thing too much for my mom to handle. The pain was excruciating. Six o'clock, seven o'clock, still no doctor; eight o'clock came and then, exhausted, I either fainted or fell asleep. I'm not sure which.

About 11 A.M. I woke up to pounding at my door and realized that I was still alive and that the pain had passed! The day clerk at the desk had come to check on me. "Do you still want a doctor? Can we take you anywhere?" I said, "Well, the pain has passed, I don't know what to do."

They got the nurse again. This time she checked me fully. She thought it possible that I had suffered a mild coronary from dramatic weight loss compounded by infection, days of sweating, dehydration, and not eating. But she thought it far more likely that I had merely suffered massive indigestion from the combination of eating only once every two or three days, followed by two meals and the antibiotics.

She detected nothing alarming about my pulse, heart-beat, or blood pressure, but urged me to see Sánchez. I promised to see him, but didn't. In Mexico they don't let you out of a private hospital until the bill is paid in full. Getting in to see Sánchez would be easy, but since I was broke, getting out again would be the problem.

I rested for the remainder of that day and evening. Mercifully the chest pains didn't return. I passed the next several days taking it easy and eating only one bowl of soup a day. On Tuesday my luck changed. The sweet-faced lady at the desk came back to the room to tell me my cashiers' check for two hundred dollars had cleared. One of the Banco de Comercio's managers was a relative of señor Morales, the hotel's owner, and had called. I went right over to the bank, about twelve blocks up the Serdán, and collected twenty-five hundred pesos.

Relieved, I returned to the Hotel Rubi and immediately paid that month's rent, the laundry and nurse's bill and put another 1600 pesos ($130) in the hotel safe. From the desk I went to the bar and consulted Jesse about what to do next.

72

He said, "Well, I think we should go to the Banco de Sonora and open an account there for you. That way you will have credit." I didn't know it then, but that simple act was to have a dramatic effect on my future relationships in Guaymas.

five

CARVING A NICHE

Later that day Jesse walked me up Avenida Serdán to the Banco de Sonora, near the Colmenar Restaurant. I was somewhat reluctant to part with the money in my pocket—it meant rice and beans. But Jesse had taken charge, suggesting I open a small savings account with a thousand pesos, eighty dollars.

On the way I again expressed a preference to use either the Banco Nacional or the Banco de Comercio, which had cashed my check. Those banks had better international connections. But Jesse insisted on the Banco de Sonora, explaining that it was a local bank and could more easily establish lines of credit for me with nearby businesses. I was soon to discover that there was also another reason.

We entered the Banco de Sonora about three-thirty, after it had reopened from the midday siesta. In those days businesses in Sonora were open from about nine until one, then reopened from about three-thirty to six or seven in the evening—a custom that has faded as standardized business hours have overtaken much of Mexico.

There were several teller lines and, as one of them came open, I moved toward it. But Jesse nudged me away to another, longer one, staffed by a young fellow who stopped occasionally for drinks at the hotel. We waited in his line until our turn came.

Jesse addressed the teller as *primo*, or cousin. Since this term was used to address both dear friends and true kinsmen, I never knew whether this guy was really Jesse's cousin or a friend. Jesse explained that I wanted to open a savings account, a *cuenta de ahorros*. "*Muy bien* (Fine)," he said. Jesse told him I was a *norteamericano*, living in Guaymas indefinitely, who wanted to establish a small account and add to it later.

The teller asked me to produce my tourist card and another form of international identification. I handed him my card and passport, which I had just retrieved from the Hotel Rubi's safe. There were forms to sign and questionnaires to fill out. He even recorded the serial numbers of the two five-hundred-peso banknotes I deposited to open the account.

Then the teller announced, "I have to, by law in Mexico, record a beneficiary." Without thinking I turned to Jesse and asked, "Jesse, would you serve as *mi beneficiario* (my beneficiary)?" He looked shaken and asked, "Have you no other family?" I said, "Yes, but you're right here. You would see to things if something happened to me."

After a pause he agreed and gave his full name for the record. This is how I learned Jesse's Christian names, privileged information on the street. The poor guy also had to sign other forms, vouch for me, and stand behind my account. As a stranger, I needed someone with an account at the bank to sign for me in order to open my own.

Jesse had known this. In fact I would have had to do this in any of the banks in town, as part of an old-fashioned system where one customer signed for another. Usually it was a family member or close business associate who did this, so it added a dimension of closeness to our relationship when I suggested he be my beneficiary.

When it came time for Jesse to sign the card, he shooed me away as he and the teller huddled secretively. That made me nervous, but I noted, with relief, that my card was perfectly filled out when the teller handed it back. It occurred to me that Jesse might not know how to read and write. A bit later he talked about his lack of "schooling," but I never knew the facts—and still don't.

When we finished, I suggested, "Let's stop at the Colmenar and have a cup of coffee; say hello to Max and Mercedes." Jesse knew Max; he did not know Mercedes. As we walked he whipped out the comb he always kept in his shirt pocket and touched up his James Dean. He always did this to regain his "cool." Had he been born in the States, he'd probably have ended up as an agent for someone like Brubeck.

At the Colmenar we sipped our cafés con leche and exchanged pleasantries with Max. Juanito appeared and I got another knockout ten-peso shine. Then Max shooed Juanito away so we could talk. Jesse was upbeat, ebullient, commenting that I had made him my beneficiary at the bank. My account was just eighty dollars, a thousand pesos, but everyone knew (and knew that I knew) that people had been killed in Mexico for less.

At the time, that amount was about a month's wages for field hands and unskilled labor. But I had no sense that anyone I knew in Guaymas was shifty, dangerous, or ominous. I was actually safer in Guaymas than in most American cities of similar size, but money matters equaled "trust," and in Mexican society trust made an impression.

Max warmed up then. Jesse explained to him, "Oh, we had this trouble with the money and Davíd stayed at the Casa Blanca for a while and didn't eat." Max responded, "But Davíd, my friend, why didn't you say so, you could have signed for your month's food, paid what you owed, and started another month's account." I responded, "Oh, I hadn't known that, or I would have asked."

Right then and there Max took out a sheet of paper and said, "Sign at the bottom and I'll keep your tab for the month. Whenever you eat, just sign for each meal. All you need is your signature, and each month you can pay me. Nothing to it!"

What a breakthrough! I was being offered credit and, as a bonus, became one more small connection in the millions of person-to-person relationships that make Mexico, Mexico. Jesse nudged me to go ahead and sign. This feeling was wonderful! No more lying awake at night with that tight, nauseating ache in my belly from eating once every second or third day! No more shaking when I tried to light a smoke. Max went away smiling as I said, "Bring us another round of coffee."

Then Jesse looked at me out of the corner of his eye and asked, "¿*Viste?* (Did you see?)" I answered, "What?" He said, "*Ya sabes* (You know)." I said "No, what?" He said, "*La firma* (the signature)." So I asked, "No. Is there something wrong? Did I do something wrong at the bank?" He said, "Oh, no!"

and was quiet for a minute, then looked up with a big smile and said, mostly in English, "As your *beneficiario* I think I should tell you that you're full of bullshit. In the bank I was slow with the documents, and you saw."

He continued, "I was born in the village of El Fuerte. My mother's family, the Gradillas, were decent people but poor, you know? I had light skin and reddish hair, *canelo*. That's how I got my street name. I was just a boy, you know, when I went over to the 'other side.' I went to California. I thought I'd make it big. But I didn't pay enough attention to schools, all that stuff.

"I made money on Catalina working the tourist boats, but after a lot of years and a lot of girlfriends, I didn't have much. I was still doing the same work as when I arrived as a boy. So I saved a few thousand pesos and came back to Mexico, to Guaymas. I got a little house, a wife, and work as a bartender. I learned American drinks on the other side."

Max and Mercedes were off in another corner of the Colmenar, noticing that Jesse was speaking in English, which was quite unusual, but not prying. Then Jesse whispered, "But you don't tell anybody. I don't read and write so good. It's hard for me, and I'm too old to learn. Especially you don't tell Negro!" Surprised, I blurted out, "You mean Negro Jacinto? But he's your friend." He said, "No, no, *el otro* (the other one), Negro Morales, patrón of the Hotel Rubi."

I said, "Oh, no. It doesn't matter to me. It's of no consequence at all. It's not my business." He was nervous, a little sheepish. In a minute I said, "After all, I can't make drinks. What the hell, we all have things we do well and other things we don't do so well." As he pulled out the comb, Jesse smiled and said, "Okay."

Later I reflected on this conversation. Here was this guy, each day squaring up accounts in the bar with the owner of the hotel, ordering fairly large quantities of liquor, tallying bar tabs, and relying more on memory than on book learning. Can you imagine what kind of memory skills Jesse must have had to conduct his ordinary business and maintain this facade?

I had seen him a number of times in the Hotel Rubi, standing there at the bar when there was no business, "reading the newspaper." Maybe he could read it, but some of it must have been a show. I had even seen him reading Duffy's Bartender's Guide, "looking up" drinks that tourists requested in the bar.

After coffee, we went back to the Hotel Rubi and Jesse opened up the bar. He said, "You know, you need to make some money. You can't just sit here and spend money in Guaymas." I said, "Yeah, I know. I've been thinking about that, but I don't know what to do about it. I don't have working papers."

He said, "Well, you need to go to the border and bring back things to sell here." I said, "Wow! What do you mean?" He said, "Well, contraband." Every day in the Guaymas newspapers they were talking about *contrabandistas* (smugglers). I said, "*¡Mierda!* Jesse, I'm no renegade." He said, "No, no! Not drugs. Not guns. Nothing like that—fans, blenders, radios, calculators, canned milk for mothers. People need those things here. It would be a *service*. Here we call that *fayuca*."

I said, "You're kidding!" He said, "Oh, no! You think about it. You got a little bit of *plata* (money). You say you have more money coming from the other side. You should go to the *frontera*. Cross over to Tucson and buy some things at good discount stores, come back and sell them here in Guaymas. Make a little money. Have a little *negocio* (business)."

I said, "Well, how in the hell would I get past the customs people and the federales up there?" He said, "I don't know, let me think about that. There are ways. You can pay, you know." I said, "Well, federales scare me." "*¡Claro!* (Of course!)" he said, and quickly changed the subject to talk about a new floor show at one of the local "nightclubs" in the *zona*, the red-light district.

Later I walked up the Serdán to the Colmenar and tried out my brand new credit on a dinner of *camarones borrachos*, shrimp marinated in beer and garlic. Fruit salad on the side. Wonderful!

I chatted with Mercedes. She was always personable. And attractive. The nice eyes and big smile added considerably to my visits at the Colmenar. Max had already gone home. I signed for the meal. No problem. The formality of my original signature for Max had been just that, a formality, but an important one in Mexico. It felt very good to have a restaurant credit and money in the bank.

Feeling stronger, I took a turn around town. I walked up and down the *malecón*, the harbor's seawall promenade, listening to the water and enjoying the sounds and smells of Guaymas. I felt better and I had a little money. I was grateful to have a relationship with Jesse and a friend like Enrique Velarde.

About eleven that night, I treated myself to a *malteada* (malt) in the Copa de Leche. They put an egg in it for me. Strength food! I took it upstairs to the roof, which overlooked the harbor and was furnished with tables and comfortable chairs. It was lively, couples chatting and necking.

Guaymas was a gorgeous port. The harbor was picturesque, the shrimp boats bobbing slowly at their moorings and the lights rippling in the water. It was hot, but the breeze on the roof was refreshing. The nearby mountains, backlit by moonlight, looked like black paper cutouts.

The harbor's promenade, with its patterned tile walkway, runs about a thousand feet along Avenida Serdán before angling away from downtown. Every hundred feet or so, old-fashioned streetlights jut up from the tiled balustrade along the waterfront. A row of large rocks protects the malecón, disappearing into the oil-stained water. The harbor itself is protected by a long outer peninsula, so dramatic tidal surges are rare, unless there is a hurricane.

I was in a good mood that night. A few good meals had rebuilt my strength and chased away some of my depression. If you have never suffered chronic hunger, it is easy to underestimate its effects. For the first few days your belly rumbles and you're shaky. Later you get tired, so tired that you become numb. Then you can't think. Finally you get depressed and quit caring.

After the malt, I wandered back to the Rubi's bar. Still leery of alcohol, I settled for an Orange Crush. Eva was there. We talked and laughed as I danced a wobbly cumbia with her, trying to get my land legs again. Afterward I ambled through the long, dark hallway to the lobby, back to room 21, and got ready for bed. After showering and dressing, I turned on my little fan, hung a wet towel over it, and put an ice-cold soda on the table next to me., Then I thought about the border, Jesse's contraband negocio, and my fear of federales.

My new room was cheerful, clean, and safe. The glass-roofed garden outside its doorway offered a soothing haven.

After Ecuador and the last few weeks, both my mind and body had badly needed this. Still, I couldn't break the habit of washing, dressing fully, and sleeping on top of the bedcovers, ready to step into my Red Wing boots and slip out a door or window on a moment's notice.

I'd actually had to do that a number of times during nearly seven years of sleeping in hammocks, graveyards, and two-dollar hotel rooms in places with names most Americans could neither have pronounced nor imagined.

My memories drifted back to 1965. That winter I had gone down to Coatzacoalcos, on Mexico's southern gulf coast, to hunt for Olmec ruins. Once there, figurines from an oil camp called Sánchez Magallanes began to show up on the local black market. I went to the camp.

It was an amazing place. Guys walked the dirt streets wearing six-guns, and the "barber shop" consisted of two open-air barber's chairs strategically situated in the middle of a wide, dirt lane. I say strategically, because they gave a great view of proceedings in the local whorehouse, which had been set up in a series of unwalled tents sixty feet away. The girls were much too young for me, and I was just twenty.

On the other side of the street another sprawling unwalled tent housed the bar and billiard parlor. A wooden hotel stood on a low rise about seventy yards from the tents. I headed for the hotel, passing a small detachment of heavily armed federal police (federales) who were patiently lined up at the whorehouse to bang several of the fifteen-year-olds for free.

The fact that they took off their pants while screwing the girls, but not their wool blouses, duty caps, and pistol belts, added enough drama and poignancy to the scene to warm the hearts of law-and-order freaks everywhere. What a show!

In short Peckinpah could have filmed *The Wild Bunch* any afternoon, simply by pointing his cameras at the bar and billiard complex, then turning them across the street to shoot an X-rated film that would have handily outsold *Debbie Does Dallas*. So I rented a second-floor room with a view of the tents. Bad move.

About three in the morning, the door to my room came crashing open. Three drunken federales spilled in, took everything, including my boots, and gave me a beating for good measure. Then they left, laughing. All they missed were the hundred-peso notes I kept in each sock. The liquor must have dulled their efficiency.

By morning my face was purple and swollen. But no shoes was my biggest problem. So I bought a cheap pair of *huaraches* (truck-tire-soled sandals) in the street below and took a series of third-class buses back to Mexico City, dressed only in pants, undershirt, socks, and huaraches.

Back at the University of the Americas, just outside Mexico City, news of my misadventure got around quickly. "Roadmap" Adams, a young expatriate who hung around the campus, took me in hand and showed me the drill.

Rooms with two windows are best. You've got to have a roof or balcony to get out onto if you're not on the ground floor. He even gave me a thin, polished hardwood wedge to drive into the doorjamb of hotel rooms (I still have it). Always get a chamber pot so you're "in" once the door is wedged. Push the bed against the door, if possible. Always dress before bed, boots ready to step into, a small duffel of essentials next to the boots. Include sandals, just in case.

From then until the Casa Blanca I had followed Roadmap's hotel protocol to the letter. His system had saved my ass in Salina Cruz on the southern Pacific Coast of Mexico. Also in "Teguce" (Tegucigalpa), Honduras, and again in Tampíco, Mexico (rough town!). It worked. I didn't need it in gentle, gracious Guaymas, but survival habits die hard. So did my fear of federales.

The next day, Saturday, a letter from home finally reached me at the hotel. I shook as I opened it, fearing yet one more piece of bad news. Instead it contained a five-hundred-dollar check from my mom and assurances that both she and my brother, John, were okay. I said a quiet prayer of thanks.

Mom wasn't flush. A subsidy of that size was a huge sacrifice for her. I was grateful. Now I was in the bucks, but I couldn't cash the check that day. The banks were open only until about lunchtime on Saturday, and the mail had come too late. So I asked señor Morales to put the check in the safe behind the front desk till Monday and decided to go out and have a good time.

I drew a hundred pesos from the safe and walked down the long hall toward the Rubi bar, where Jesse advised me, "You have credit here." Everywhere credit was popping up like magic; people knew that money had arrived. Five hundred bucks—that was more than five months' good wages in Guaymas, at the time.

That night I went across the street to the Chapúltepec pavilion, a huge raftlike dance floor that floated in the harbor. I ordered a Coca Cola and grabbed a small table. The Saturday night band was going full bore. When Enrique came off his shift at the Rubi bar, he walked over to join me. This

83

was the first chance I'd had to really get to know him outside of the bar.

He was a real sweet guy. Early twenties at the time, he was nice-looking, always immaculate, usually sporting a fresh, meticulously pressed white shirt, black pants, and polished dress shoes.

Because he was the one who had come to get me from the Casa Blanca, I "invited" (translates, "I'm buying") Enrique to have Coca Colas or beers and dance. He accepted. As I look back on it, the graciousness of Guaymas folks was simply remarkable. I'd invited Enrique to order anything he wanted, but I was drinking Cokes, so he drank Cokes. It reminded me of high-school dates, when your partner carefully ordered the same thing you did so as neither to offend nor upset the price structure.

84

We had a great time. He knew many of the local girls; he was a "catch," I'll tell you. There were a lot of girls there that were interested, eyeing him and waving. After all, he was clean-cut, single, and had a job. After a couple of cold Cokes, he danced, and I followed suit.

Boy did I dance. I must have danced with twenty different girls—tall or short, skinny or chubby, light or dark, quiet or giggly, it didn't matter. In other words, I danced with every *chica* who said, or nodded, "Yes."

We danced for several hours, lights sparkling and the dance floor rocking in the water to the beat of the music. Every time the pavilion rolled too far, the girls screamed and fell into their partners "by accident." The guys cheered on cue. As I said, it sure beat watching a lava lamp cut slow farts in a darkened room. The music was varied—cumbias, rancheras, and paso dobles, even a few late-fifties jitterbugs.

It was a great scene.

Between dances Enrique talked more about himself. He had a sweetheart, was saving money, and thinking about marrying her in the next year or so. He said she was nice, well-raised, and *seria* (sensible). So I asked, "Aren't you going to get in trouble for being here?" And he said, "Oh, no. Not with you. I'm on good behavior, besides some of these girls are my girlfriend's girlfriends. I can dance a few dances. It's okay."

As the night wore on I tired, the dance still in full swing. We left around midnight, climbed the wooden gangway up to the malecón, and crossed the Serdán to the Rubi. Before walking home, Enrique stopped to say goodnight to the taxistas at the Sitio Rubi.

He had a habit of balancing on the edge of the curb and talking while flexing his heels, his back to the street, rocking back and forth. He smoked filtered Winstons and would take puffs to the rhythm of this rocking. After each puff he'd extend his arm straight down, cigarette in his fingertips, and smartly flick, flick, flick the ashes behind him into the gutter, take another puff, and repeat his characteristic movements, punctuated by a bright, bubbly laugh. Anyone who knew him could spot him two blocks away from this distinctive curbside "cigarette dance."

After he left I was still in an upbeat mood, so stayed to bullshit and pitch coins with the taxistas at the sitio. They lived in their own world, with its proprietary customs. Like other sitios in Mexico, the Rubi's consisted of a call box, a bench, and about seventy-five feet of curb.

Like taxi ranks everywhere, each taxista took his turn. One would take a fare out and then return to the back of the line. The Rubi's day and night cars altogether totaled a dozen cabs. But there were usually no more than four or five drivers on shift at night. All but the most senior drew lots to see who would work shifts of twelve hours, either day or night. The *veteranos* had preferential rights to Saturday evenings and Sundays, the real moneymakers.

The owner of the sitio, the actual taxi stand, held the franchise issued by city hall. About half the Rubi's drivers owned their own cars and paid a percentage to the sitio owner. He maintained the telephone and placed the advertising in the phone book. Others owned a car but no taxi plates, so paid to use someone else's. Young taxistas who owned neither car nor plates shared the day's earnings fifty-fifty, after paying for gas.

Veteran or apprentice, drivers slept on the hoods of their cars during the night, since many also held day jobs. By 3 A.M. you'd find these guys stretched out with a little pillow up against the windshield, their legs dangling over the taxi's hood. Most of the cars were late fifties to early sixties Chevies, Fords, or Plymouths.

I enjoyed the sitios along Avenida Serdán. The taxistas knew almost everything that went on in town; no one's business escaped them. Drawn to the camaraderie and the "action," or *movidas*, of the street, they counted in their ranks some of Guaymas's brightest and most interesting storytellers.

That was the night I "met" Lupita, the itinerant shoeshine girl who hung around Avenida Serdán. I had seen her around the Colmenar a few times. She looked like she was about seven or eight years old, but the taxistas insisted she was about ten—a scrawny, dirty little thing and undersized for her age. When she wasn't around, some of the men would crack jokes about her. They sometimes called her Lupita "la gatita" (the little alley cat). She had an insincere bravado about her that reminded me of the younger reform-school kids I'd once worked with in the States.

Lupita drove the taxistas nuts, constantly seeking attention. She taunted them, swore like the sailors on the waterfront, and tormented them endlessly to buy her *chicles* (chewing gum). Sometimes she made very grown-up comments to the men. But she was just a kid with a little girl's voice.

None of the men there ever messed with her. But she often got under their skins. Then they shooed her away. She hung around the shrimp-packing plant across the street. Apparently she made her life in the street.

That night she came by selling chicles, one of her various enterprises. I usually saw her with Juanito, the crippled shoeshine boy who did my boots at the Colmenar. During the day she protected him and helped hustle customers on the street.

Now alone, she spotted me, a fresh target, and fired her best shot, shouting, "*Ay Güero, ¿me quieres por un ratito?*" (would you like me for a little while?) This was the hookers' standard business hustle, meaning "do you want to come to my room with me?"

Wow! She was like something right out of a Dickens novel. Embarrassed, I turned to her reflexively and scolded, "No! If you talk to me like that again *(otra vez)* . . . I'm gonna rap you on your buns, your *nalgitas.*" One of the taxi drivers turned to me and said, "*¡Bien dicho; bien dicho!*" (Well said!).

They considered it "proper" that I chastised her. But she had winced as if deeply hurt when I barked at her. I felt like I had come on too strong. She could be amusing in one instant and wildly inappropriate the next. She scampered off into the night and disappeared.

The taxistas talked about how they were embarrassed by her. This was the underside of Mexico that doesn't look so good to Mexicans themselves. Here was this street urchin, a little girl, with no place to go.

One of them, a little guy called "El Burro," who always wore a plaid shirt, explained her to me. "Well, they say her mother left her here years ago and never came back. She's an orphan and she lives in the street, *en la calle*. It's hard to understand these things. It's ugly, *feo*, but that's the way life is sometimes." I'd been embarrassed in another way—by her sexual innuendo—so had barked. She really looked hurt when she ran off. Shit! I still had little Lisa on my conscience.

I killed a few more minutes there, tossing ten-centavo pieces against cracks in the sidewalk and listening to the taxistas' reflections on social problems in Mexico. Social policy under a streetlight on a corner in Guaymas at 1 A.M., just yards from the water and the sounds of the dancing in Chapúltepec, was ordinary. Then Jesse came out of the Rubi. He'd finished closing the bar and stopped to talk, smoke a cigarette, and bullshit.

He was still on his "little negocio" theme. He said, "Davíd, you really ought to make a trip to the border to buy appliances and bring them back." And I said, "Well it's not such a bad idea." One of the taxistas butted in, "Yes, that would be easy for you to do." I asked, "How would that be easy? Paying off the federales?" And he said, "No, no. If you immigrate to Mexico, you're able to bring your household goods with you, duty free."

I bit, "Oh really? How would I convince anyone that I was moving to Mexico?" Before realizing his mistake, he said, "Well you have this fiancée in Empalme . . ." And I said, "Yes, but I don't anymore." And everybody kind of went, "*¡Ayeee!* Sorry!" Someone muttered in the background to "shut up."

It was a terrible faux pas. In Mexico you don't rub in the cabrón thing. To retrieve the situation Jesse stuttered, "I know! We get you a lady friend to go to the border with you and say she's your wife, coming back to Mexico with your household goods. You make a little bit of money. People here can tell you the things they want you to buy for them in Tucson." As he pulled out his comb, I thanked him for the advice.

Back in my room I showered, dressed, and cranked up my little fan. I sat at my table and wrote a letter to my mom, then made entries in my journal. Digging into my footlocker for paper, I spotted the used Pentax camera I'd bought in the States to take to Ecuador when I was a graduate student. I decided I'd stop at the Kodak shop the next day on my way to the Colmenar and buy some film. I wanted to take a few pictures around Guaymas. It was so pretty and full of flowers.

I went to bed feeling good. I was alive, I had some money out in the safe, I'd eaten and had a great time dancing, then bullshitting with the taxistas in the street. My mood was dulled only by the nagging feeling that I'd come down too hard on Lupita, the street urchin.

The next morning I was awakened by tapping at my door around 10:30. It was already blazing hot. I opened the door, and one of the hotel's day clerks announced, grinning, "You have someone who wants to see you!" I told him I'd be out in a minute.

I dressed quickly and went out to the lobby. The clerk jerked his head toward the street, still grinning. I didn't get it till I turned to look. Be damned! It was little Lupita, waiting outside on the curb. I hurried out, but she scampered away. Jeez! I waited, then turned to reenter the lobby. That's when she rocketed toward me from around the corner and handed me a small bunch of hand-cut bougainvillea.

God knows what courtyard wall she'd climbed to get them, but three beautiful sprigs of bright, red bougainvillea were wrapped neatly in a piece of newspaper, secured by twine. As she darted toward me and shoved the flowers into my hand, she muttered, "*¡Lo siento!* (I'm sorry)" then zoomed off again.

Dumbfounded, I stood there holding her bright red bouquet. A couple of the taxistas stuck their heads around the corner, winked, and joked that I had made myself a *novia*, a girlfriend. This embarrassed me all over again. Obviously these guys weren't the same ones who had been on shift the night before. They hadn't been "briefed."

I took the flowers to my room, got an Orange Crush bottle, filled it with water, and stuck them in it. I set the flowers on my writing table. Pretty. I stared at them for a long time. These were the first flowers I'd gotten from anyone since my senior prom in 1962, at age seventeen. I was touched.

It was 11 A.M., ninety-eight or ninety-nine degrees out, and heading for triple digits by noon. The "cold" tap's water was already warm, so I managed an unsatisfying shower. As I redressed, clothes already sticking to me, I caught one quick glimpse of an impish face at my back window.

Lupita had somehow managed to pull herself up and stick her nose into my back window. Her eyes wide, she spotted the little spray of flowers in the soda bottle, smiled, and disappeared. I didn't see her up close again for several days.

It was already Sunday afternoon, so I went out and walked up the Serdán, taking my camera with me. I stopped in the empty Kodak shop, glad for a premium chance to hit on the curvy little clerk. I asked her for a date. Icily, she asked how my fiancée was doing. Bet she knew Iliana's sister! I bought a roll of film, strolled out too casually, and twenty paces later sat down to eat at the Colmenar.

Dating was a riddle in Guaymas. Iliana was gone but not really. I was far too "hot" physically and emotionally for my customary café con leche, so I chugged a cold Orange Crush and lit a cigarette, my version of Jesse's ritual with the comb. It didn't help.

On the upside, Max was nearby and immediately became fascinated with the camera. I had decided to load it and get my mind off the date I wasn't having while I waited for my food. The camera had only been used a few times because I couldn't get film for it where I worked in Ecuador.

At the time Mexico was a country starved for foreign manufactured goods. In the late sixties cameras, fans, blenders, and many similar items still were not produced there in either the quality or the quantity needed to meet demand. Despite that fact there were embargoes on many foreign products.

Max wanted to buy the camera. First he offered a thousand pesos, eighty dollars. For a moment I thought about photographing the fine, old colonial houses in town. Then I thought about food. I had no compelling need for the camera, but I hesitated, and he quickly bettered his offer, "I'll give you twelve hundred pesos." Nearly a hundred dollars! I could have a fried egg with my rice, beans, and tortillas every day for two or three months, and have enough left over for coffee and cheap Delicados cigarettes with that much money. I sold him the camera.

Doing the deal powerfully reinforced the notion that maybe I should go to the border and buy stuff to sell locally for a profit. That's when I began to think about it seriously. Max disappeared into the back room and came out with twelve hundred pesos, just like that. I stuck that lovely roll of bills in my pocket and wandered the Serdán, thinking about the future. Later I returned to the Rubi and put a thousand pesos in the safe.

It was late Sunday afternoon and I had money for gasoline, so gassed at the Pemex station on the Serdán and headed for Empalme. I had business with Lisa. I shook as I drove. Why is it so much worse to be rejected by a kid than an adult? But no one was at the house. Relieved, I headed back to Guaymas.

Again on the Serdán, I drove the old Rambler down to the point where the harbor curved west, away from downtown and toward Baja. A narrow, sandy area ran between the pavement and the water, dotted with palapas, the traditional, palm-thatched huts. Families crowded most of them, seeking shade. Kids and ice-cream carts were everywhere. This was the public beach in Guaymas—free, but no bathroom facilities. On Sundays it would fill up with people, popsicle vendors. and food carts.

Unlike the folks at Primaverales, these poorer families didn't invest in bathing suits. The adults hiked up their skirts or rolled up their pantlegs and waded out into the water. The kids dove in wearing just underpants. I hung around, watching the kids, then got in the car and drove on to the rugged outer peninsula that encircled Guaymas's harbor.

Several small motels and a trailer camp there catered to occasional American tourists. One was the Guaymas Inn, which specialized in shrimp curry, expensive when compared to rice and beans, but it was a fabulous meal.

At dusk I drove back to the Rubi, parked, and went to the upstairs balcony to watch the moon rise and the dancing across the street at Chapúltepec, which ended early on Sundays. The breeze up there softened the heat, so I lounged in one of the big wooden rocking chairs, dreading going down to sleep because it was just so damned hot inside. As the summer days lengthened, the heat was building up day by day.

It was early July and the heat had reached such proportions that simply walking around at night was surrealistic. All along the streets, especially in the barrios, people had set up hundreds of folding burlap cots in order to sleep outside, adjacent to the street. After nine or ten, you simply couldn't walk on the sidewalks in large parts of Guaymas because they were overflowing with the cots.

Late afternoon temperatures were often 108–110°F. By July adobe and concrete houses had become ovens, after soaking up weeks of blazing sun and heat. At times when there was no breeze, it would still be over 90° at midnight. When there was a sea breeze, the temperature might drop 25° to only 85° at midnight.

Because of humidity from the sea, Guaymas simply didn't get the huge temperature drops in midsummer that one expects in a desert environment. On rare occasions when the prevailing winds came from the east, blowing an offshore breeze out of the Sonoran desert, it would cool down into the seventies at night and be lovely outside.

Desert breeze or not, by mid-July these thick-walled houses would get hotter and hotter, until eventually two-thirds of Guaymas was sleeping outside. The other third had larger houses with interior courtyards to sleep in. The arrangement of cots, like Guaymas folk themselves, was gallant. The women's and little girls' cots were lined up against the adobe walls, with the men on the outside, exposed to the street. I sometimes walked the side streets at night, getting vicarious pleasure from seeing the families nestled together on the sidewalks.

On Monday afternoon, I went to the bank, depositing half the five hundred dollars from home into my savings account. I had paid two months' rent in advance and also had three thousand pesos in the safe at the Rubi. Life began to settle into a pleasant routine. I felt comfortable for the first time in more than a year and began to really enjoy myself.

94

It was about this time that a daily ritual started in the hotel. I would generally get up at 10:30, bone-dry from sweating all night, and go straight to the old bar to have a couple of ice-cold Orange Crushes. I began reading the Guaymas newspaper in the bar.

One day I was playing around, reading the news aloud at the end of the bar, asking Jesse to correct my pronunciation as I read. He asked me to speak up so the other patrons could hear. I felt stupid at first, my Spanish being only average. But the customers liked it. So I read aloud many days, the regulars treating it as my "Spanish lesson," and purchasing my Orange Crushes. I suspected that some of the local guys around the hotel had a hard time reading the newspaper, too, as they puzzled through the flowery Spanish that journalists often used.

This transformed into a daily ritual between noon and one, which was the beginning of most people's siesta. Quite a number of the taxistas, fish-vendors, and local merchants gathered at midday in the old front bar of the Rubi, usually drinking just Coca Cola or a beer before lunch. Often ten or fifteen men would stop by before lunch, and I would read the *noticias*, the news of the day, for fifteen or twenty minutes.

I remember one newspaper columnist in particular, who styled himself "Diogenes" and fancied himself a philosopher. He went in for very formal Spanish in his columns. I would usually have my big black English-Spanish/Spanish-English dictionary to look up words I didn't know. I also got help from the audience—they appreciated the fact that here was a gringo trying hard to pick up the language, working at it and reading the papers.

In a true twist of irony, a gringo was reading Spanish to men who spoke it beautifully, often eloquently. But among the regulars some struggled with the written word because they'd dropped out of school early to work. The Rubi audience ranged from prosperous, sophisticated, and well-educated to laborers and vendors who had worked every day since they were twelve or thirteen.

This ritual added a rhythm to my weekdays, expanded my circle of acquaintances, and polished my Spanish. It, like my room, made me feel "at home."

In the course of these newspaper readings, I discovered that many of the local men were really tuned in to the world around them and hungry to discuss politics, philosophy, current events, and differences in culture.

Favorite topics included the local economy, the emerging drug trade, national politics, and relationships between the United States and Mexico—especially the ongoing cultural and economic tug-of-war between the two countries.

Rich, revealing discussions on culture, race, politics, getting along in the world, and standards of "right" and "wrong" all took place.

During these sessions we exchanged views and information. Some would ask me about where I grew up. But no one pried too closely for the specifics of my family background, lest they uncover something embarrassing. In Mexico the first rule of discourse was never humiliate—so questions were gracious and general.

People would say, "Well, what is done here in Guaymas ..." I would respond, "What is done where I grew up in West Virginia . . ." The Guaymenses were fascinated with West Virginia—an area of the United States that was not like Tucson or Los Angeles or what they had seen of New York at the cinema.

The state was a poor, semirural workingman's world where some people couldn't read and write. Few owned new cars. I had classmates whose entire families slept on one mattress on the floor of a shack back in a hollow. These were facts of life that patrons of the Rubi could relate to.

Some were surprised to hear of this "other" America. Others may even have questioned the authenticity of my accounts of the U.S. government's massacre of coalworkers' families at Cabin Creek or the "coal wars" at Matewan. But they could relate. Everyone was still stunned by the Mexican army's massacre of students at Tlatelolco in October of '68.

Through these discussions I discovered that Mexicans and Americans are fundamentally different in one respect. The guys at the bar admitted to having prejudices. For example, they tended to see Americans as loners—arrogant, driven, greedy, and not very family oriented. Some conceded that they weren't too hot on gringos. But the stereotypes they had never seemed to apply to the norteamericanos who they actually knew. I concluded that in Mexico, people are going to find you likable if you are a likable person, wherever you are from.

Americans, on the other hand, will profess to have no national or racial prejudices. They'll say, "Oh no, Mexicans are fine," but they often despise the individual Mexican they interact with. Individual Mexicans often meet the stereotype that Americans secretly have, but deny. So my view was that, while Americans usually profess to accept all classes of people, they often despise individuals for their "personal failings." In contrast, Mexicans tend to despise entire classes of people but take individuals as they find them.

Even the proprietor, Hector Morales, showed up frequently to drink a beer and listen. He was about five feet three and slender. The jet-black bags under his eyes made him look sleepy and detached, but he was very sharp. When he approved of a particular argument he would turn up his bottle of Carta Blanca, suck it straight down, slam the empty onto the polished wood bar, nod in approval, and walk out. Conversation over.

97

six

A WIFE FOR EDWARD MEYERS

A few days later Edward Meyers popped in to the Hotel Rubi during one of our noon newspaper sessions. I was surprised to see him, because he always stuck like glue to the trailer camp out at Primaverales. Now he had hunted me up at the hotel and motioned me to a stool at the empty end of the bar. "Buy you a beer?" "No thanks, Ed, I'm just drinking sodas. What's up?"

He said, "I want to talk. Do you remember the night I talked to you about finding a wife here? You brushed off the idea, but I am really lonely and I need to find a wife. Please help me find a wife here in Guaymas. You got connections, you know local people . . . some widow lady, somebody. I've just got to have someone or I am going to die here by myself. That's all there is to it. I can't make it. I can't make it by myself."

As before, I paused. Then he blurted, "I'll pay you. I'll pay you five hundred dollars." Man, he was really hurting.

Feeling rotten, I said, "Well, Ed, let me think about this a couple of days. I won't say 'no,' but just let me think about it, then I'll come out and see you at the trailer camp."

He said, "Two days, two days." I said, "Okay, okay. I'll be out in two days, no more." He thanked me profusely and shuffled out the door, looking worn down, gray, and desperate.

Jesse heard some of this and came over, pretending to wipe off a bar stool. He asked, "Everything okay? What did that guy want?" I told him it was just an American who hangs out in the trailer camp at Primaverales. And he said, "Oh yeah, I've heard of him. He's got a big truck or something." I explained, "Yeah, that's the one. He's a widow man and he wants me to help him find a wife here in Guaymas."

Jesse asked, "What's the matter with the guy?" I said, "Nothing, really." And he said, "Well, is he some kind of convict, or what?"

"No! He has a couple of laundromats in the Los Angeles area and his wife up and died on him recently. His kids are grown and out of the house. He's just a lonely son of a bitch, sitting around drinking rum and just doesn't have anybody." "Is that all?" asked Jesse. "Well, maybe he drinks too much, but I don't think there's anything wrong with him, except loneliness," I conceded.

"He's got these laundromats and he's got people hired that run them and nobody needs him. So he's sitting down here, escaping, trying to get away from where his wife died and all the memories."

Jesse said, "Well, what's the matter then? In Guaymas we've got widow ladies. They gotta eat, too; they're lonely, too. Did the guy say he'd pay you?"

I answered, "Yes, but I don't know how I feel about that."

He said, "Well, you know, don't be so fussy. You gotta do things for people. That's what makes the world work. You gotta do things for people." So I said, "Are you serious?" He said, "Yeah!"

I asked, "Well how would you go about helping him?" and he said, "Well, I remember some years ago, a *norteamericano* came down here and advertised in the paper, saying he wanted a wife." I said, "Jesus! Did it work?" He said, "Yeah, I think so. There were rumors that it did. I don't know anything more. But you could try that. In the big city papers, people advertise, looking for a wife or a girlfriend or something like that."

Later on that night I drove on out to Bacochibampo Bay and stopped at the Hotel Miramar to consult Negro Jacinto, who was working there. "Negro, what do you know about the American guy down at the Primaverales trailer camp—the one who owns the big truck?" He said, "Oh yeah, people talk about him. They say he's lonely, *un viudo*, a widower, or something."

I said, "Well, he's asking me to help him find a wife and Jesse said something about advertising in the newspaper. What do you think? Would that be a terrible thing to do?" He responded like Jesse had. "Well, no. Maybe he doesn't find anybody. But what harm? What harm would there be in this? You put an ad in the newspaper and you say at least how old the guy is, and you're not lying or anything like that, maybe. There are many widow ladies in this town. They might like to marry somebody. What's it hurt?"

I discovered that the local mentality turned toward the practical in certain matters of life. Very interesting. Here I was mincing around with my sense of the romantic, and everybody else was saying, "be sensible."

I left the Miramar, went down the beach, and answered Edward Meyers, "Okay, I'll help you out. We'll put an ad in the newspaper." He seemed elated and repeated, "I'll pay you five hundred dollars if I get a wife, or even if I get somebody who wants to live with me." I said, "Well, let's not get too flagrant. Let's just see what happens." So we wrote up an ad for a weekly paper in Guaymas, which read roughly as follows:

SEÑOR NORTEAMERICANO.

DE 48 AÑOS. BUSCA UNA ESPOSA.

ESE SEÑOR VIUDO ES DECENTE

Y HONRADO

Y BUSCA VIUDA O SOLTERA IGUAL.

The ad read, "North American gentleman. Forty-eight years old. Seeks a wife. This widowed gentleman is decent and honorable and seeks a widow or single woman, either one." It went on to say, "Contact at Playas Primaverales, Friday between one and three in the afternoon." It gave the phone number at the Primaverales bar, for appointments. That was the ad. Afterward I went back to the Rubi and thought about all this, nervously.

So on Friday I went out to Primaverales around noon. Manuel was ticked off about the ad. First, it had raised eyebrows in the daily newspaper office and they wouldn't take it, so I placed it in one of the free, weekly broadsheets that contained mostly advertising. Now Manuel was nervous that Cleopatra, the owner, would see it and object. I should have asked first, so I apologized and Manuel softened up.

I didn't know what to expect. We planned to set up "interviews" for Saturday if there were any actual phone calls. I drank a couple of cold Orange Crushes, lit a cigarette, and leaned against the bar.

At about 12:45, unbelievably, the phone started ringing off the hook. I must have taken twenty to thirty phone calls, writing down people's names, addresses, and phone numbers—whatever they would give me—and set up a number of appointment times starting at noon the next day.

I was careful to explain to each of the callers that yes, this was legitimate; I was simply an agent for this guy because he was a paisano; I spoke Spanish and was familiar with Guaymas. I described Edward as an ordinary North American, a small businessman who was recently widowed, very lonely, spoke a little Spanish, and was from the Los Angeles area.

About eleven the next morning Ed and I returned, got a table and several chairs from Manuel, and set them up under a thatched lean-to near the little restaurant next door. Ironically, I was only fifty feet from where I had first met Iliana. I wondered if she was okay.

I snapped out of the nostalgia, took up a post on one chair, and put Edward behind the other. I paid a couple of the shoeshine boys to direct anyone asking for us to the palapa near the footbridge. We were only eighty feet away, not hard to spot.

As long as I live I will never forget that Saturday. By noon people started to show up. Some came by taxi, some by bus, and one group in a private car.

The first to arrive got off the bus. A dark, heavyset man, clean but poorly dressed, he had two grown women and a girl with him. One looked to be his wife, a women of about forty, the other a few years younger. The girl with them was very attractive. These folks looked beaten down, wore cheap shoes, and carried the woven nylon shopping bags that marked their economic station.

I was acting as interpreter. They came up and started to talk to Edward Meyers as I translated. "*¿Cómo está usted? Yo soy señor Ruiz,*" and I would say, "How do you do, I'm Señor Ruiz," then back to them, "*¿Cómo está usted? Yo soy Edward Meyers,*" back and forth.

Initially I found it really embarrassing and thought to myself, "Holy shit! How did I get myself into this?" That's when Edward told me this was giving him "new hope," so I went on.

Edward and I had assumed it was the younger woman in her thirties, standing apart from the others, who was to be introduced. But throughout the conversation they kept referring to "Elenita," little Elena.

103

Confused, I turned to the younger woman standing off to the side and asked her directly, "*¿Es usted Elena?*" (Are you Elena?) "No, no. Señor, Elena is my daughter," pointing at the girl. Uh oh! The girl was only sixteen or seventeen!

Elena was the pretty, teenaged girl, looking nervous in a little off-white top and faded pink pants! She was just a cute kid with her hair pulled back. But they had come to present her to Edward. A kid too young even for me! And our ad had screamed, in big print, "forty-eight-year-old widow man." There was nothing fakey about it. I was stunned!

I said, "One moment, I need to explain the situation in English. . . ." "Edward, they're talking the girl for you. If this is what you're up for, you need to know I don't feel good about it at all." And he said, "Which one are you calling the girl?" And I said, "The little one in the pink pants." Edward paused, looking confused, "Shit, she's a baby! She's way younger than my daughters!"

I went on, "Well, that's whose looking, that's who they are bringing to you." And he said, "Oh, no! I'm not up for that. I'm not trying to marry some little girl. She's cute . . . I might have a fantasy once a week when I look at Playboy and drool over one of their nineteen-year-old pinup girls, but I'm not going to do something like that!"

I shushed him, "Don't sound agitated! Let's not have these people feel that they've done something inappropriate. Let me just get their names and end this." He nodded. I turned and explained that Mr. Meyers was very pleased that they had come and thought that the *Señorita*, Elena, was a lovely girl, perhaps just a little shy, but he would like to be introduced to her formally. So I presented her formally to Edward, then told him to stand up and say *"Mucho gusto, señorita,"* which he did.

104

While Edward smiled graciously, I explained that we were going to talk to a number of people and asked for their address. I continued, "If Mr. Meyers would formally like to ask your daughter for a date, we'll contact you in a day or so. If not, it will probably be that he has found someone else that he would like to invite for coffee or a walk. Meanwhile, we are very honored, Elena is obviously a precious, young *señorita* and very sweet." They smiled and nodded.

Then I offered, "For your kindness in coming here, may we invite you to have a cup of coffee and dessert in the restaurant?" They said, "No thank you," so I walked them back over to one of the taxis and said, "Well then at least let us see you back home correctly." I hustled them into the back of a cab. They were looking quite nervous so I quickly paid the taxi driver fifty pesos and told him to drive them home. They were from the farming hamlet of San José de Guaymas, several miles outside of town. Poor country folk.

We had a few minutes to compose ourselves, so I had coffee sent over from the restaurant. The next meetings were easier. We met several women in a row who were pretty clearly "semipros," to put it kindly; tough, slutty-looking characters in their thirties or forties. Your classic well-used women.

The first one, gaunt and hawk-nosed, had a big scar down one side of her face. The second wore her hair done up in a ratted beehive, flashy red skin-tight pants, and a black top. She didn't look good in them.

Again Edward was cordial, and I went through the ritual of "thank you so much," . . . Edward also paid the taxi fares for both of these. This was costing money! When the day was over he had spent about fifty bucks on taxi fares and desserts.

After the second of these dubious ladies left, Edward said, "Well, we can expect just about anything. I'm prepared for anything." But he sounded animated for a change and actually laughed as he said it. Progress. I wrote down people's names, anyway, because I thought he might change his mind later on. Take out the lady in the red pants. Not my problem.

Then we had another wait. We had listed a bunch of folks from the Friday calls who assured us they would come. Clearly a number of these were going to be "no-shows."

Then another couple brought a daughter. Both times when these young girls showed up, "Dad" appeared to be the motivator. I didn't know whether their mothers also thought this was a good idea, but this was getting to be sociologically interesting. This girl was in her early twenties and, taking a guess, probably already had a kid somewhere. Her group also looked hard up. But the girl was sullen, really sullen. I don't remember much else except her looking sullen and disdainful. She obviously didn't like the looks of Edward at all—or me, for that matter.

Poor Edward! And he had gotten himself all cleaned up for this. I'd got him out in the sun for a few days. He hadn't had a drop to drink and was in fresh clothes. He even eased off the cigarettes and had knocked off a couple of pounds taking brisk walks up the beach. He was up for this. Some of the grayness was gone. The guy had been right to the bottom and was now hoping.

Then we had another odd group. A grandmother in a splashy print dress. She was fat and waddled. Her stockings were the kind that went up to the knee and had rolled partway down. Her hair was all done back in a braid. The woman with her appeared to be late thirties, quiet and Indian-looking, in a pale gray dress, but had only one arm.

She had lost her left forearm. So she wore a long-sleeved dress, the left sleeve pinned down over the stump of her arm. Still she was a handsome woman, with strong features and jet-black hair worn braided in back, Oaxaca Indian–style. These folks certainly had a central-Mexico look to them.

They also had a girl with them who appeared to be about eighteen or nineteen. I didn't pay much attention to her, because the woman with one arm really caught my eye. This also answered my question if it was always a man who was wanting to push one of these girls into an arranged marriage. Apparently not—here were grandmother, daughter, and granddaughter—three generations of women. Edward lit up at once, started talking and became animated. At first I thought he was beginning to like the idea of one of these teenagers. Simultaneously the grandmother started making introductions and asking questions about Edward. Sharp old gal, nobody's fool at all. Finally I asked her who was to be presented to Mr. Meyers. Again it was the youngest.

Edward interrupted, "Find out if she's available!" And I asked, "Okay which one?" He said, "The one with one arm; the one with one arm." So I turned to Grandmother and asked, "Is this other lady your daughter?" She said, "Yes, this is my daughter *señora* Epifania. . . ." I pried further. "By any chance is she a widow or divorced lady?" Grandmom said, "Oh, yes!" So I turned to Epifania, asking directly, "Are you a *soltera* (single lady)?" She hesitated, looking perplexed, then answered, "Well, yes."

Meanwhile Edward was pleading with me over my shoulder the whole time, "Ask her if she'll go to coffee with me. PLEASE, ask her if she'll go to coffee with me." And I said to him, "Okay, the one in the gray dress with one arm, right? No mistake?" He said, "Yes."

107

So I turned to Grandma and said, "Señora, I want to thank you for the introduction to your granddaughter, the señorita, but señor Meyers would very much like to invite your daughter, señora Epifania, to coffee tomorrow."

It was frighteningly quiet for some seconds. I didn't know whether lightning was going to strike, the grandmother was going to be offended, or the youngest girl was going to cry.

Then all at once, Grandma beamed, the young girl sighed in audible relief, and Epifania answered the invitation with a stupendously rich, warm smile, then blushed! A striking fortyish woman just blushing intensely, her eyes cast down.

The granddaughter giggled. And I said, "Well have we offended someone?" Epifania answered, "No! I would be more than honored, 'enchanted,' to go to coffee with the señor."

Then she made a quick, instinctive movement to hide her bad arm, covering it with the good one. She obviously didn't know what to do next. So I invited Grandma to take the granddaughter into the restaurant. I hustled them to the door, seated them, invited them to have whatever they cared for, and asked one of the ladies there to take care of them.

By the time I got back to the tables, Edward was working on this woman in his bits and pieces of Spanish. Actually he was not doing such a bad job. They were already breaking the ice, both of them nervous as teenagers. But the richness and warmth of this woman's smile had brought out the long-lost little boy in Edward Meyers, who was a nice, gentle guy. There was a spark there. It was almost like seeing two high-school kids, neither wanting to hurt or be hurt.

She liked what she saw; he liked what he saw. And they were both big enough to know that neither one of them was perfect. On the one hand you have a fortyish, one-armed lady. On the other, a desperately lonely middle-aged guy with a spare tire. But they talked animatedly for about fifteen minutes.

I did a good bit of the translating back and forth—"where are you from," and "where are *you* from," etc. Her whole family was originally from south of Guadalajara but had been living in the Guaymas area for some years. Epifania's husband had been a shrimper, *camaronero*, lost at sea some years before. She did not go into details. She seemed pleased that Edward was widowed—no "ex" to deal with.

108

So they set a coffee date for the next day. I suggested that they go to El Pollito restaurant in downtown Guaymas, neutral territory, have coffee, and take a Sunday stroll, as was customary on a first date. I asked her if she would like us to send a taxi for her. She declined, but assured us she would meet Edward at El Pollito, about three.

I also asked her if she wished to have a chaperone for tomorrow. She said "no," but indicated she would like to keep the date just *"por el centro* (downtown)."

I explained that to Edward. He said, "That's just fine. We'll have some lunch, we'll take a walk." I conveyed that, then told Edward, "Don't bring your truck; don't take her anywhere in your vehicle. Stick to the center of town. Don't get anxious or grabby with her—that's just not done here." He said, "Okay." She collected her family and left in a taxi, still smiling.

Edward went back to his truck. Several more people came, and I took their names and talked to them, but Edward didn't want to see anybody else.

Afterward I went to the bar, drank an ice-cold Bohemia beer, lit a smoke, and relaxed. It had been one heck of a day. I'd never been involved in anything like this before. Manuel and the others wanted a report. "He chose an Indian-looking woman. About forty. Widow. One arm. Handsome. Nice smile." The barmen looked at each other, surprised. One, named Jaime, exclaimed, "I saw her. Nice face." "That one," I confirmed. Manuel was relieved. *"Propio, bien hecho, Güero.* (Suitable, good job, Güero.)" Whew!

After my break I went back to Ed's truck and found him puttering around in a euphoric psychological dreamland. I said, "Okay, enjoy the moment, but let's take you downtown and get you a *guayabera*, dark pants, and get you done up to look local. First, you've got a spare tire, and a guayabera is going to look great on you. Second, you want this woman to know you care enough about this date to wear new clothes, something a little different." He said, "Okay."

We went downtown right then and got him fitted out with a couple of guayaberas and a new pair of dark pants. The stuff he had with him in the truck was all gray and verging on threadbare. I told him, "No booze; absolutely no booze." He was good for his word, he didn't drink a thing.

I asked if he wanted me around the next day or anything like that, and he said, well, it would help if I could give him some moral support when he came down to El Pollito. I said, "Okay, fine. Don't bring your truck. Come in a taxi. Don't scare this woman by making her think that you plan to drive her off someplace."

The next day, Sunday, I went and met him about two. He was spotless. Haircut, polished shoes, and all decked out, he looked great in the guayabera. It was sparkling white, pleated down the front, and took twenty pounds off him.

I complimented him, "Ed, you look great! Now go down the street and get some flowers to set on your table." So he did. He walked down to the little flower stand right on the corner of the plaza, came back with some flowers, and sat down.

As women the world over, Epifania was about ten minutes late and really had him jumping. When I spotted her coming down the Serdán in a taxi, I hightailed it across the street, then walked down to the Copa de Leche after I saw her go inside El Pollito. I faded out of the scene, hoping it would go alright.

I shouldn't have worried. Lunch that Sunday was just the beginning. They dated. Oh, did they date! They went everywhere around town for the next several weeks. News spread among the working-class women. People out at Primaverales thought it was neat. Epifania was a widow and crippled to boot. There were only certain kinds of work she could do.

As it turned out she worked in one of the little cleaning establishments in town, pulling the clothes in and out of the vat of the dry-cleaning fluid with her one good arm. Her little family was barely making it. It must have been tough to lose her husband and the income a shrimper could make in a good year.

In spite of her bad luck, she was a warm, upbeat person. Edward needed that, so the two of them got along very well. Considering the language barrier, I was surprised at just how much they seemed to be enjoying each other. Whether or not they fully understood each other, they laughed easily and touched gently.

Edward came to me at the Rubi about two weeks later, telling me that he had proposed to marry this woman, but didn't know what to do about arrangements, the daughter, the grandmother, etc. So we arranged a little parley at her house on the high road above Guaymas, in a district of humble concrete and tin-roofed houses perched between a rocky cliff and the road.

Epifania's house consisted of one big room divided into front living room and rear sleeping quarters by a large sheet hung from the ceiling. Edward confided later that he was stunned by her humble surroundings. But they kept everything in their small house spotlessly clean. I suspected that

Epifania had wanted Edward to see her as she really was. No fantasies.

They talked about marriage. About what to do with the daughter, Granny, and the rest of the family. The grandmother wanted no part of the States. The granddaughter might have, but she didn't get a vote. Grandmom had a younger sister in another house a hundred feet away. It was also a tin-roofed concrete room divided in half. There was an uncle and someone's ten- or twelve-year-old son. So there was an extended family unit here. Removing any worker from it had significant consequences.

I suggested that Edward ask if the rest of the family would like to stay where they were for the foreseeable future, then find out if Epifania wanted to go to Los Angeles with him, at least for an extended "honeymoon."

I suggested he offer to send eighty dollars, a thousand pesos a month, to help with family expenses. He liked the idea. This moved things to the need for a private conversation with Epifania about money, arrangements, and practicalities. I indicated that, and the others left the three of us alone to talk.

I explained to Epifania in Spanish that Edward offered to send eighty dollars per month to replace some of her wages. She thought for a while, then asked if a hundred dollars monthly could be sent to her mother. Edward understood and agreed quickly. Yes, he had proposed to her. Yes, she wanted to get married. She did not want to get married in church—she wanted only a civil ceremony. I translated.

That was fine with Edward. No big splash, then dinner for friends afterward and some music. Done! The matriarchal families in working-class Mexico are so easy to deal with, compared to the male-focused ones.

The others returned. Finances settled, everyone agreed that the eighteen-year-old daughter was going to stay in Guaymas with Grandma and the rest of the kin, for a time. Since she was still in school, that seemed to please everyone.

In Mexico when a woman of mature years who had daughters of sexual age remarried, whether widowed or divorced, the girls were often packed off to relatives or a convent. This was a long-standing tradition in those days. The presumption was that the new husband would naturally try and seduce the daughters who, after all, were not related to him by blood. However naughty it might be to screw his step-daughters, it wasn't incest. The reckoning was that no real "macho" man in his right mind would pass up even a remote chance to take on a fifteen-year-old virgin and break her cherry.

Though this prospect was based far more on fear than on reality, the fear that stepdaughters would be at sexual risk was once a rampant "urban myth" with real psychological horse-power in Mexico.

They reached an understanding that day. Edward was going back to the United States to make arrangements, would come back in about ten days, and they would be married in two weeks. After the ceremony they were going to have an informal dinner at El Pollito. They were going to get married midweek so they could reserve the restaurant, have friends in.

Then they planned a honeymoon in Hermosillo, which was near enough that if Epifania had any last-minute panics it would be okay. If that went well Edward would take her over to the other side a week or so later. Finished, I walked down to the Rubi, enjoying the steep descent through lively neighborhoods of older houses and brightly flowered patios.

The next few weeks unfolded in a flurry of deal making, border crossing, and nightclubbing, as I established a new life for myself. Edward Meyers came back on schedule. On a scorching hot Wednesday afternoon in early August, they had a short, ten-minute marriage ceremony at the Civil Registry.

During the ceremony I prompted Edward in Spanish. He was done up in a nice gray suit with a striped tie. He had so hoped his brother would come down with him, but had returned alone. I suspected then, and knew later, that his family really had not approved. Afterward we went to El Pollito on Avenida Serdán, where a lovely buffet dinner was waiting.

114

They laid on a nice feed—spicy grilled chicken (the house specialty), baskets of chilled shrimp, rice and beans, cold fruit salads, and homemade mango ices for dessert.

They had gone light on the liquor, one round of *brindis*, the formal toast made with a very light planter's punch. I had continually warned Edward that his heavy rum drinking simply had to stop if he didn't want this woman to leave him.

A surprising number of Epifania's friends from the barrio and dry-cleaning establishment had shown up. They were all invited. So it was a gay occasion. You could tell that these poor working women, most already knocking at the door to middle age, thought she was lucky. And the two of them clearly thought they were lucky—each had gotten a second chance at the companionship they feared was lost to them forever.

As the party broke up, the married couple left their guests. Edward thanked me profusely and tucked an envelope in my shirt pocket as they headed out the door. He had not brought the refrigerator truck back. Instead he had returned in a blue Ford sedan. The newlyweds waved goodbye from in front of the restaurant, then honked their way up Avenida Serdán in harmony with local custom, heading north to Hermosillo for their honeymoon.

Epifania had been wise. She had asked Edward to settle a modest sum of money on her that she could keep in the bank in Guaymas, along with some cash to keep with her always in case of emergency. This he did. He also bought her some new clothes. She liked gray, and wore a gray, satiny dress on her wedding day. I liked her. She was warm and direct. He was gentle and grateful.

They made a nice couple. I felt good about the whole thing. And I got my five hundred dollars, becoming a man of means by ordinary Guaymas standards. I was up to nearly fourteen thousand pesos, split between the safe and the bank, and was soon to have more coming in.

115

While Edward was in the States making arrangements to marry Epifania, I created the little negocio that Jesse had proposed. With some very unusual help . . .

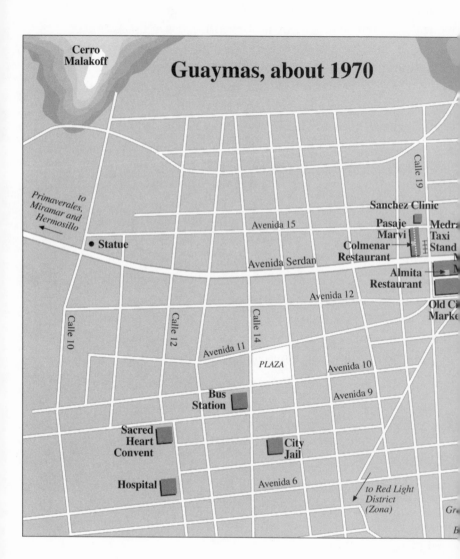

Guaymas, about 1970

Cerro
Malakoff

to
Primaverales,
Miramar and
Hermosillo

• Statue

Calle 19

Sanchez Clinic

Avenida 15

Pasaje
Marvi

Medra

Colmenar
Restaurant

Taxi
Stand

Avenida Serdan

Almita →
Restaurant

Old C
Marke

Avenida 12

Calle 10

Calle 12

Calle 14

Avenida 11

PLAZA

Avenida 10

Avenida 9

Bus
Station

Sacred
Heart
Convent

City
Jail

Hospital

Avenida 6

to Red Light
District
(Zona)

Gre

B

116

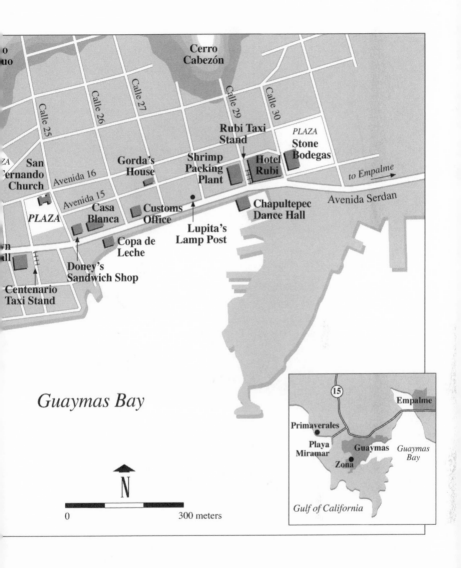

Cerro
Cabezón

Calle 25
Calle 26
Calle 27
Calle 29
Calle 30

Rubi Taxi
Stand

PLAZA
Stone
Bodegas

San
Fernando
Church

Avenida 16

Gorda's
House

Shrimp
Packing
Plant

Hotel
Rubi

to Empalme

PLAZA

Avenida 15

Casa
Blanca

Customs
Office

Chapultepec
Dance Hall

Avenida Serdan

Copa de
Leche

Lupita's
Lamp Post

Doney's
Sandwich Shop

Centenario
Taxi Stand

Guaymas Bay

N

0   300 meters

15

Empalme

Primaverales

Playa
Miramar

Guaymas

Guaymas
Bay

Zona

Gulf of California

1. The author in 1968.

2. San Fernando Church and bandstand on Guaymas
Main Plaza (early 1970s).

3.   Hotel Miramar (early 1970s).

4. Miramar Beach, looking toward Playas Primaverales.

5. The much-changed Hotel Rubi, 2002.
(Photo by E. Ehrmann © 2002).

6. View of the Rubi Bar. Harbor is to the right out of view. (Photo by E. Ehrmann © 2002).

7. Reunion lunch at the Almita Restaurant, ca. 1995.
(l. to r. the author, "Negro" Jacinto, and "Canelo."

8. Mercedes (center), and family, 1994. Olga, her daughter (second from right), is the author's goddaughter. Mercedes was carrying her when the author left Guaymas.

9. A typical dirt lane and poorer barrio on the outskirts of Guaymas.

10. Ruin of the old Río Rita in the 1980s.

seven

A WEEK FILLED WITH WOMEN

The evening Edward Meyers first visited me at the Rubi, I was killing time, *matando un rato*, in the rear, paneled bar at the south end of the hotel, where Jesse was bartending. It wasn't busy so I was studying one of the regulars. He was known on the street simply as "El Alemán," the German.

He was a big, heavyset guy in his fifties, with a beer belly. He was an "engineer" of some type at the city waterworks. A drinker, dice player, and inveterate cusser. His Spanish was tolerable, but he could never say the word *cabrón* (cuckold, son of a bitch) correctly, so pronounced it *cabón*, no "r."

His every sentence was punctuated with *"eeh cabón; eeh cabón,"* and the regulars at the bar found it hilarious. If you are a male in Mexico, *cabrón* is immediate, "must-learn" vocabulary, as basic as "food," "toilet," "beer," "woman."

Not only was el Alemán a trash mouth, he was into porn. He was always showing off the miniature pornographic comic books that some working-class Mexican men relied on for the kind of fantasy sex they would never actually experience.

These comics featured stories of passion and forbidden sex acts graced with copious hand-drawn sketches of the lush, eager, narrow-waisted women who would do *"everything"* to please their man—fill in the specifics with your own imagination.

So Alemán was middle-aged and into this sort of thing. Occasionally he came to the Rubi and would sneak off with Eva or one of her girlfriends in the *ambiente* (sex for rent scene).

This particular night he showed up late. Not long after he arrived Marta came in and sat next to him—obviously an arranged meeting. And just as she did the first time I saw her in the Hotel Rubi, she ordered Castillo rum, drank it down in shots, then chased it with ice water.

I had fantasized about her since before going to Ecuador. In Ecuador, starved for food, clean water, warmth, companionship, even oxygen at eleven thousand feet, I had, I confess, mentally composed several of my own imaginary comic books with her as the main story line. I've already mentioned that I'd seen her again briefly on the beach at Primaverales on a recent Sunday.

I recognized her instantly when she came in. She was still wearing the very same gray-striped blouse and dark skirt that she had worn the first time I saw her. Though she looked more threadbare and less elegant now, my reaction to her was the same—the sensation of a hard right hook to the gut that left me breathless, radiated upward to my brain as a desperate, primitive need, then rushed down to my groin.

It was totally involuntary, and only some women could generate it. Most women don't actually understand male sexuality. But Marta understood SEX, not just sex, and stimulated raw, primitive DESIRE, amplified by the lush scent of vanilla. When she walked into a room, guys didn't "think" anything. Most simply got an instant hard-on.

Marta had lost weight since I had first seen her. I guessed her at twenty-three or twenty-four years old. She was dark-skinned, with nice expressive eyes and wavy brown-black hair, the color they call *café-castaño*. She had long, delicate fingers and knockout legs. As she talked to the German, I was drawn in by the sounds of her sensual, throaty voice. I was later to discover that that voice could get very harsh.

I rolled dice halfheartedly and nursed my beer, while surreptitiously keeping an eye on her as she talked. El Alemán's back was to me, but her face was toward me, about twenty-five feet down the bar. Once when I sneaked a sideways glance, she was looking right at me, the same way she had that day on the beach at Primaverales.

Our eyes met for one fleeting moment. I had been caught! She smiled, then turned back to the German before he noticed. I caught her looking at me again a few minutes later. Then she began to drink heavily and become more absorbed with El Alemán.

They talked softly, drinking steadily, she belting down the Castillo rum, he beers. Eventually he got up to go to the bathroom and make a telephone call from the public phone booth in the dark hallway to the lobby. While he was gone she nodded toward me, smiled, and said, *"Buenas noches."*

I returned the greeting. She looked at me intently and started to say something, but the German returned. He handed Jesse a wad of pesos. Marta carried the partly drunk bottle of Castillo with her. It dangled languidly from her hand as she sauntered out the door with the German and disappeared into the night. I watched, both jealous and aroused.

Jesse came over, wiping up the bar, and suggested it was about time to close up. It was. There wasn't much business. There were only three or four of us there, prevailing on the house while we nursed beers and tried to shoot five "aces" with the dice for fifty centavos a game. As he cleaned up I pried, "Jesse, what can you tell me about the girl with Alemán, the one they call Marta? Is that her real name?"

He said, "Well, as best I know that's her name, but *en la calle* they call her La Flaca (Skinny). "What's her story? Is she a *vieja* (hooker)?" I asked. He answered, "Well, *de vez en cuando* (every now and then). *En la calle* they say she has family to support."

I pressed, "Does she ever work in one of the houses in the red-light district, the *zona?*" He said, "No, *nunca* (never)." I continued to pry, "Well does she go with the German often?" He said, "No, only a couple of times. And she gets drunk before she goes and does it, and I think he pays her a lot of money."

I commented, "Well she's real attractive." He said, "*Claro, que sí* (of course she is), and she needs a boyfriend. You ought to take her out sometime."

By then it was after eleven and Negro Jacinto floated in through the door that opened onto the side street by the empty stone bodegas. Negro was in a real "up" mood. He was about five feet five, cherubic face, infectiously bubbly, and always gracious. He said, "Davíd, I'm glad to see you're looking good. They say *en la calle* that your money came and you're feeling better. *¡Qué bueno!*"

I said, "Thanks, I feel worlds better." Jesse butted in quickly telling Jacinto that I was hot for Marta, and she had just left with the German. His exact phrase was "*está pegado con la Marta* (he's smitten with Marta)."

Negro chuckled but said, "Well you be careful, you know? She's a working girl and is in *el ambiente*, now and again. Be sure you know what you're getting into if you take her out."

Negro, sensing my mood, asked, "Do you want to go nightclubbing?" I said, "Sure, but I thought the Pleamar (High Tide Club) was closed." It was the only club we had visited together, and the federales had temporarily posted a "closed," *clausurado*, sign there. Jesse said he'd like to go out, too. Negro suggested, "Well, we can go on out to the *zona de tolerancia* (the red-light district)." He said, "*Sí*, have you been there before?" I nodded.

Though I had been there before, I had never had a grand tour. He continued, "We'll go see a floor show." I asked, "Who has a good show?" He said, "The Río Rita. First quality. Good as the Pleamar." I said, "Okay."

Planning ahead, Jesse said, "*¡Mira!* (Look!) I'll go with you in the Rambler. We'll follow Negro, because he might not want to come back too early tonight. Taxis are expensive in the *zona*, so we'll take both cars." We agreed, and Jesse closed the bar.

The closing-up procedures in the Rubi bar were always a scream. Jesse went through his usual ritual of not wanting to be the last one out of the room when the lights were turned off. He was a real freak about ghosts, certain the bar and old hallway were haunted. We held the front door for Jesse and made the mad dash up the dark hallway to the lobby, laughing

132

the whole way. Once there, Jesse dropped the cash box into the lobby safe.

Now safe from the pursuing ghosts, we packed into the cars. Jesse and one of the regulars got into the Rambler with me. I pulled up behind Negro's Ford and followed it to the red-light district. The zona was not far, perhaps three miles, but it required a zigzag route on unmarked dirt streets and was hard to find.

This was intentional. The zona attracted as little attention as possible from the town's respectable residents, and crowds of sailors couldn't find it on their own. An obscure route also enabled the taxistas to make handsome fares for the trip. There was a brisk trade each weekend in taking men, and some of the girls who worked there, to and from the "night-clubs."

Our drive started out on a paved avenue on one of the city's main bus routes, then turned off into a series of wide, unmarked, rutted dirt streets. Soon the lights of Guaymas vanished, and we rolled slowly into a district that was eerily quiet except for the occasional dogs barking—no streetlights, no pavement, no street signs. Few lights in the houses.

The hush and darkness were interrupted occasionally as taxis passed us going the other direction on their return to town. We took one final turn behind Negro's immaculate turquoise-over-black '54 Crown Victoria and suddenly emerged onto a large, brightly lit square surrounded by neon and nightclubs.

The red-light district was its own village with a number of clubs laid out in a huge square around a central plaza, partly filled in with buildings housing laundry, bodegas, and simple open-front restaurants. Situated at the outskirts of town, the zona nestled smack up against the spectacular bowl of mountains that separated Guaymas from Bacochibampo Bay and Primaverales.

We got out and mounted wide steps up to the Río Rita, the largest nightclub, which dominated one corner of the square. As we entered, a modest floor show was in progress. This was a weeknight—the jazziest shows were on Friday and Saturday nights.

Still, it was a surprise to discover how big and how busy the place was. It sported a decent five-piece band, twenty to thirty girls, midweek, and twice that many men drinking, talking, or checking out the cute singer on stage.

Almost immediately Jesse and Negro introduced me to the manager. Alonzo Chang was a legend among the taxistas and cantineros, who knew him as El Chino (the Chinaman). He stood about five feet tall and was nearly five feet around the waist. He perched on a large stool at the end of the bar, orchestrating everything and compulsively downing highly sugared Mexican Cokes, one after another.

He was a jolly, outgoing guy, simpático. His mixed Mexican and Chinese ancestry had earned him his nickname and was an echo of the Chinese immigrants who had once come to Sonora to build the Pacífico railway, which ran through town.

We watched the show, one set only, no repeats on Thursday night. There were dancers, singers, and one stand of jokes, as at the Pleamar. I drank one super-sweet Mexican Coke and had a good time. But I was still thinking about Marta as Jesse ragged me about getting hot and bothered, *calientito*, for her. He was right. I was absolutely choking on testosterone.

Two minutes later Negro introduced me to one of the girls, who came to sit and talk with him for a few minutes before she moved on. Her name was Elsa. Her nickname was La Chuleta (Porkchops). Her name obviously referred to the knockout view I got as she walked away to drink at another nearby table.

Had she been a fashion model in the States, she could instantly have doubled the sales of any line of jeans she modeled. Here at the Río Rita, she had to settle for doubling her price on Saturday nights.

Most of the girls at clubs like this were more ordinary, so made a good bit of their money by drinking tea water laced with liquor, just like the B-girls who worked the French Quarter in New Orleans. The waiters would leave them a token, called a *ficha*, for each drink they and their male hosts consumed. At the end of the night they were paid several pesos for each ficha. At the Río Rita mixed drinks, *cocteles*, were fifteen pesos. A beer ten. Pricey!

The beers most commonly served were long-necked Coronas or Superiores, which everyone called *jirafas* (giraffes). In those days the jirafas were considered nightclub beers and were rarely served in upscale, mixed company. It is now amusing to watch the prosperous graduate students sucking them down in the pubs around our university, lime slices speared on toothpicks and balanced in the necks, just as they were served in the Río Rita thirty-odd years ago. Chang would have been impressed.

After a while Jesse asked if I saw any girls who caught my eye. Negro said, "Yes, you have money. Have a good time. You've been lonely for a while." Actually, I had spotted somebody. Across the room, near the band, sat a very attractive girl, mid-to-late twenties, tall and stately, dressed in a simple but classy black evening gown.

I said, "Yes, that one over there in black is very classy looking. Do you suppose she'd come over for a drink?" Negro waved her over and introduced me to her. Her name was Francisca. I invited her to sit down. She accepted. I bought her a drink, got another soda, and we chatted. She was pleasant and spoke elegant Spanish—virtually no street-slang.

As we talked, she asked if I was the norteamericano who had been living in a hammock out at Playas Primaverales. Surprised, I admitted I was and asked her how she knew. "Your boots are unique. The *taxistas* talk." Then she gave me a gentle lecture about how one can't just be living on the beach. I laughed.

She asked me what I did for a job. I told her I was an anthropologist, but just now was resting up in Guaymas. She wanted to know if I had a university degree. I told her I had already finished my master's in the States.

She told me she had once been a nurse in Mexico City. In turn I told her I had gone to university in Mexico City when I was twenty. That clicked for her. She liked talking about the "D.F." (federal district) and had thought my Spanish was tinged with a Mexico City accent.

She said my Spanish was nice . . . it reminded her of home. Flattery. I wanted to ask why she had given up nursing and come so far north to Sonora—and the life of a B-girl in a club here, three hundred miles from the border, but I didn't.

We turned to light chatter, talking and laughing. I was having fun. Suddenly Negro said he was going to leave the table to talk to a friend and asked to be excused. Next Jesse quietly slipped off, with the excuse that he was going to the men's room and would be right back, which of course he wasn't.

As soon as we were alone, Francisca said, "Well, Davíd, would you like to go with me to my room *por un ratito* (for a little while)?" I said, "Well, gee, I don't know." And she said, "Come on, it'll be only a hundred pesos (eight dollars), and I will be real nice to you. You're nice, I'll be nice to you."

I said, "Okay," and thought, 'What the hell.' As we stood up from the table and turned to go, I spotted Jesse and Negro sitting together on the last two stools at the end of the bar, talking to Chang. Quite aware of my doings, they both turned and grinned at me, then Jesse closed thumb to forefinger to give me a subtle "okay" sign. Obviously they had engineered the situation.

We walked through a big archway at the back of the dance floor to a little room in the adjoining corridor. Once in the room, I gave her a hundred peso note.

Francisca was gentle, joking and teasing. She could tell I was nervous and a little shy. She took off her gown, but not her slip and underclothes and started pulling my shirt out of my pants to unbutton it. She kept up a gentle chatter, teasing me about sleeping on the beach, repeating that a nice, educated guy shouldn't be wasting his life. That I ought to find a nice girl, get married, go into business, do something productive.

Then she said to me, "You know, Negro and Canelo, they're great people, they'll take care of you. You listen to them. . . ." The serious moment past, she went back to teasing me while she expertly finished unbuttoning the shirt, "Don't you like the Mexican girls?"

I retorted, "I like them a whole helluva lot, why? What do you think I'm doing here right now?" She laughed hard and grinned. Next she began kissing my neck as she unhooked her bra. Oh, my!—this was not going to be painful.

Just then I heard a loud "pssst-pssst," the harsh, urgent hiss one uses in Mexico to chastise errant waiters or stop buses in midtraffic on the Reforma. It had come from the doorway to her small room. I thought, "Holy smokes—what's going on?"

Then came an insistent "rap-rap-rap" at the door, and I thought "Well, now what?" Francisca turned and answered the rap, "*un momentito* (just a minute)." Opening the door on a crack, she stuck her nose out cautiously. Apparently she didn't like what she saw. In an instant she slammed the door shut, turned to me, and ordered, "*¡Ándale!* You've got to get out of here!"

As my fears gathered, she began buttoning up my shirt about a hundred and fifty times faster than she had unbuttoned it. There was a commotion in the hall, with laughing and talking. It didn't sound like federales. The next thing I knew, another girl darted in, grabbed my arm, and pulled me into the hallway.

Okay, I admit that I had begun to panic, but at least it wasn't cops or two goons with a knife. Instead it was a cute little hooker pretending to lick my ear, while dragging me toward the dance hall, forty feet away. She had obviously done this before and was good at it. I really had no choice in the matter.

Calming down, I was still wondering why I was getting a hooker's version of the bum's rush when a very distinguished gentlemen passed us in the hall—nice suit, silver hair. I thought I knew him from somewhere but wasn't certain, so didn't say anything to him. He smiled vacantly and walked on past, not paying close attention to us.

When we got to the front room Negro grabbed me. The little hooker disappeared immediately as Negro walked me to the end of the bar and sat me down. He went, "*¡Por Dios!* That was so close!" At the same time, Alonzo Chang, the manager, was carrying on "*¡Ay, que bárbaro!* (Horrors!)" and wiping the sweat from his forehead in exaggerated terror. Finally I said, "Will somebody tell me what's going on?"

Jesse came over, laughing his buns off, and informed me, "You just about got caught." And I said, "Got caught by who? Cops? What the hell's going on?" He said, "No, no, no, no. Didn't you recognize that guy going in there?" And I said "Well, he sure as hell looked familiar. I know I've seen him somewhere." Jesse said, "You've seen him at the hotel! That is don Francisco."

"He's the one who owns all the Pemex stations around here, and la Francisca is his steady date. He is her steady client, and has been seeing her two or three times a week here for years. She's not supposed to be with anyone else. But he doesn't usually come this early in the week. He usually comes on weekends. His wife must be out of town or something."

I asked why it was such a big deal. After all, this is a night-club. This is the zona! He said, "Oh, no! She is RESERVED." I gaped, "You mean, she never takes other clients?" He said, "No. She cheats on him, when he's not here."

I groaned, "Well, *¡Mierda!* I sure didn't get my money's worth." Negro asked, "Well, did you pay her?" I said, "*Claro que sí.*" And he said, "Well don't worry about it. She'll see you later. It'll all work out. I think maybe we should go next door."

The three of us went next door to a club called the B-47. We had a couple of drinks there to calm down, and Jesse combed the "cool" back into his James Dean. Then, as predicted, Negro asked me to take Jesse back to town. He wanted to stay on a while. So, following Jesse's street directions, I drove him back at about one o'clock in the morning and dropped him off at a corner near his house.

He was not yet at the stage where he wanted me to see precisely where he lived. This is common in Mexico. Life en la calle is open, informal, and easy. Life *en casa* (at home) is more private and protected.

I parked at the Rubi—there was a rare empty spot smack dab in front of the graceful archway into the lobby—and stuck my nose inside, but nothing was happening, so I walked around the corner to the taxi stand. A group of the taxistas were still there talking and pitching coins. Though a weeknight, it was early enough that a few fares from the nightclubs or late buses might materialize.

In spite of the drinks I was still wide awake after the episode at the Río Rita, and hungry. Several of the men asked how our trip to the nightclub had gone. I said it was "okay," but not as exciting as the Pleamar. To which they responded in Spanglish—go back on Saturday night with the cantineros, Jesse and Negro, and it will be *"¡super bueno!"*

I was still talking to El Burro and Mateo, when little Lupita, who had given me the flowers, popped her head around the corner of the wire gate to the shrimp-packing plant across the street. I had gotten glimpses of her several times a day since the flowers, but only at a distance. She usually vanished as quickly as she appeared.

The taxistas had told me they thought she slept either in

140

the plant's workyard or on the roof. Activity there was irregular in the summer. It was long past the prime shrimp season, and the packing plant went at full tilt only several times a month when a shrimper would come in with a load of *camarón de luna*, the small shrimps usually harvested at the full moon. Then they'd run a couple of shifts to get everything frozen and processed quickly.

Immediately the men started ragging me again about here's my novia, sticking her head around the corner. She was only fifty feet away. These guys had ragged me ever since the Sitio Rubi day crew had seen her bring me the stolen bougainvillea, the morning after I had first scolded her.

Given the night's fiasco at the Río Rita, I figured the whole town would know about it by morning and was in no mood for more kidding. So I said, "No, she's not my girlfriend. She's my *mandadera* (errand girl).

141

Lupita appeared to be just a kid. In spite of appearances, though, she really "acted out"—a saucy, raunchy denizen of the street. That she was my mandadera was a surprise to both of us. Someone said, "Oh well, that explains why she was looking in your window and keeps asking where you are." I said, "Yes, she runs errands for me."

It is not uncommon in Mexico for a businessmen, even a taxista, to have a favorite shoeshine boy who also runs errands. It was much rarer that mine was a little girl, simply because there were so few girls on the street. I don't think they really thought she was my girlfriend, but I was getting ragged about it and just didn't need it.

Lupita heard and came scampering over from across the street, just as raunchy and as tart as ever, saying "*¡Ya ven, cabrones, soy la empleada!* (See, you sons of bitches, I'm the

employee!) *El Güero es mi patrón* (The Gringo is my boss)."
Again I scolded her, off-handedly, "None of this *cabrón* stuff."
And she said, "*Sí patrón* (Yes, boss)."

I told her, "Come around tomorrow morning and I will
have more errands for you." Immediately she became more
formal and subdued, "Oh yes, of course—until morning,
then." And disappeared again into the night.

Several of the guys looked at me, grinning, obviously prepared to tease me a bit more. Then old Mateo, who had a son
with cerebral palsy and was by far the most sensitive of the lot,
said, "I worry for her; soon she'll be too old to be a little girl,
and she's too young to be a woman. She simply should not be
on the street."

I asked Mateo, "What's the story with her?" He said, "I'm
not certain. But they say her mother came to Guaymas with
her a few years ago and then left her here when she went to
Baja." He said, "Those are just rumors, things that one hears
en la calle." I nodded, "*He oido* (I've heard)."

He continued, "It would be good for her to have something to do." I agreed, and we turned to other topics. I thought
all I had done that night was to create a face-saving situation
for both me and this kid, by claiming she worked for me. After
calling the taxistas *cabrones*, a very risky maneuver, Lupita
didn't reappear, for fear of retribution.

Still hungry, I asked Burro where I might get something to
eat at this hour. He suggested the Almita, across from the city's
old market, about twelve blocks away. I started to walk but he
offered me a cheap fare, since he had gotten a call to fetch a
prescription from the all-night pharmacy, then deliver it.

His trip would take him within feet of the restaurant, and
I could jump out. As we drove up the Serdán, along the

142

malecón, we passed Lupita standing under a streetlight near the packing plant, staring out across the harbor. She was alone but seemed not to notice us. Burro, seeing me look puzzled, told me she often stood at that spot—that she was "*un poquito rara* (a bit odd)."

We passed in front of the Supermercado Morales, the town's first modern supermarket, and turned left at the corner. Burro dropped me at the curb and pointed to the wide, lit entryway of the restaurant, in a narrow lane behind Morales. I walked in, took a table, and was surprised at the boisterous crowd—men who had obviously been nightclubbing, mixed with truck drivers and cantineros who had closed their bars.

I checked out the menu and ordered a small *milanesa* (a breaded "veal" cutlet), refried beans, lettuce and tomatoes, and a toasted roll. Spectacular! The restaurant smelled wonderful in the hot night. The scents of cilantro, chiles, fresh fruits, and hot coffee were circulated by the big fan set up out on the sidewalk, facing inward. The fan also drew in other exotic scents from the old market across the street—vanilla, chocolate, saffron.

143

I had been sitting there about thirty minutes when Negro Jacinto breezed in with Alonzo Chang. They were happy to see me and came over to sit down. I had mistakenly thought Negro had stayed out at the Río Rita for one of the girls. Instead it was for an early morning breakfast with Chang. They didn't order, but food appeared quickly and magically. Apparently they were regulars.

I started to say something about the earlier events at the Río Rita, but Negro subtly shook his head, "No," and swiftly changed the subject to a funny story about tourists out at the

Miramar Hotel, where he worked. I was learning that events in the zona were never spoken of publicly *en el centro*.

Negro ate his eggs quickly and Chino took off on foot. I got a ride back in the Crown Victoria to within two blocks of the Rubi and went to bed. It was a struggle to sleep in that heat, but my little fan and wet towels helped.

In the morning the cleaning girl came in to do my room about ten, but she wasn't alone and didn't know it. The minute she opened my door, I groaned. There right behind her was gritty little Lupita, La Gatita, now my employee. Obviously I had stuck my foot in my mouth the night before. I told them both to get the hell out of the room and give me five minutes until I could get dressed, throw on some fresh clothes, and go outside.

Lupita was standing beneath the courtyard's rear window, waiting for me. She was wide-eyed and expectant. Marisol, the cleaning girl, went on into my room, looking over her shoulder at me disapprovingly. Just as I started to talk to Lupita, the pleasant-faced woman who often ran the front desk came back, wagging her finger at Lupita, telling her she shouldn't be there.

I turned to the señora very nicely (she was always so pleasant) and told her that I was in the process of asking Lupita if she could run some errands for me. I asked if that was against the rules. I'm not certain that it was completely within the rules, but it was such an unusual request for a norteamericano guest in the hotel that it wasn't turned down.

She answered, "Well, I'm sorry. I didn't realize you had business. She sort of hangs around." I said, "Yes, I understand that, but I think this will be all right. If you don't want me to see her here in the future, I won't." She said, "Oh, no, no.

That's alright, but she shouldn't be just hanging around here all the time." I said, "I understand that."

So I turned and talked to Lupita right there in the corridor. She kept calling me "patrón." I had learned to deeply detest the nuances of that title in Ecuador. Finally I said, "Do not call me *patrón!* That does not suit me." She said, "Well, can I call you *jefe?*" I said, "Well if you insist you can call me *jefe* (boss). But I much prefer that you just call me *Güero.*"

She said, "Okay. But you have proper names, too—señor Davíd Stuart," pronouncing it "Astuaard." I asked her how she knew that, and she answered, "It is my business to find out things." I said, "Very well."

With a pleading tone in her voice she continued, "Well, last night you told me I was going to work for you." I said, "Yes, that's true," responding quickly so as not to make this little kid feel terrible. And I did feel sorry for her. Ratty or not, she was a street urchin; she was homeless.

She had been on the street so long she was obviously wise to the ways of the world, but she was still a kid. And she was quite a sight. She wore a dirty, faded pale blue dress that buttoned up the front, sporting several little tears in it. And when I say "dirty," I mean filthy!

The dress was also far too short for her. Occasionally one runs into parents who costume their little girls in dresses that are just too short, midthigh, thinking that it's cute for a girl that age. Well, Lupita was obviously a ten-year-old girl wearing a six- or seven-year-old girl's cast-off dress. Bare feet, no shoes. Her feet were cut up, and she was dirty.

I asked her if she had any family in the Guaymas area. She said "no," looking away, and offered no further comment. I asked her where she lived, and she told me, "in the street," as others had told me. After some prodding she said she often slept across the street near the *empacadora* (shrimp-packing plant). That the night watchman would fall asleep, then she would climb up into the stacks of boxes and would find a place to sleep. Then she said, "Well, if I'm to work for you, I must know what kind of work it is that you do and what you want done."

Improvising I said, "I arrange things for people; so if there is any business that I should know about in this town that has to do with my countrymen or things like that, you just let me know. At other times I will want cigarettes or my clothes taken out to be cleaned or messages sent to people, and you will deliver the messages." I elaborated for effect, "And the messages will always be confidential. I will write them in a little note."

Actually I was thinking I could send her up to Negro's house now and again when I wanted to meet him for a drink or something like that, instead of one of the shoeshine boys who hung around the Rubi's barber shop, and why not? She sought clarification.

"So you would arrange things? You would get your countrymen out of jail or something like that?" I said, "Yes, things like that." She kept elaborating and I didn't discourage her, "And I suppose you translate; you're a translator?"

I said, "Yes, I also write letters for people who need letters written in English and translate English letters into Spanish." I continued, "If there seem to be people who require my services, you let me know. At other times I will simply have you run errands for me, do things that I require. I have no wife, so there will be things that I require."

She said, "Very well. And what about my salary?"

Thinking that this wouldn't really amount to much of anything except a token sum for her I said, "Well, how about five or six pesos a day?" She said, "No, that's not enough. I must have ten pesos a day to start." Irritated, I said, "Every day! THIRTY days of the month? . . . And how am I to pay you?"

She said, "Daily. You pay me daily." "Well, I don't want to do that. I'll pay you weekly, six days of wages, like everyone on *sueldo* (salary). But if you're going to be my agent, you've got to clean up. You're not presentable. You need a bath."

I had to be blunt with her. Dirty, raggedy, and very smelly, with matted hair, the kid was offensive "as is." Who knows—she might actually look normal if she were all cleaned up. At least she was interesting! Still, I couldn't imagine how a stunted ten-year-old could actually make a living on her own in Mexico. Later I was to find out.

The way I meant to leave it was with the mandate, "Take a bath and get cleaned up!" Irritated, she was quiet for a moment then insisted, "Well then, I need an advance on my salary." Her tone was determined, if not defiant. The kid sure had spirit.

I figured, 'What the heck,' so I gave her fifty pesos and told her to come back for work only when she was properly cleaned up and had news for me. I repeated that she could not be my agent looking the way she did. She scowled, but took the money and shouted "*¡gracias!*" over her shoulder as she darted away through the lobby before anyone could catch her. That was that for the day.

I reentered my room, thinking 'Well, I've made an ass of myself and thrown fifty pesos away.' But she really had an appealing quality. I could still picture her big brown eyes staring through the window a few nights before, after I placed the bottle of red bougainvillea on my writing table. About then a wave of deep empathy for her welled up in me.

I had paid her the fifty pesos, had employed her, and figured, 'What the hell, I'll pay her for a while till I decide to put my foot down and work up the nerve to tell her to buzz off.' So that was that.

Later that day I was reading the newspaper in the hotel's public bar and drinking my Orange Crush, when the nice little taco man who worked the neighborhood popped in. He always brought a large, blue enameled tin full of goat meat tacos for sale. These consisted of grilled meat folded in a corn tortilla, topped with chopped onion, tomato, jalapeño, cilantro, and a dab of lime.

He always greeted us with a wide smile and "tacos MAG-NÍFICOS de cabrito." And they were magnificent. In Mexico pursuit of the best taco is a form of street religion. I have been a devoted practitioner for forty years, and, I assure you, this gent was the high priest. If he'd had money or a backer he would now own the largest chain of taco stands on the planet.

But he was just one of the thousands of grindingly poor characters who endlessly worked the streets of Mexican towns with tins of tacos and wore huaraches instead of shoes. Our taco man had only a piece of commercial fishing cordage for a belt. He couldn't even afford a leather one. He was clean, but tattered. Stoop-shouldered, his graying hair was always brushed straight back. He smiled a lot. Poor but proud. Only God knew why. . . .

That day I pondered the situation with Lupita as I ate his tacos. In my own mind it was complicated and about "the Truth." Just the night before, Edward had come and asked me to help him find a wife. So I hadn't altogether lied to the kid. I was very soon going to be arranging things, just as I had told her.

The seeds of this had actually germinated earlier, when I used to hang around Playas Primaverales and direct tourists to the doctors, help them order dinner, or write out the Spanish version of their U.S. prescriptions to take to the local pharmacists. I often accepted free meals. If somebody said, "We're so grateful; can we buy you a meal," I'd say "yes."

And, upon further reflection, I had actually begun saying "yes" years before, as a college kid of twenty in Mexico City. There I often helped lost or befuddled tourists, and they would say, "Oh, let us buy you a drink, or dinner," and I'd let them.

Now Jesse was urging me to "do things for people" locally and let them pay me, if they offered. If one considered free meals and beer as precedents, then perhaps it was a natural thing for me to do in Mexico. Satisfied with my own rationalizations, I went back to my room and updated my journal.

Later I walked up to the Colmenar and had a bowl of soup with café con leche. I chose a table out in the *pasaje* to catch any hint of breeze. The Sonoran summer's heat radiated off the street in front, rising in boiling waves of distorted air. As I ate I talked to Mercedes and Max, the owner. It wasn't just my tender gringo hide—everyone was hot and sweating! The whole town was praying for a cooling breeze to provide relief.

In the poorer barrios the late morning greeting among familiars had changed from "*¿Has comido?* (Have you eaten?)" to simply, "*¡Ay, qué calór!* (Wow, what heat!)" But in downtown Guaymas, where one assumed that food was not the main issue, men were beginning to greet familiars with "*¡Agárrate la onda!* (Catch the wave!)" or "*¡Qué onda!*" The "wave" greeting had started in the sixties down in Mexico City among the smart set, as an exhortation to "be cool! be hip!"

Here in Guaymas by-the-sea it had taken on a third layer of meaning, because wave action in the bay meant cooling breezes. Its second meaning among the sailors and camaroneros already derived from the rhythmic slap! slap! slap! and dipping motion of a boat's hull as it plowed through the waves. On the Serdán, it meant "be hip, get cool, get laid," all rolled into one.

In colloquial Spanish, where double entendres are highly regarded, triple entendres can reach mythic proportions. "*¡Agárrate la onda!*" was a gold-plated "three-fer" in the summer of '70.

150

My days had taken on a satisfying structure. That day I was up around ten, an Orange Crush in the front bar of the Rubi. Noon newspaper readings, conversation, and more Orange Crush, sometimes the goat tacos, then a slow walk uptown to the Colmenar.

Along the way it was appropriate to greet nearly everyone in sight, friend and stranger alike. Courtesy required a pause at each sitio. I usually stopped at the Rubi, Centenario, and Medrano to shake hands, chat, and "grab the wave"—find out what was happening on the street. Then on to late lunch at the Colmenar, more greetings and conversation.

Later I was to discover that this was known as *serdaneando* (doing the Serdán). Men of affairs, both prominent and humble, invested several hours daily in making their rounds, taking the pulse of the town, maintaining relationships. In recent years *serdaneando* has taken on a newer form, as young folks who have access to cars drive endlessly back and forth along the main drag. We now know it in the States as "cruising."

By early evening I had made it back down to the Rubi, where I checked in at the sitio, then the barber shop, before taking an hour's fitful nap in my room. I was surprised this day that not one word of last night's "almost got laid" fiasco at the Río Rita had come up at the sitios. That morning I had mentally braced for a major ragging before working up the courage to make the day's rounds.

After my nap I bought several tacos from a cart near the hotel, then climbed to the Rubi's balcony, where I watched a spectacular sunset over the harbor and entered more of the day's events in my journal. I liked the view and the big, old-fashioned rocking chairs up there. As I rocked I could hear the men below at the sitio and the bustle of the waterfront. It was my private hour.

151

By dusk, about nine, I was in the hotel's rear paneled bar, as usual. There weren't many customers around. A couple of businessmen who should have been home with their families were drinking and complaining about the summer slowdown in commerce.

By midsummer both the money from the shrimp harvest and American tourists had vanished. So these two were moaning about how *piojo* business was. *Piojo* means "body louse," so business was "lousy." Almost exactly the way we use it in the States.

While we were sitting there playing a halfhearted game of dice, don Francisco walked in. Jesse stiffened and nodded quickly toward something behind me, while simultaneously drawing the tip of his forefinger to his lower eyelid. In Mexico this gesture means "Careful! Watch out!" Obviously he expected trouble.

I turned just as don Francisco sat down and ordered beers for the house. There were perhaps five of us, so it wasn't a big deal. We accepted our beers and all thanked him very kindly. He chatted brightly for a while with the group, then turned to Jesse and said, "Canelo, you should introduce me to your *norteamericano* friend. I saw him with you the other night." Nervous, Jesse introduced us, stuttering slightly.

As we shook hands, he said, "I am Francisco X., pleased to know you." I introduced myself and said, "Oh, yes, I've heard of you. You are don Francisco. You own the gasoline station El Corsario. I hear people speak well of you." He smiled and asked what I was doing in Guaymas. I told him that I had returned from work in South America, to visit friends, and was staying on to relax and enjoy Guaymas.

After we traded formalities, he said, "Yes, really, you look very familiar. I'm sure that I saw you last night." I said, "Yes, perhaps I did see you in passing. I noticed how distinguished you looked. I was at a nightclub. It may have been you that I saw, I'm not certain, at least it was a gentleman who looked rather like you."

Staring, he said in a sardonic tone, "Now I'm sure it was you." It was quiet for a long moment. Jesse was nearly as stressed out as I was.

But don Francisco was in control, enjoying himself. He was accustomed to power. Tall, handsome, distinguished, and rich, he spoke the elegant, old-fashioned Spanish several of my professors had once used in Mexico City. My mouth was getting dry. I licked my lips. He noticed.

Satisfied, he pulled out his wallet, opened it, and extended his hand to give me a hundred-peso note. "I am reasonably certain, *casi seguro*, that you dropped this in the hallway last night as you passed me. Either that, or we are *cuates.*"

His voice gave no emotional clues. I didn't know what to do next, so cast one eye toward Jesse, who nodded, almost imperceptibly, indicating I should accept.

I accepted the money graciously, thanked him in my best Spanish, and asked if I couldn't buy him and the others a round of drinks with the money. He smiled again and said, "No, thank you." Explaining that he had to be on his way home, he shook my hand pleasantly and walked out the door.

I turned back to the bar after the door closed behind don Francisco. Jesse was actually shaking by the time I asked him what was going on. He pulled out a bottle of tequila and poured both of us a shot.

153

He said, "He's trying to find out whether or not you screwed Francisca. He must have realized that she was going to do it with you and that his visit broke it up. At least he hoped that he broke it up—and he knows as well as anyone in town that the standard fee is a hundred pesos. Thank God you took his money. Maybe he wanted reassurance that you hadn't slept with her, or maybe he wanted to see how you would respond—and you handled it well."

I told Jesse I was stressed out and found the whole scene very weird, *raro*. He agreed, still shaking. I asked if don Francisco did this sort of thing often. He said, "No, no. This is unique! I don't know what to make of it."

Worried, I asked Jesse if he thought don Francisco would make trouble, like pay to have my legs broken. He said, "No.

He's not that type. He's very *culto*, cultured. He wouldn't make that kind of a stink over a hooker—beneath his dignity.

"On the other hand, if you were to go near one of his daughters after he's seen you in the *zona*, and he's got several gorgeous daughters, then maybe you'd get real trouble. If he's really angry, you may get visits from the *policía*, checking your passport, auto insurance, stuff like that.

"That's how he would use his power if he wanted to make trouble for you. Guaymas is too small a town for anything like violence. There is no one here who would hurt anyone for money. We're poor here in Guaymas, but not that poor. That's border stuff, maybe Mexico City or Guadalajara, but not here."

Then I asked, "Well, what did he mean by 'we're *cuates* (twins)'?" He said, "Well that is used in several ways. Usually it means very close friends, but sometimes is said when two guys are screwing the same girl. Besides, if anybody gets in trouble, it will be Francisca, not you."

154

I said, "Well, *¡mierda!* I didn't know what I was getting into last night." Pulling out his comb, Jesse said, "Don't worry about it too much. She's a big girl, that's just between the two of them." But I did worry about it.

That night at closing time nobody went nightclubbing. I wandered around the waterfront for a while but, still troubled, took my old gray Rambler and drove out to the Río Rita again. I got lost twice on the way. It was a while yet before I fully learned the route.

I pulled up to the club, entered, and stopped to greet Alonzo Chang. I asked him where Francisca was. He said, "Well, sit down and have a drink." I said, "No liquor, I just want a Coca Cola and wish to talk to her for a minute, if possible. No business. I can't stay long."

Chang disappeared and Francisca came out, wearing the same black dress, high-heeled black pumps, and silver belt. She gave me a great big grin and hustled me over to a table, sat me down, and said, "Look, I owe you a hundred pesos." She reached into her dress, pulled out a hundred-peso note, and returned my money.

"I hope you're not furious at me, Davíd. El Chino was kind of mad. He doesn't like trouble of that kind, but my Francisco doesn't usually come in until weekends. I enjoyed talking to you, and I do take clients every now and then."

I listened but said, "I don't think you understand—everybody's giving me a hundred pesos tonight. I saw don Francisco, that's what I came to tell you. He also gave me a hundred-peso note and said he thought I had dropped it in the hall last night." She sat there goggling at me, dumbstruck, then began laughing—laughing herself senseless. It was not the reaction I had expected.

She called to Chang, who came quickly. He asked, "What's going on? What's the matter? What can I do for you?" She said, "You give us two drinks, real drinks. I'm buying. I want to talk to my friend, Davíd here." I said, "I really don't want a drink. I'll have Coca-Cola." And she said, "Okay, *bueno*, whatever you want," but reminded Chang to bring her a real drink.

Once she had her high-ball and had taken a belt, she wanted to hear all about the don Francisco conversation at the Hotel Rubi. "*¡Cada detalle!* (Every detail!)" I recounted the scene word-for-word, as best I could. I told her I was concerned, that I hadn't meant to get her in trouble.

She said, "Oh no. He's merely jealous. He'll be mean . . . he'll yell at me and stay away . . . he's not going to hit me or anything like that. He'll just throw a fit and won't come back for several weeks. It happened like that once before."

And I said, "Well, you gave me the hundred pesos back. I don't know how to give him a hundred pesos back." She said, "You come on with me." She put her arm around my waist and took me on into the back corridor, the same room that I'd been kicked out of the night before.

I protested, "Wait! I don't want problems." She assured me that Francisco was gone—he'd told her he had business en el centro. Had I been that business? Still I was nervous, so she ducked out and told Chino she wanted to go across the street. He okayed it.

In the Mexican clubs, if a girl left the premises, she (or her client) ordinarily had to pay a fee called the *salida*. This amounted to an "exit fee" for the house, to compensate the loss of her commerce. There was a little "motel" across the street, where some of the girls actually roomed. It belonged to the club and was a big moneymaker for the owner, Pepe L. She took me over there. These were her private quarters.

This room was larger, and nice. It smelled clean. Stuffed animals graced the bed. As I looked around, she said, "Okay, I have returned your hundred pesos and Francisco gave you a hundred pesos. Right?" I nodded. She said, "I want one hundred pesos." I asked why. She said, "Well, you are going to spend *un ratito* (a while) with me. We had a deal, and that's all."

She picked up where we were the night before when the rapping at the door brought proceedings to a grinding halt. She smelled good and was lovely to look at. About half an hour later she stopped, got up, and went into her little shower room to clean up. I was starting to get dressed when she came back out again, wearing a different negligee.

She offered me a cigarette and said, "Now, I want something else from you." And I said, "Well, what?" She said, "I want the other hundred pesos that don Francisco gave you." Again, I asked why. She said, "I'm going to fuck you with don Francisco's money. The son of a bitch has it coming." So I laughed and handed over the second hundred-peso note, which was don Francisco's, and spent the rest of the night with Francisca.

About five o'clock in the morning she woke me. A big pitcher of café con leche and some sweet rolls, *panes dulces*, had been sent in. She was amazing. While I drank the coffee and wolfed down sugar-coated sweet rolls, she was planning the rest of my life.

She gently scolded me all over again for having lived on the beach and having no clear direction. In essence she said, "You need to make a place for yourself, you need to have a job, you need to get a wife, a house, babies."

157

I chuckled, then she got dead serious. "Let me give you some advice. I think you should be dating *señoritas*, nice girls, here in Guaymas. If you want to come to the Río Rita and have a good time, drink a Coca-Cola or a beer and watch the floor show, that's fine. But tonight, our all-night date, that's the beginning and the end of it. You just be my friend and a friend of the house. We girls here aren't right for you."

You be my friend, not my client. This had also been a theme with Eva at the Rubi. Frankly I didn't understand it, but I told her I'd respect her advice as best I could and would be honored to be her friend. She smiled, touched my face affectionately, and I left a little after five. Her word was good. In the months to come she was a real friend to me when I most needed it.

As I walked out to cross the street I saw Chang standing by the steps in front of the Río Rita, near my Rambler. I asked if he needed a ride to town. He accepted and hopped in.

Immediately he began talking about Guaymas, about how important dignity was, and how to preserve it. He explained in the abstract how easy it was to maintain dignity even in a small city like Guaymas. It depended on respecting others' secrets. I suggested that might be difficult in a place where everyone appears to know everyone else's business.

He retorted that "appearances" and "reality" were two different worlds. I told him I didn't quite understand. He expanded the thesis that most secrets were inevitably exposed by the very one who most needed to keep them—that bragging gave others the right to gossip.

I asked if silence would generally be respected with silence. He said, *"Claro, que sí."* I asked if that might apply even to the private affairs of a norteamericano. He smiled and said, *"Cierto* (Certainly)." The lesson over, he started telling jokes and laughing.

He got out on an empty cross-street near the Serdán, where no taxistas would see us. The veil was already dropping. I was never to hear one word about that night. I drove on to the Hotel Rubi and parked by the bodegas to avoid the taxistas and went to bed a little after five-thirty in the morning.

The next morning about ten, I was on my way to get an Orange Crush, when Lupita went "pssst-pssst" from the sidewalk in front of the archway to the lobby. Wow! Lupita was wearing very different clothes. Using the salary advance, she had apparently bought herself the street-kid equivalent of a "makeover"—"new" clothes, rubber flip-flops, neatly brushed hair. She had also gotten herself a bath and cleaned up.

The pair of rubber thongs were blue, the kind that you get in the dime stores. But these looked slightly used, so she had likely paid only a couple of pesos for them. She had on a little striped V-neck cotton top with no sleeves and a pair of boy's khaki pants with an elastic waistband.

I commented on the pants—they were a dramatic change from the filthy little dress that was too short. She said she had wanted to buy a dress, but couldn't afford one because she had also bought underclothes. I later found out that there were a couple of used clothing places in Guaymas run by social agencies. Her hair was brushed, trimmed, and held in place by two little blue plastic barrettes. Even her nails were clean and trimmed!

I was surprised and impressed. I told her so. She looked really different—quite presentable to be my agent. I told her that, too. She seemed pleased. She looked just like an ordinary cute kid, with nice big eyes. Still she was a handful. Then she cussed one of the shoeshine boys who teased her on the way past. That broke the momentary illusion. I scolded her for that. She scowled but said she was ready to go to work.

159

I told her, as best I recall, "Okay, there are several things you can do for me. First, I need some clothes mended, cleaned, and pressed," which I did need. "So I need to find me somebody reliable and dependable to care for my clothes—and inexpensive. A widow lady, a poor lady, somebody who takes in clothes, but very reliable."

She said La Gorda could do that for me. "Okay, fine," I said. "Also, I need to find the newspaper office. I need to place an ad." She said, "Okay, fine, I'll take you up there. You follow me in a few minutes." I said better an hour or so—I was expected in the bar. "The third thing is . . . I want to know something about a person. This is confidential, between us. If you talk, I'll fire you."

She nodded gravely, telling me she understood. She appeared to be taking the "job" seriously. I continued, "I want to know about a girl who comes here occasionally for drinks in the evening, one called Marta." I described Marta to her. She said she had seen her, the taxistas called her La Flaca. She knew which one. I said, "Correct. I want to know where she lives and if she's married. Can you find out and tell me?"

She said, "*Sí*," then looked at me bravely, holding her breath, and asked if I was in love. I said, "No, I just want to know about this woman. Don't ask questions; just do as I say."

So I stopped inside again and went down to the public bar, got my Orange Crush, read the newspaper. She hung around outside. I came out after a while and we went up the street toward the weekly "newspaper's" office near the town hall to place an ad for Edward Meyers. When I entered she disappeared, so I went in alone.

Finished, I went from there on up to the Colmenar and had lunch. While I was sitting there Lupita passed by with her charge, Juanito, the crippled shoeshine boy. I shouted. He came back and did a nice job on my Red Wings. But Lupita didn't come with him.

That surprised me. Instead she stayed mostly out of sight, somewhere in the narrow street at the rear of the Pasaje, near the entrance to the Sánchez Clinic. Several times she stuck her head around the corner for a moment, checked on us, then disappeared again. She was a hard one to figure out. She was like a human yo-yo, here and gone, here and gone.

After the shoeshine, I went serdaneando, working my

way back to the Rubi, an Orange Crush, up to the balcony, and time to work on my journals.

Later that evening, as was my custom, I was matando un rato while perched on my favorite stool in the paneled bar at the Rubi. That was one of the evenings when we had some food delivered by one of the taxistas from the little outdoor stand next to the city jail. They specialized in ham and cheese *tortas* (sandwiches). These were dry-"grilled" in an old waffle iron, with avocado, homemade sauce, chile, and onion. They were delicious, but I was distracted and jumpy. All through this period I was nervous over the Edward Meyers business.

It was late evening when Lupita came waltzing in the side door of the paneled bar by the bodegas and started toward me. Jesse was relaxed in one of his characteristic poses—one he favored when business was slow. Slouched forward, one loafer on the top rung of a bar stool, he balanced on the other leg and smoked a Winston, while telling "parrot" jokes.

Usually Jesse was calm and cool—he nearly always wore a white or pin-striped American-style dress shirt, sleeves turned up neatly, tails out, and khaki pants with penny loafers, just like an American college kid. But the sight of a street kid in his bar got him agitated. He started waving her away with the back of his hand, "*¡Sácate!* (Scat!) *¡Lárgate!* (Get out of here!)"

I tried to plead her case, asking Jesse to let her come in; that she wanted to talk to me. He refused, explaining that these street kids were "bad business." That she was far too young to be in a bar with grown men, drinking. I even told him she was running errands for me.

No deal! There was simply no use in protesting. My friend, Jesse, had put his foot down! She upset him profoundly.

As I went out the door to talk to her, Jesse already had the comb out, restoring his "cool." Lupita was angry at being thrown out and began cussing up a storm. She first called Jesse a *pinche cabrón* (a truly nasty epithet), then it got even worse. I scolded her, telling her that the bad language wasn't acceptable. She scowled again and got down to business.

Lupita couldn't read or write and admitted she had never been to school. Nonetheless she was an inherently smart kid. On top of that she had apparently spent the best part of her life on the street, fending for herself. She had two juicy bits of information for me and told me to get out the pen and small notebook I carried everywhere. A habit from field days.

Man! The heat was unbearable out on the street, especially after the cool bar. I began sweating. The temperature was mid-nineties. The night air appallingly still. The massive stone bodegas thirty feet away radiated intense heat. We walked fifty feet to the Serdán and stood under the streetlight at the corner and hoped for a breeze. No luck.

Lupita had gotten Marta's address and told me that Marta lived with an "aunt" and another older guy who she thought was the aunt's boyfriend. She said Marta had a little boy, but that there was no husband or boyfriend, as best she knew. She gave me a street address, which I wrote down. Since she couldn't read, I wondered how she did that, but said nothing.

I asked if there was a telephone or anything. And she said, "Well, no. *¡Por Dios!* What do you expect?" Defensive, I said, "Well, just asking." I told her she had done a super job. She grinned. But she had more to convey.

"Also, Güero, there is an American couple. The guy is in the city jail. They wrecked their car and hadn't bought

Mexican insurance, and the woman is in the Sánchez Clinic. Her back is hurt. I think you should know about this." I thanked her and put my notebook away, ready to go back into the cool bar.

She made no move to go, and was looking expectant, a specialty of the street kids, so I said, "Well I'm not going to advance more money. You got four more days to work now." She retorted, "three," that I had hired her the night before.

I told her, "Okay," that she had three more days to work for the fifty pesos. She looked pathetic and said she had spent all her money. I asked if she was hungry. She nodded "yes," animatedly, so I told her to wait there a few minutes and we'd go get something to eat. She said she'd like that; she'd wait for me.

I went back inside, where Jesse was getting ready to close. I told him she had run some errands for me and hadn't had anything to eat. I asked where I could take her to get a meal. Jesse said not to take her to any of the bars at that time of night, then suggested the bus station. He reminded me that they had a twenty-four-hour counter that served good, cheap *menudo* all night.

I piled Lupita into the gray Rambler and took her up to the bus station—the same one where I had first arrived from Ecuador. It was bright and still busy at eleven-thirty. We took two stools, ordered menudos (thick tripe soup), and leaned on the counter. She was excited at the prospect of eating in a restaurant and told me she had heard the taxistas talk about the menudo here, had always wanted to try it.

In fact they had spectacular menudo in that place. It was a specialty. They served a large, steaming bowl of menudo with hot corn tortillas rolled up on three sides of the plate, under the bowl. With the menudo came a little cheesecloth sack of herbs. It contained partly crushed cilantro (coriander) seeds, onion, garlic cloves, and dried, red chile seeds—all tied up with a long string, like a tea bag. The usual procedure was to dip the spices into the steaming menudo to steep, while the boiling hot soup cooled. Usually ten minutes was about right.

By the time ours came Lupita couldn't wait. She dunked in the condiments, having watched the other patrons do it, then lit into the bowl of menudo like you would not believe. She finished her bowl and the three tortillas in about fifteen minutes. I gave her a couple of my tortillas, then let her finish my bowl.

She was still hungry, so I ordered a plate of *frijoles maneados con queso* (refried beans hand-stirred with white cheese), a tasty specialty that can only be gotten at home or in real Mexican restaurants in working-class districts. Between the lard and melted cheese, it might not qualify as health food, but it's the best way you can ever eat beans. I shared the frijoles with her. She wolfed her half right down.

God almighty! Where did she put all that food? And she had the table manners of a wharf rat. I got on her butt about shoving the food in her mouth, her elbows on the counter and her head nearly inserted into the soup bowl. I was gentle, but firm about it, not scolding as I'd been the first night with the taxistas, when I really dumped on her. At the counter I simply asked her to sit up straight and get her elbows, "*codos*," off the counter, that it didn't look good.

Miraculously she complied. She straightened up, looking a little self-conscious about it, and smiled nervously. I nodded in approval, gave her the "okay" sign, and she smiled again, relaxing. She was less businesslike and warming up a bit.

Finally full and feeling chatty, she asked, "Are you going to go look for this Marta?" And I said, "I told you, don't ask questions." And she said, "Well, okay. Is that a rule of being at work?" "Yes," I answered. She said, "Well, did I do okay?" I said, "Yes. Fine! You've done everything I've asked.

"I'm pleased. Now, tomorrow I want you to send a clothing lady to me at the Rubi to clean and mend my clothes." She said, "I'll take them for you." I nodded, "Okay," and lit a cigarette. She watched intently as I smoked, studying me as I had studied El Alemán. Finished, I asked, "¿*Lista?* (Ready?)" She nodded, so I paid the bill and we went out to the car.

I piled her into the Rambler and headed back downtown. I offered to take her all the way down to the Rubi, but she said, "no," she had things to do in el centro. What business she had downtown at that hour of the night was beyond me. Perhaps she simply didn't want me to be seen taking her back down to the Rubi, where the taxi drivers would start ragging us again.

Once back on the Serdán she asked me to let her out right by the Mercado Morales, the only store that qualified as a supermarket. As I pulled to the curb, she bailed out of the car.

The corner was dead quiet. At this hour there was nobody out except for taxis and an occasional police vehicle patrolling the Serdán. Most people had already gone to bed. Many of them were sleeping on cots out along the residential side streets.

She got about fifty feet then came back, stuck her head into my open driver's window, scowled, and said "Güero, you are a strict *cabrón*, but I will try to do as you ask. This is my first job—it is important!" Having got this off her chest, she smiled radiantly at me.

I retorted, "*¿Y tu? Te sientes mejor?* (And do you feel better?)" As she darted away, she shouted "*¡Mucho!* (much better!)" over her shoulder. Now we were even.

As she disappeared, I got one last glimpse of her. Just before she rounded the corner of the Morales market, she stopped, took off her little thongs, and tucked them under her arm. Then, looking free again, she scampered down the street and disappeared. That was the last I saw of my new man-dadera, close-up, for several more days.

The next day I went out to Primaverales with Edward Meyers, interviewing callers. After the interviews and helping Edward buy some new clothes, I went hunting for Marta with the address Lupita had given me. She had it right. I found the house easily, in the old San Vicente neighborhood. It was another modest dwelling, quite like Epifania's.

Marta wasn't there, but the "aunt" took the message that I wrote her, asking if she'd like to go out for coffee soon and reminding her that I was the norteamericano, the güero, staying at the Rubi. I hoped for a response, but had to get back to the hotel and clean up for my own Saturday night.

eight

SETTING THE COURSE

I had spent Saturday afternoon helping Edward Meyers prepare for his Sunday date. But Saturday night was mine! I had an invitation to an upscale "roof dance" at the Miramar Hotel, courtesy of a young physician named Jorge, who I met at the Rubi barbershop. Ironically it had been anthropology that brought me the invitation.

Our first conversation in the barbershop had been about ecological theory and the role of energetics in cultural evolution. He was intrigued by my ideas about "power" and "efficiency" and even more by the fact that I actually expected one day to publish them and "found a theory" of my own.

This met Jorge's definition of *cojonudo* (ballsy) and fixed in his mind one singular difference between Mexican and North American university education. In Mexico one carefully, even piously, toed the line "professed" by the faculty, whereas norteamericano students dreamed up new ideas to advance knowledge and got degrees for their effort.

It's not that simple—chapped lips are a basic requirement for survival in both systems—but he loved the imagery and contrasts.

In Guaymas I ran into quite a number of people, not only the highly educated but also barbers and tradesmen, who absolutely relished discussing big ideas. Given how many conversations among men in the States turn on openers like "How 'bout them Packers," I was just ecstatic at the intellectual climate in Guaymas.

Social and economic topics were often discussed on the street. So the young doctor had first become interested in me intellectually, then as a person.

Thus when Jorge got a coveted invitation to a roof-terrace dance at the Hotel Miramar, he had asked me to be his guest. The dance was to "present" a group of local girls from upper-class Guaymas "to society." I was excited. Jazzed!

168

He came by the Rubi about seven, as planned. I was waiting, decked out in my best guayabera, black pants, and polished dress shoes. Ironically, he was sporting a striped Van Heusen dress shirt and khakis—the American Ivy League look. He didn't have a car, so I had gotten the Gray Rambler all cleaned, polished, and ready to go.

We drove out to the Miramar, where Negro worked. The entire south wing of the hotel jutted out dramatically toward the sea. An outside stairway led up to a grand terrace on the roof—little used except for big parties like this one.

The Miramar was delightful. A combination of beach, hotel blocks, separate houses, and cobblestone lanes graced with magnificent bougainvillea and flowering tropical plants, the property was a miniature paradise a hundred feet from the sea.

We arrived around seven-thirty that evening, a gentle breeze wafting in from Bacochibampo Bay. It intensified as we mounted the stairs to the roof, carrying with it the smell of salt air mixed with the perfume of available girls on the terrace above us. Yum!

I greeted Negro on the way up. He told me that I was mixing with the *cabezas grandes* (the big shots) and to have fun. I told him I wanted to see how the other half lived around Guaymas, and to check out the girls. He grinned, "Oh boy. You stay away from don Francisco's daughters!" Though no one had talked openly about the fiasco at the Río Rita or don Francisco's subsequent visit to the Rubi, a whispered awareness of these events must have been going around.

We emerged onto the roof garden overlooking the sea. The tops of tall palms swayed in the gentle breeze, and a bright orange-red glow announced that sunset was coming on.

169

The terrace was gorgeous, its floor laid out in patterned *terrazo* tiles. A balustrade encircled the dance floor. Tables with large green parasols had been set up around the margins. An animated crowd of 100 to 150 young people from the better families in Guaymas was milling about.

The bar stood in one corner, staffed by a phalanx of waiters in stiff, white tuxedo-style shirts and black cummerbunds, fresh towels carefully folded over each left arm like badges of office. A five-piece combo band next to the bar played Cole Porter tunes and jazzy big-city dinner-club standards.

As the crow flies we were only two miles from the Pabellón Chapúltepec, floating in front of the shrimp fleet. In social terms the distance was at least two full light-years.

We went to the bar—drink anything you want was the drill. *¡Suave!* (Cool!). Cuba libres were ubiquitous. They also offered imported whiskey—blends, sour mash, and Scotch. I was awed. Two bottles of American whiskey would have covered my month's rent at the Rubi.

I recognized one of the cantineros tending bar there. His name was Eduardo and he usually worked downstairs in the Miramar nightclub with Negro. Like the Rubi's Enrique, he was a nice-looking, clean-cut fellow in his early twenties. Unlike Enrique, he didn't smoke and wore an expensive gold ID bracelet. I asked him to make my Cuba libre easy on the "Cuba" (rum), with lots of lime. He was surprised to see me, but quickly regained his distant professional demeanor.

Standing at the bar I surveyed the crowd. These party-goers looked very different from most of the people I saw on a day-to-day basis. This was upper-crust Guaymas and obviously the product of a distinct gene pool. I was stunned at the number of tallish girls with light skin and medium- to light-brown hair, some with touches of true blonde. There were even true redheads. Several pairs of hazel eyes checked me out as I checked them out.

These kids were much less mestizo-looking than the ones I saw every day downtown. Good grief! They looked so, uh . . . WHITE!

The girls were all done up in party dresses, but favored much more subdued colors than the poor girls wore. These señoritas were into pastels—pinks, blues, yellows, and lime—not the same shocking primary colors worn at Chapúltepec.

Marta would not have blended into this crowd at all. Her dark skin, threadbare clothes, and "come-take-me" sexuality would either have cleared the terrace or brought the chauffeurs up from below to hustle her away. The young women at this event were products of both careful breeding and meticulous packaging. The contrasts momentarily unnerved me.

Everything here was more refined. There were even several "little black dresses," lots of pearl jewelry, and a fair amount of gold. Most of the girls appeared to be in their teens to early twenties. Most of the young men, also lighter and much taller than average, appeared to be in their midtwenties to early thirties. Nearly everyone in this crowd had nice teeth and clear skin!

A table of well-dressed adults dominated a corner of the terrace facing the ocean. These were the hosts and hostesses, our chaperones for the evening. I don't remember their names—I never saw any of them again. Young Doctor Jorge introduced me properly as "señor Davíd Stuart, *maestro de antropología*," and we went through the obligatory process of shaking hands all around.

The adults were gracious and elegant. Several distinguished-looking gentlemen were wearing their best guayaberas. Another wore a formal white tuxedo shirt, pleated down the front, and a silver-gray bow tie with matching gray pants from a morning suit. It was simply too hot for full-dress tuxedos, *trajes de etiqueta*. Their female companions were matronly, well-dressed ladies wearing lots of jewelry.

These were the moms and pops who had put on the dance party. This affair was the Sonoran equivalent of an upper-crust East Coast cotillion in the States. In both cases the goal was exactly the same—to invest in the daughters' futures, get them into the "right" social network, and ensure dynastic survival.

Once the introductions were over Jorge and I were free to join the other young men cruising the girls. Rather like genteel sharks circling the *carnada*, baitfish, out in the bay.

I found the party fascinating. What a contrast to the Serdán and my friends. It seemed utterly surreal that I was at the Miramar sipping free drinks on a decorated terrace overlooking the sea. I went to the railing above the cobblestoned parking lot to check out the scene below—Mercedes, Lincolns, and big Ford LTDs. Chauffeurs were opening doors for the young folks as they stepped out. What an amazing sight in Guaymas!

According to the waiters, some of those cars had come from as far north as Hermosillo. Others had come from Ciudad Obregón, eighty miles south on the Pan-American Highway. In those days there were about four hundred thousand families in the state of Sonora. The hundred-odd households represented on the Miramar terrace probably accounted for more than half of the state's wealth.

I enjoyed several dances with a young woman that Jorge introduced to me. She was polite, a good dancer, and her hair was soft. Wrapped in Chanel No. 5 and a pale yellow dress, she was all of nineteen.

Too soon she rejoined her school of baitfish—the large cluster of young women on one side of the *terraza* who were obviously available. Another group was mixed, young marrieds and others who had brought their own dates. The young doctor and I were part of the smaller crowd of single guys. You never get odds like this in the States!

After the Yellow Dress left, I wandered and mixed. This was a friendly group. A number of the others, male and female, came over, asked me questions about who I was, and chatted. Frequently they asked if I was married. Did I have a wife in the States? A fiancée? I'd say, "Oh no, I'm a single guy, *soltero*," and a practicing field anthropologist.

Several complimented my Spanish. They were either being kind or were subconsciously comparing me to the average American tourist. Quite a number tried out their English on me. Several spoke it well. A few had studied in the States, mostly Arizona and California prep schools. One fellow told me that he was a student at St. John's in Santa Fe. His English was perfect.

These kids were nicely dressed, well-spoken, and well-raised. It was a genuine "pinch me, I must be dreaming" experience. The people, clothes, cars, and chauffeurs were a surprise to me. I had seen all this in Mexico City when I studied there, but not in northwest Mexico.

Behind closed gates and high walls there were powerful families with big houses, fancy cars, and lots of servants. They just weren't obvious, day-to-day. I danced more. Happy.

About my fourth dance, I asked my partner her name and gulped at her answer. Oh, dear! This had to be one of don Francisco's daughters! For a moment I had visions of something hideous happening to me. I had already partaken of his private vieja, old lady, out in the zona. Now I was doing what Negro had warned against—messing with one of his daughters. Worse yet I was dancing with one of them on the roof of the Miramar, in front of a hundred people. This was going to get around.

Jesse and Negro had not been kidding me—she was a fine-looking young woman of about twenty, pretty as a picture. She looked far more European than Mexican. With her honey-brown hair, nice features, and dark hazel eyes, she would have blended in perfectly on the streets of Paris. Nicely dressed, she wore a long, tasteful string of pearls at her throat.

173

I had a fondness for pearls, and these were probably worth more than a year's rent for my room at the Rubi. A few inches below the pearls, firm young boobs peeked out from her little black dress. Advertising, you know. I assumed Mamá was anxious to get her into a high-class breeding program. As she walked away I was relieved, but checked out her legs anyway. Mamá had no reason to worry.

I took another break, lit a cigarette, and watched the sunset. As I puffed I thought about the Almita, the sitios, Marta, and little Lupita. One world was full of taxi drivers, shrimpers, waiters, bartenders, and street kids. The other one, currently on display, was inhabited by clear skin, pearls, Chanel No. 5, tuxedo pants, and good teeth. What contrasts between life on the malecón and life among Sonora's young elites! But both worlds intrigued me, and I saw no reason to choose.

The whole party scene seemed magical after the Casa Blanca. There was even a nice buffet with cold shrimp and snacks. Free food! I sensed my luck changing. As it turned dusk, the waiters lit brass lanterns all around the terrace. These cast flickering orange lights, breathtaking against the indigo-blue twilight sky.

The band took a break while the waiters brought up black beans with cheese, fruit plates, and cold shrimp salads, standard "uptown" party fare. I ate black beans and shrimp, feeling totally content for the first time in years. I shouldn't have indulged myself.

As I chatted with several of the guys, don Francisco's daughter and the young doctor still nearby, a well-cared-for twentyish girl walked over and started talking to me. I had just begun to introduce myself when she interrupted, "Oh yes, I know who you are. You're the *norteamericano* who had the girlfriend from Empalme who used to work in the little restaurant at Primaverales." Surprised, I said, "Yes. How did you know that?"

She smiled, "Oh, it caused a great deal of comment at the time. Do you still see her?" I said, "No. I haven't seen her in some time." Still flipped out over the collapse of my engagement, I tried to be nonchalant about it. It didn't help.

She pressed, "Oh? Where is she now?" Getting louder, her tone was sarcastic. People turned and looked. I answered as calmly as I could, "Oh, I'm sure I couldn't say," then indicated vaguely that she had gone away for vacation or, perhaps, had taken another job someplace. Apart from being chickenshit, trying to be casual and pretend Iliana was of no interest simply didn't work.

She looked me in the eye in front of everyone and said loudly, "Well, you are much better off. After all, what did you expect when someone of your station, *puesto*, became involved with a girl of the servant classes?" Eyes glittering, her tone was defiant. I realized that I was expected, indeed socially obliged, to agree with this little bitch and repudiate Iliana.

In Mexico this is known as *desconociendo*, denying or refusing to acknowledge someone. And I was already halfway there with my disingenuous "vacation" comment. Desconociendo someone means to utterly ignore their existence.

That is what a reputable family man does to his Saturday night vieja from the zona when he walks past her on the Serdán, unseeing, at midday on a Monday. The girls in the zona ranked that as equal to being beaten in the pain it inflicted.

In Mexico there is a whole social syndrome involved with desconociendo. Judas did it to Christ for thirty pieces of silver.

And mestizo Mexico did it for four centuries by denying the Indian half of its heritage. So denying your relationship with someone in Mexico evokes powerful symbolism and emotions.

She was waiting. It was hushed around us. I decided I would rather be damned than give this mean-spirited little harpy the satisfaction of denying Iliana. In the next instant I feared that if I said anything at all other than "yeah, she was just a wench, who cares," I was going to be social toast among the assembled.

Conflicted, I hoped more silence would resolve the situation. I *was* interested in dating some of these girls and didn't want to pay the price. But silence didn't work. Eyes still glittering, she continued to stare, then demanded an answer. Wow! This chick was plain mean. That's one thing Iliana had never been.

So I smiled. In fact I beamed, "Well, I did not think of her that way. I found her company very charming." She retorted in feigned innocence, "Oh I'm sure, and I didn't mean to offend you. Girls of that class can be very roguish, *picaresca*, and coquettish." Yikes! That was below the belt.

Picaresca in this context was a nasty double entendre. The word does mean "roguish" in formal dictionary Spanish, but the phrase *¿la picaste?* is widely used in Mexico when a friend is asking, "Did you sleep with her?" The stateside equivalent is, "Did you score?" Its meaning blends in with the verb *picar*, which means to peck or sting, as in sting her with your prick.

This was too much, even for many of the kids in the crowd. They may have been a touch pampered, but they were not mean. A number turned away. I had been put down far too bluntly by this character, who felt she obviously could get away with anything.

I responded simply, "To me, the señorita was very charming," putting smiling emphasis on the word *señorita*. In this way I emphasized my former fiancée's virginity. Obviously this was bullshit. Every taxi driver and half the waiters on the roof knew Iliana had left me, pregnant by another man. For some seconds there was horrified silence all around us. I guessed that Iliana's pregnancy had traveled from taxista, to spouse/cleaning-lady, thence to at least some in this crowd.

In that exchange I won an "A" (locally, a grade of "10") for gallantry. By emphasizing her virginity, an epic lie, I later discovered I had won a double "A" with the waiters who were traveling through the crowd and tending bar at the time.

This for three reasons: 1) these latter *were* the "servant class"; 2) it was *their* daughters, or wives, these young rich guys were banging when they went out *gateando* (screwing the servant girls), then denied it; and 3) my lie about Iliana's virginity was so unexpected and so outrageous precisely because she had put "horns" on me by having sex with someone else (every Mexican guy's worst nightmare). My defense of Iliana was taken as ballsy, cojonudo, noble, showing corazón, and a bit *loco*, crazy. In short, I was one hell of a stand-up guy.

At the moment, of course, I didn't realize any of that. What I did realize over the next few minutes was that my defense of a "servant girl" had ruined my chances of dating any of the upper-class girls in the Guaymas area. I was no longer a welcome applicant in this breeding program. Pfft— I had just popped out of the toaster. Done.

I drifted away from the Mean One after that. Gallantry aside, I had just chosen between social worlds in Guaymas.

For a moment I panicked. I had come back to Mexico to be included, not excluded. I lit a cigarette and composed myself.

I stayed on for about another forty-five minutes, chatting here and there with the guys as if nothing had happened. But whenever I got too near the school of *carnada*, lovely backs turned toward me, the young things suddenly absorbed in deep conversation with their girlfriends. I had not wanted to leave quickly after an exchange like that. Pride. But they were already spreading me with butter and jam. Time to go.

My young doctor friend decided to stay on and get a ride with someone else, but I left around ten. It was a pretty night. Once downstairs I stuck my head in the dinner/nightclub and talked to Negro. The upstairs dinner served, he was getting ready to leave. I told him I'd meet him down at the Hotel Rubi.

Of course he asked, "Well, how did you find it amongst the fancy-dressers, the *caprichos?*" "Well, different, *raro.*" He said, "Well, it takes all kinds." That was my one fling with a dance party among the upper-crust of Guaymas.

I left, cranked up the Rambler, and drove back to town, thoughtful. The evening's incident forced me to review pieces of my life. I had been living in odd enough circumstances since my dad's death. I had been pursuing an impoverished student's life in poor places like Ecuador. That had been my choice. All the Mercedes sedans in the car park at the Miramar had brought back a flood of memories from my earlier life.

My father had been a physician and prominent in medical education. We were never very prosperous, much less rich. Academic medicine simply didn't pay much in those days. But I remembered the arranged dates with spoiled doctors' daughters and social pretensions that I didn't want to deal with again. I had walked out of that world when younger and discovered that night that I still didn't belong in it, not even in Mexico.

As I drove toward town, I was contrasting the Miramar dance with the social scene a week earlier, when Enrique Velarde and I had gone dancing at Chapúltepec Pavilion with the working-class girls—the tall girls, the short girls, the chubby girls. Frankly I had enjoyed Chapúltepec and its people more. And the women much more.

I simply couldn't yet sort out where I belonged in Guaymas, which I had thought had been a "no-man's land" for me. I wasn't trying to become *mexicano*, like Jesse or my other friends. I was obviously norteamericano. Hell, that's what my street name, Güero, meant. It's a polite way of saying gringo.

But I sure didn't belong with the rich folks in Guaymas. My ruminations, of course, meant nothing, even though they were important enough to enter in my journal. Meanwhile Guaymas society was operating to the beat of its own drum.

It was still early for a Saturday night—not too late to do something else. Back at the Rubi, I talked to Jesse. He was getting ready to close up, even though it was only about eleven—business was *muy piojo*. Then Negro came in from the Miramar and asked, "Do you want to go out to the Río Rita with us?"

I answered that I wasn't in the mood for the zona. That I had been looking forward to the dance on the roof, but it proved disappointing. He reminded me that there was dancing going on at the Chapúltepec and at another club up the street, called El Taconazo. El Taconazo was notoriously rowdy.

Negro insisted, "You should go dance and have a good time." I was vacillating. I felt generally safe in Guaymas, but I had been in Mexico long enough to know you don't want to be the only standout gringo on a Saturday night in a place like the Taconazo, where everybody's had too much beer and is feeling rowdy.

About that time the Miramar's Eduardo, who had just finished tending bar at the dance, came in and started making comments about the "incident" up on the roof of the hotel. He was chattering about how I had stood up for my former fiancée. Man alive! He was wound up about the whole thing. Even Jesse and Negro were beginning to react about the so-and-so cabrones, the rich SOBs.

180

I'd never heard any of this before. It was deep-seated class hostility from the underside up. With Eduardo and the waiters, I had won points by defending Iliana. I downplayed it, but "the incident" had stirred up forces I didn't control. Still, they sensed I was embarrassed, and the conversation ended.

I asked Eduardo if he was headed home, and repeated that Negro and Jesse had urged me to visit the Taconazo and go dancing. He said it was a rough bar, but that there was a much nicer place to dance, on the roof of an old hotel building right around the corner of the malecón.

He stepped outside and pointed it out to me. I had walked past the place and seen kids hanging off the roof on weekend nights, but hadn't realized that there was a public dance club up there. He said, "I'll get my wife and meet you there at midnight." It was then eleven-thirty. I said, "Great!" Negro drove Eduardo to his house to save time.

I lit a cigarette and walked up the Serdán, passing Lupita

under her streetlight. I waved. No response. I kept walking, passed the Copa de Leche, then angled left, following the bend in the malecón.

After dropping off Eduardo, Jesse and Negro took off— a new Saturday night floor show in the zona was too much for them to miss. According to them, some new *artista* named Mariquita was going to dance at the Río Rita—they acted as if it was equal to the World Series.

Eduardo showed up as I sat on the seawall in front of the hotel he had pointed out. He not only brought his *señora* (wife) but her unmarried sister as well. It was my first "blind date" in Guaymas.

The sister was "single," but already had a child. She was pretty and a nice, warm person. They asked if I minded. I told them I was dying to dance and would be enchanted if she granted me a few dances. No problem. She smiled and took my arm, and the four of us went upstairs.

181

From about midnight till after two in the morning, we danced in the disco up on the roof. Lots of life and color. The place was packed with several hundred working-class revelers, both singles and young marrieds. My partner's name was Leonora. She was upbeat, laughing, and dancing. I felt great. I was comfortable.

There was no sexual or social tension. What a relief! It wasn't a heavy date, it was just, "come on, I know this guy. Dance with him and have a good time." It turned into a nice night near the more ordinary end of the social spectrum.

Leonora and I probably got in twenty dances. We laughed, flirted, swapped lies, and drank Cokes. Several of the girls I had danced with the week before at the Chapúltepec were in the crowd. They waved and giggled. But Leonora was my "date," so I didn't leave her at our table to dance with anyone else.

The four of us were escorted to a corner table overlooking the harbor that the waiters had set up especially for us. In Mexico when you ran with taxistas, you got cheap fares. With cantineros, the cover charge was waived. With waiters, you got THE table and snappy service. There was no band here—straight deejay. The cover charge was nominal, but the house got rich selling icy Cokes at three times normal price to the several hundred sweating dancers crammed up there on a roasting hot Saturday night.

I loved the sound, the motion, the colors—the girls in bright blues, shocking pinks, pure yellows, even lime-green dresses. The guys universally wore black pants and white shirts, or guayaberas, with their blue bandanas folded under the collar, to protect it from sweat, just as I did. Everybody was dancing and laughing, a striking contrast to the cordial, but more subdued ambience of the roof-garden party.

This scene was what I liked. This was where I felt comfortable. This was real. It was also spontaneous, sweaty, bawdy, lively, and unaffected.

Better yet nobody here was going to say, "And by the way, whatever *did* happen to that little tart who walked out on you, knocked-up with somebody else's baby?" I wasn't going to catch that kind of grief here. It was not going to happen, simply because too many of these kids' lives included complications that they didn't need to talk about, either. They weren't rich—most things were beyond their control.

In fact, 80 percent of Mexico went through life with so much beyond its control that there were many things one never asked about, that one did not rub in somebody's face.

It was just not done. The first commandment in properly raised Mexico, prosperous or poor, was "Thou shalt not humiliate another." Only the truly rich seemed immune from its dictates.

In working-class Mexico this dictate required that layer upon layer of secrets be kept, that folly and misadventure be hidden away in dark mental closets, and that daily life be neatly compartmentalized. Those closets, compartments, and secrets preserved sanity, dignity, and order in daily life. I was already learning the compartments and sensing the layers.

About 2 A.M. we departed. I left good tips for the waiters, then called a taxi from the Rubi. El Burro came in his old, beat-up Chevy. I paid the fare for Eduardo and his ladies, thanking Leonora profusely for the dances. I never dated her again, but I saw her from time to time. She was always pleasant and very warm. No goodnight kiss, but I got a nice little squeeze on the arm, shook hands, and helped her into the taxi.

Tired but hungry, I walked up to the Almita, since I was already more than halfway there. The wide, brightly lit door-way was a beacon for the late-night crowd. Ana María López was the night manager. Late nights she was cook, waitress, and hostess all rolled up into one. Multiple roles apparently suited her, for she was also warm, funny, courageous, and sexy.

I ordered the same milanesa plate I'd eaten before. That was the last time I ever had to order. Thereafter it arrived magically. I was scooping beans onto my tortilla when Jesse and Negro made their entrance.

"Big Floor Show! You gotta go with us next week and see this Mariquita. *¡Muy manguita!* (sweet and juicy, like a mango)." We made it a date.

Again Jesse pushed the idea that I "import" items for sale in Guaymas. Negro agreed, but ate quickly and left a few minutes before me.

Jesse began to trade salty "parrot" jokes with other patrons. The "parrot" jokes all began with the phrase *"el pinche perico dice . . ."* ("the frigging parrot says . . .") then moved into clever stories, usually sexual, with hilarious endings. They were all the rage in Guaymas at the time. When he got into those it was endless. So I got up to go.

I turned left exiting the Almita, after saying goodbye to Jesse, and walked along the narrow lane behind the Morales market. Refrigerated trucks were just beginning to show up for early morning deliveries. These carried products like sides of beef, freshly slaughtered calves for veal, and loads of fresh fruit.

About seventy-five feet past the Almita, the tortilla factory that supplied both the Morales and the stalls in the city market had already opened its doors in preparation for morning production. The factory occupied a space only eight feet wide but nearly sixty feet long, which housed a big tortilla press. At the moment they were preparing the *masa* (dough) and would soon begin making tortillas for sale in the surrounding markets.

As I passed the entrance Lupita came darting out of the narrow recess at the mouth of the tortilla factory. She was still wearing her "new" striped V-neck top and khaki pants. She asked if I had seen Marta, the girl whose address she'd given me. She asked again what business I had with Marta. I repeated that it simply was not her business.

She persisted, sounding like a kid begging mom for candy at the supermarket. She actually tugged at my sleeve and bounced up and down as she pleaded, "Oh come on, tell me!

After all, I work for you." Finally I said, "Well, I heard from her and asked her to meet me tomorrow (Sunday) for a walk on the plaza. Big deal, okay?"

She knew I didn't want to talk about Marta, but kept it up, compulsively. Exasperated, I asked why she was so curious. She said she needed to know. Finally I barked, "¡Ya!" (Enough!)

She shut up for a second, then reminded me, "And remember, I told you that there was this American lady with the hurt back up at Clínica Sánchez and that the husband was in some kind of trouble? You ought to do something about it." Again I promised I would see to that after fulfilling my obligation to meet Edward Meyers at El Pollito—now just twelve hours away.

She also told me she had heard the taxistas talking about a group of American men who'd come to go fishing. They were staying at the Hotel Miramar and had been asking the taxi drivers to tell them how they could find the red-light district.

I asked what that had to do with me. She told me the gringos didn't trust the taxistas and wanted to go themselves, so I could drive them out to the zona and make money. I reminded her that I had an "arrangement" with Edward Meyers that would earn money. She was quiet.

Thinking the conversation over, I started walking again. I expected Lupita to disappear, but she began walking alongside me. I asked, "Where are you going?" She said, "I am going to walk to the Hotel Rubi with you." I asked, "Why? Suppose I want to walk alone?" She said, "Well, I want to talk to you." Amused, I humored her, "Okay. What do you want to talk about?"

She said, "Well, I heard you, Canelo, and Negro talking in the Almita." I said, "Well, damn you, what were you doing, listening?" She said, "Well, yes, but I work for you. That's my business." I was fascinated with this kid, and at the same time she was a truly exasperating character. She started tugging at my sleeve again as we walked. "Okay, since you are now listening to my business. What did you hear and what do you think of it?"

My mandadera weighed in, "Well, I think Canelo is giving you good advice. You go to the border. I heard him tell you, you have money and should go to the border. You buy fans, you buy blenders, you buy appliances, and you make money."

I said, "Why are you so concerned about me making money?" She said, "Well, if I bring you business, then maybe you would give me a raise." Playing along I said, "Well, okay. You bring me business, enough business, and I'll give you a raise." She nodded, "Shall I tell the taxi drivers that you'll take the gringos out to the red-light district?"

I told her the taxistas were my friends and I wouldn't steal their business. She retorted that I could pay the taxistas their regular fare to the zona and take the gringos there. That if I charged double, I'd still make a profit. You have to give the kid credit—she was both smart and persistent. I said, "No!"

She shut up for a few minutes, and I picked up the pace. Then another tug at the sleeve. "When you go to *la frontera* (the border) will you take me with you?" I honestly don't know what I was thinking at the time. Perhaps it was a continuation of the "stupid" streak I had started earlier that evening on the roof of the Miramar. Heck, the streak could have started early that afternoon, with arranging Ed Meyer's impending date.

Whatever the case, I answered, "If I buy fans and such in Nogales or Tucson, I'll take you with me. I promise." She asked, "Do you swear to that?" The pleading tone in her voice really got to me. I said, "Yes. *Te juro* (I swear). I'll take you." She actually stiffened, then began to vibrate, "Well, I can help you. I can help you." So I said, "Fine." Her physical reaction was simply amazing.

She walked all the way down the malecón with me, chattering a mile a minute the whole time. She was buzzed and still vibrating. Beyond excited. She began prying again, "Do you always eat at the Almita? Will you always be eating at the Almita?" I said, "Well, I like the food there and all. Have you eaten?"

She said, "Yes, I ate today." I asked, "What did you eat?" She answered, "I ate beans and tortillas." Curious, I asked, "Where did you have beans and tortillas?" She said, "Well, up in the street behind your room. There's a *señora*, La Gorda, who prepares me a meal when I have money. I buy my tortilla and beans in the afternoon for two pesos."

Surprised, I asked where, and told her I didn't know that there were any restaurants in that block. She said, "No, no. It's not a restaurant, it's just a house." I said, "Well do you sleep there too? Is that where you live?" She said, "No, no. I have my own place." Now I pried, "Where is that?" She said, "Well, that's my secret place." So, I let it go. I assumed from the taxistas and her earlier comments that it was somewhere around the packing plant.

Then she said she'd heard I'd been going to the zona, the Río Rita. Her tone was curious. I didn't respond immediately, fearing the Francisca business would be her next topic. After another pause, she asked if I had any girlfriends there. I said, "No," and asked her not to press me about such things. I reminded her, "You're my employee. That's all." She said defensively, "Well, I just don't want to see anything bad happen to you. I'm *encargada*, I've taken on the responsibility for you."

Whew! I saw it as exactly the reverse. I felt responsible for her, but said nothing. This is just the way things "happen" in Mexico. Obviously she imagined that she was going to be my protector, just as she was for the crippled shoeshine boy. We had walked about two-thirds of the way down to the Rubi, when Lupita stopped vibrating and announced, "Well, I've got to go now." She scampered off into the night and disappeared up a side street.

Back at the Rubi, I turned on my little fan and spent a few minutes noting the day's foolish streak in my journal. Surprisingly, I got a really good night's sleep. Midmorning Sunday, I awoke and got ready to meet Meyers at El Pollito. It was time to prepare for his date with Epifania.

I met Edward, sent him to get flowers, then waited with him till his date appeared before I slipped off. I stood across the street for a few minutes to make sure everything was okay, then walked the two and a half blocks to the small plaza in front of San Fernando de Guaymas, the church where I was to meet Marta "about four in the afternoon."

Smoking, I lounged against the plaza's white Victorian bandstand and watched as folks came out of the church from late mass. The little girls wore white lace dresses, most accompanied by older women wearing black lace head-scarves. There weren't many grown men coming out, but a number waited for their women on the plaza. Some played checkers on homemade boards, using soda caps for the "black" and "red."

I began to wonder if Marta would really show up, but waited, watching people and listening to the ice-cream vendors' sing-song chant, "*¡Heladitos! ¡Heladitos!*" Guaymas's main plaza was picture-postcard charming—the white iron benches and dense, carefully trimmed trees offered a leafy haven from both relentless sun and the cheerful chaos that generally ruled in el centro.

Long after I had mentally abandoned hope, a throaty voice floated over my shoulder, "*Buenas tardes, Davíd. ¿Cómo estás hoy?*" Marta had used the familiar form of Spanish with me. A good sign.

I turned to her, expecting her to be as smooth and assured as she had been at the Rubi. Instead she seemed shy and hesitant. This wasn't what I had expected. But nothing else had changed. She was wearing the same striped gray blouse, black skirt, and flats that she'd worn nearly every time I'd seen her. I returned her greeting, "Oh, Marta, I'm glad that you came. I hoped that you would come." She said, "I told you that I would, Davíd."

189

She wanted an ice cream. Then we walked, stopping to listen to some John Philip Sousa marches in the park dedicated to the three presidents old Guaymas had given the nation. We talked, got coffee, and agreed to go out again soon. After a drive along the water, we took a taxi from the Sitio Centenario to her house. As we were about to part she questioned me about the little girl who'd come to her house to ask if she lived there.

I told her it was Lupita, my mandadera, and that I had asked the kid to locate her, if possible. Marta wanted to know if I liked little girls and what type of relationship I had with the errand girl, referring to Lupita as a *chamacona*. That's what guys on the street call girls who are fully developed but not yet marriageable—in the States we say "jailbait."

I answered, "None!" and looked so weirded out that she shut up. She gave my arm a squeeze and turned to get out, but couldn't control her anger. "Don't *ever* send *la mandadera* to look for me again!" Her voice had transformed from throaty to raspy and hard. Uh oh! She was more complicated than I had reckoned. The taxista glanced nervously over his shoulder. I shrugged.

I watched her go. Staring at her legs was getting to be a destructive habit. As she stepped through her door, she hiked her skirt unexpectedly, giving us a quick shot of soft upper thigh. The driver uttered an involuntary "*¡A todo madre!*" (Wow! The whole nine yards/Done right!) then turned to apologize. I smiled, shrugged again, and asked him to take me to the Colmenar. I was hot, hungry, and frustrated.

nine

YOU GOTTA DO THINGS FOR PEOPLE

Halfway to the Colmenar, I changed my mind and asked the taxi driver to take me back to the Rubi. It was simply too hot to eat in town. I took the Rambler out to Primaverales where I bought a taco to go with my Orange Crush and watched sunset from the footbridge. The sound of the surf always calmed me. I smoked one of my last Pall Malls and thought about going over to the States for fans and blenders. Perhaps it wasn't such a bad idea.

Relaxed, I drove into town about eight, parked in the narrow street behind the Pasaje Marví, and walked down to the Colmenar. Business had been slow for a Sunday and they were already cleaning, ready to close early. Max had gone so I ordered a bowl of soup and chatted with Mercedes, gently working in the idea of "importing" small commercial items from the States.

Mercedes, always pleasant, was positive, telling me that Max needed two new fans and a good three-speed blender for malteadas. She indicated that it had become more difficult to acquire such items, since several of the local *fayuqueros* had recently switched to true contraband—drugs and guns.

That's when she asked if I was planning to "put down roots" in Guaymas. Without even blinking, I answered, *"Sí."* She smiled, commenting that it was natural, since I had so many friends in town. I thanked her and drove back to the Rubi.

Jesse was in the air-conditioned paneled bar. The place was nearly empty, so I pressed him for details about the fayuca. He reminded me that a businessman acquaintance of his needed a new air conditioner and promised he'd ask around quietly about how one obtained the necessary import papers. He was pleased that I was considering a trip to the States, reminding me, as he had with Edward Meyers, that "you gotta do things for people."

I nodded and Jesse pulled out a notepad, suggesting that I start a list of items to purchase in Tucson. When I actually started taking notes he became animated, ending our conversation with, "That's it, then you are going to the other side!" He paused, then asked why I had changed my mind. I answered that I didn't want to be hungry again. He smiled and nodded.

Back in my room with an Orange Crush, I thought about Marta and wrote in my journal. Man, it was hot! I got up to resoak the towel hanging over my fan. As I arranged my makeshift air conditioner, I heard a rattling at the screen facing the packing plant. I stuck my nose to the screen and heard, "psst-psst!" Lupita! Rather than talk in front of the taxistas, I told her to come to the window on the back street and I'd let her in.

I opened the rear window and she scrambled in. Lupita surveyed the room carefully, picking through everything until I told her to keep her hands to herself. Then she sat at my writing table and stared at my journal. I went to close it, but she asked if I had been writing. I nodded. She asked if it were a letter. I said, "No. Just today's events." Amazed, she admonished me that nothing "interesting" had been happening lately.

Defensive, I told her people "respected" writing. That one could often "influence others" through the written word in ways that face-to-face communication might not. She nodded, as if she were listening.

Done, I smiled, "What did you want?" She got right to the point, "Are you going to go to the border, *la frontera?*" I said, "Well, I am thinking about it. Jesse might help me with import papers." She said, "Oh. I know how you do that. You go to señor X at the tourism office."

I told her, "I already ran into him once when he signed a check for me." She nodded, "You pay him a tip, *propina*, and he'll get the papers for you that tourists use when they come to San Carlos or Miramar in the winter. They bring their refrigerators and their fans and things, then take them back to the other side when they close their houses. He can arrange that for you."

I asked, "Are you sure?" She said, "Yes. Do you want to meet him?" I said, "Sure." She said, "Okay, I will arrange it." I asked if it would cost a fortune. She didn't think so, but said she would find out—that was her job. She was deadly serious. And I was beginning to take her seriously, as well.

That decided, she reminded me that I had been remiss— the American couple still needed help. The guy was in jail and the woman at the Sánchez Clinic, her back injured. She said,

"You ought to see them." I said, "I told you I was busy this weekend, but I will go tomorrow." She said, "Okay. I'll meet you at the Sánchez Clinic. When are you going?" I said, "Okay. I'll see her tomorrow afternoon, at two o'clock."

Finished, I shooed her out, "Now it's time for you to go!" She was cruising around the room, then bouncing up and down on my bed. Irritated, I said, "Out! Out!" She teased, "Don't you like me?" I said, "Yes, I do like you. But you are my employee and you don't belong in here tonight. Sneak out quietly and I'll see you tomorrow at two." She giggled, climbed over the head of my bed and went through the window, then was gone.

A moment later someone pounded on my door—unusual at that hour. My most unfavorite deskman. It was frigging fat Ramón, leering. "I thought I heard someone in the room with you." I grinned, "Well, come in Ramón. All I can offer you is a warm 7-Up." Ecstatic, I had the son of a bitch aced!

I guessed the fat prick had been listening at my door but hadn't heard enough. It was heavy and old-fashioned, and the transom was closed. He entered, officious, and nosed around, saying, "I was sure I heard someone in here."

I said, "No. A couple of the taxi drivers at the sitio were ragging La Gatita outside my window a few minutes ago. Why?" Disappointed, he said, "Oh, that must have been what I heard," and skulked away. No forty pesos tonight. A small victory, perhaps, but a victory nonetheless.

The next day, Monday, I kept to my usual routine of Orange Crush and reading the newspaper. In the bar I talked to Enrique Velarde, asking him what he thought about going to the border. He said, "Well, if you talk to the right people . . . I would do it."

And I said, "Well, suppose I get my butt thrown in jail in Nogales or something like that?" He said, "Well, you know, we would come get you. You have money in the safe. It could easily be settled for a fine. Don't you worry about it." So that was the last vote I needed. Hecho, done!

About one o'clock I started working my way up to the Sánchez Clinic to meet the American lady. As I did my rounds, something was very different at the sitios. The greetings were much more effusive, like "¡Ay, que Güero!" and "¡Viene El Güero! (Here comes Güero!)" I was no longer a güero, I had become the güero—abrazos (hugs) and slaps on the back and cigarettes offered me at every sitio.

By the time I reached the Medrano I had figured it out. In publicly defending Iliana on the roof of the Miramar, thirty-six hours before, I may have been both a cabrón and a gringo, but I was now their cabrón. Their gringo.

195

At the clinic I asked to see the American lady. No problem! She was in neck traction, but it was only a whiplash, nothing grave. They had totaled their car, but had not purchased Mexican insurance on it. That was a basic "no-no." Now they needed to get the wrecked car shipped out of the country on a flatbed. Legally they could not leave without it— a quirk of Mexican law.

So the husband was over in the city jail, because he didn't have Mexican insurance. The woman was hysterical. This is frightening stuff for Americans, who are accustomed to "due process"—an alien concept under Mexican law.

In short, her husband was in the slammer, she was in traction, and the good Dr. Sánchez was running up a hefty bill on her. So I asked, "Do you have any money? Do you want to be in the hospital here? Shall I talk to Dr. Sánchez?" She said, "We have some money, and I just want out of here." I said, "Okay, I'll see what I can do for you."

I talked to Dr. Sánchez, who spoke lovely English—a fact entirely lost on our terrified Mrs. Smith. I asked, "How seriously hurt is she really? Must she be in traction?" He said, "Well, she ought to have a neck collar." I asked, "Do you have one?" He said "Well, yes. I'm having one prepared for her."

Obviously he wasn't rushing her out the clinic door. Every day she stayed was one more day of charges. I asked, "Could she leave this evening or tomorrow if she had a neck brace?" He said, "She could leave tomorrow." I asked, "Well, what will she owe you?" It was in the range of five hundred dollars.

So I went back and talked to the patient, "Do you have Blue Cross–Blue Shield or anything like that?" She did. So I said, "Well, you're going to have to pay this bill now and collect your Blue Cross–Blue Shield when you get home. Make sure you've got a bill from Sánchez. He can get you out of here tomorrow with a neck brace, so long as you're careful."

"I'll book you into my hotel, if that suits you, and keep an eye on you for a day or so, while I check on your husband." She said she could pay the bill and would like the hotel room arranged. She seemed grateful. Done for the moment, I split.

Lupita was waiting outside, where she informed me, "Well, it is arranged to see señor X." I said, "¡Me estás vacillando! (You're putting me on!)" She said, "No, no! He knows who you are. He knows I work for you." News had spread and my little mandadera was already acting as my official agent in the streets of Guaymas. God knows what havoc she was wreaking, but it couldn't have been worse than me being the last guy in northwest Mexico to figure out that his fiancée had been knocked up by someone else.

"When am I to meet señor X?" I asked. She grinned, "Well, he wants to meet you this evening around six o'clock at the Colmenar. You shall sit out front at a table. You will say to him, 'Oh, señor X, thank you very much for signing my check a few weeks ago, won't you sit down and have a cup of coffee with me?'" She repeated, "Out front!" I said, "Okay. That sounds good."

I figured that if the meeting actually took place, I owed La Mandadera some real respect. She'd apparently been on the street long enough to know how to arrange things, directly or through someone else. Actually I thought she had outlined a rather neat arrangement. The worst that could happen would be for me to have my afternoon coffee alone after a "no-show." Low risk. I was intrigued. This had all the makings of a B-movie plot. Cool!

I told her I was pleased, "That's good work. We'll do it your way!" She smiled angelically, then asked, "Well, do I deserve a bonus?" I said, "We shall see tonight." Then she asked again if she was really going to la frontera with me. I told her, "Yes. I gave you my word. But I don't want trouble from you on this trip."

She began vibrating again. Before she spiraled out of sight, I said, "But right now we must go to the jail. Come with me. Let's see this *norteamericano*."

I took Lupita over to the city jail in the Rambler and asked to see the American. They brought him to the front. He was thirtyish and appeared to be scared shitless. The guard asked, "Well, who are you representing?" I answered, "Well, I am talking to him for the wife. We want to know the charges and the amount of bond that must be posted." He said, "He wrecked the car. He damaged federal property (the highway pavement). He had no insurance. This is pretty serious."

I said, "I know that. Let's see what can be done. Let me talk to him. I'll contact the American Consul in Hermosillo. Obviously we must arrange to get money to resolve this." At the sound of the word *money*, it was smile time and "Well, certainly you can see him."

Mr. Smith was one seriously scared son of a bitch. Yet they'd been pretty careful with him. He hadn't been thrown into the bull pen out in the jail's open courtyard, where someone might carve on his ass. He'd been in a separate cell. I know that it was hot, stinky, dirty, and unpleasant, but he didn't have a mark on him. As Mexican jails go, he'd been at the Ritz, but he was obviously unaware of his stunning good fortune.

I told him, "You know, you're in a jam. You didn't get the insurance? Mexican law is just absolutely brutal in this respect. What do you want to do? I'm getting your wife out of the Sánchez Clinic and getting her booked into my hotel. How are we going to get you out of here?" He asked who I was. I repeated that his wife had sent me.

That wasn't good enough. He wanted the U.S. ambassador. I told him the ambassador was in Mexico City. Then he said "Get me the consul, or whatever." I told him the "Whatever" was stationed in Hermosillo and that "she didn't get down this way very often," but that I'd phone.

He insisted. So I told him the truth. "If you or a close relative either own a Fortune 500 company or are an active member of Congress, I can get the consul here tomorrow afternoon. If not, it'll be about a year unless, of course, you're Republican." Tricky Dick was President, remember?

He beamed, "I *am* Republican." I smiled back, "Great, I'll let them know in Hermosillo. That should speed it up to about a month." He realized I was serious and did a pretty good imitation of a guppy eating fish-food dinner. Then he asked how to get out.

I said, "Money." He said, "Well I've got money in the States." It turned out he was an engineer at a California electronics company. He said, "If I could just get to Tucson, I could get money from my bank." I said, "Hell, you're not likely to get to Tucson. You're likely to be here a while. They're not going to turn you loose on trust."

He whined, "Well, what do you think can be done?" I said, "You've got few choices. Your wife can't go to Tucson for money, unless you pay these folks off, because you're both on the same tourist card. You need to ship your car out of the country, and both of you must ride with it. You've got to take that car out with you." He said, "I just want to get out of jail."

199

I said, "Okay, you hold on. I'll notify the consul in Hermosillo." He asked, "Is my wife . . . I know she's in the hospital. Is she in bad shape?" I said, "No, she's got to have a neck brace because she has whiplash and some bruises, that's all. I'll have her out of the clinic tomorrow. Do you have enough money to pay the bill, four or five hundred dollars?"

He said, "No, just before they took me I gave all my money to my wife." This had been his one smart move. Delighted, I said, "Good. We'll do what we can." I consulted the jailer, who advised, "You should get him a lawyer *and* talk to the *teniente político*" (like a deputy mayor).

That made sense, so I went to Guaymas's town hall and asked what the charges against Mr. Smith were and what the fines would be. The official (I assumed the teniente) who came out to talk was very professional as he counted off the infractions—"reckless driving," "destruction of public property," and "no valid insurance."

I hedged, "This guy's pretty sure he paid for insurance at the border." He said, "Well, we don't have any *turista* insurance sticker. He had no policy in the car at the time." I said, "Well, perhaps there has been some mistake here. How do we proceed? No one else was hurt in the accident." He said, "No, but property was damaged."

I said, "I am going to contact the consul in Hermosillo." He said, "Well, are you acting as this guy's agent?" I said, "Yes. He's just a *paisano*, in trouble. These people are not villains. They haven't killed anybody. They haven't stolen anything. I understand your country's laws and respect them, but it is time now to get the money needed and resolve this situation." The teniente softened, acknowledging that if damages were paid, the situation might be reasonably disposed of.

I pressed the teniente for an estimate, "Well, perhaps twenty thousand pesos, *if* he can get the car out of the country." That was sixteen hundred dollars. "Maybe even thirty thousand pesos, somewhere in there." I asked, "Well, can we arrive at a figure?" and lied about the guy's occupation. I said, "He's only a *maestro* (a schoolteacher)."

He said, "Well, you know, I am sure we can handle this for twenty-five thousand pesos." And I said, "Well, write me that in a note, so I can explain it to the consul." He replied, "No, I don't want to write that up, because I want to check into the legality of some of this, but you can accept my word for it, that's my view on the matter."

"Good," I said. He continued, "Particularly if there's something extenuating about this insurance policy that we don't know. But these people really ought to respect our laws." I said, "Yes, I am not questioning that at all."

I walked the five blocks back to the clinic and talked to Mrs. Smith again. I briefed her, "We're looking at two thousand dollars in fines, plus costs to get the car out of the country. What's the best way to go about that?" She suggested, "If I can get out of here and call relatives, they can send money to Tucson, if somebody will just go get it." She couldn't leave without him and the car, because they were on one tourist card—a dumb thing to do in Mexico.

So I suggested, "If you trust me . . ." (as I handed her my university ID card), "I'll bring back the money." I continued, "Your husband told me that he left you with money when they took him to jail. Do you have enough to pay Sánchez and the expenses needed to sit tight here in Guaymas for a few days?" She nodded.

"I've set up an account to get meals sent in to your husband, so he doesn't have to eat jail food. I'd like some money to tip the jailers, to make sure he's treated well. How do you feel about that?"

She said, "I have the money, if they take traveler's checks." I laughed, "Oh yeah, Sánchez will take traveler's checks, no doubt about that." She smiled and I promised, "I'll come back tomorrow at noon and get you—that's when you'll pay off Sánchez's bill. Meanwhile I'll reserve an air-conditioned room at the Hotel Rubi. We'll make your husband as comfortable as possible and get his situation sorted out." She seemed relieved.

I collected Lupita, who had been hanging around outside, and updated her. She knew I was going to the border and was beginning to get excited. When I came out of the

Sánchez Clinic she had asked, "What are you going to do?"

"Well, I'm going to the border to get money for these people." Mrs. Smith had said they wanted to pay me for my trouble if I got them back to the States quickly. I had said, "Okay. This has taken my time. Whatever you think is appropriate. I don't want to join the long line of people gouging you, but if you tip me, I'd be grateful."

As I dropped her off, Lupita was vibrating again. Though it seemed unlikely that she had actually arranged a meeting, I promised her I would meet señor X at the Colmenar around six.

By six o'clock that evening, I was comfortably seated at one of the Colmenar's outside tables, sipping my coffee. No appointment is kept in Mexico to the hour or to the minute. About twenty after six, the tourism bureau's señor X came strolling by, cool, casual, and not noticing me at all.

I waved, "*Buenas tardes*, señor X. I appreciate your signature on my international draft. May I invite you to coffee or dessert?" "Why, thank you," he said, "I'm not sure I remember your name." I said, "It's señor Stuart." He said, "Oh yes, now I remember. Very glad to have been of service." He sat down.

Mercedes came out. I asked her to take the gentleman's order. He had coffee and *flan*. He sipped and talked, "I understand you are going to be staying in Guaymas a while." I answered, "Yes, I feel at home here and the people are very *simpático*." We chatted like this for fifteen minutes. In Mexico you socialize first and never go straight to the business.

He smiled as I pursued my theme, "If it isn't too much of an imposition, I would value your guidance about how a *norteamericano* might bring some personal effects into

Mexico. Is this possible? If not, I would understand that. But I have items that are personal comforts of mine."

He said, "Oh, that can be arranged. That can be arranged. Of course there are import fees for certain items, and there are processing fees for certain documents."

I had waved Mercedes away. We were alone out there at the front tables. I said, "Well, what would it cost me to bring in some of my household appliances?" He asked, "Well, what do you think might be the value of these items altogether?" I said, "Perhaps a thousand dollars. It is difficult to say what personal effects are worth."

He smiled. (Good teeth!) "The document processing and fees would be twenty-five hundred pesos (two hundred dollars)." I said, "Well, that's certainly not cheap. That is more than I expected, but let me think about it. How is the best way for me to get in touch with you tomorrow?" He said, "Just stop by the office—one o'clock." That was lunchtime, when all the rest of the staff was going to be out. So I said, "Very well."

203

I went back to the Rubi, but didn't say anything to Jesse or Enrique about these arrangements. No sense in guaranteeing too many witnesses at the trial. I drank Orange Crushes in the bar while Jesse told parrot jokes.

Later I walked the malecón, smoking a cigarette. It was hotter than hell. I was changing clothes twice a day, but still felt like I was in a men's locker room. Lupita caught up with me near the Copa de Leche and asked how it had gone with señor X. I told her his estimate of cost and indicated he would have the papers the next day. I asked her if she thought I could really sell enough to make a profit.

"Oh, yes," she said, and asked if I wanted her to find out

who needed things. I told her, "No—too visible. I'll ask Canelo." She was disappointed. I went back into the Rubi bar, leaving her outside with a promise to come back for her later.

I asked Jesse, "Who do you think would want appliances, if I go to the border? I have business to conduct for an American family." He said, "I'll ask around. Let you know tomorrow." Then paused, "So you are going to start doing things for people?" I nodded. "Well, we are going to make a *mexicano* out of you yet."

Grinning, I thanked him and retrieved Lupita. We went to the bus station for another bowl of menudo. While she wolfed down her food, I sat there with a café con leche, thinking. The TNS line bus pulled in, bound for San Luis Río Colorado and Mexicali. I thought about Iliana and Lisa, then put them out of my mind.

Lupita started to chatter about the frontera and going to 'the other side'. I broke in, "Well, I don't know how I'm going to get you across. You can go with me only as far as Nogales, Sonora. Then I'll return for you after doing my business." She was visibly disappointed, but shrugged as if to accept it.

I offered to drive her downtown. She declined. "*Negocios* (business)," she said, as she sailed out the front door of the bus station and scampered off. I went back to the Rubi and wrote in my journal.

The next day was eventful. No time for the newspaper reading. Edward Meyers left a message at the Rubi desk—he was dating Epifania and having a grand time. I'd already heard this at the sitios, but was glad for him.

At noon I picked up Mrs. Smith from the Sánchez Clinic and settled her bill, after convincing Sánchez to come down another fifty dollars. She was a free woman in a neck brace for just over four hundred dollars, courtesy of American Express.

El Burro ushered her into his taxi and took her to the Hotel Rubi, where we had reserved a spacious downstairs room in the central corridor. I met her there a half an hour later and spent time calming her down, regaling her with stories of local life. I made several calls to the consul in Hermosillo. On the second try I reached her and filled her in.

That done, I took Mrs. Smith to the big mahogany telephone booth in the hall, where she phoned relatives in California to send money to First National in Tucson. I asked if she could have them send it by wire to the Banco de Comercio. That required her family to check with the local bank.

We waited in the booth for the call back. They could handle the transfer, but estimated it would take a week. She shook her head and asked me to get the money for her in Tucson. I told her I'd leave the next day and be back in two or three. That's the way she wanted to go.

Before I collected Mrs. Smith, I'd stopped at the insurance agency in Pasaje Marví and asked what it would cost to haul the Smiths' wrecked car from the police compound and load it on a rail car, then ship it to the States. They told me the cost would be about $350. Not too bad.

She approved that at the hotel and was calming down. Then I returned to the jail and spread tip money among the jailers. I talked briefly with Mr. Smith, telling him, "We're making arrangements. Your wife's out. She's sent for money. I'm going to go to the border. I'll bring it back." He pleaded, "God, get me out of here quick." I told him we'd have him out in three days. He pleaded, "Can't you make it sooner?" I told him I'd leave the next night if everything fell into place.

I left the jail and revisited the same official to clarify the fines, telling him the American consul was advised and interested. I asked if I still needed to retain a lawyer, suggesting we could settle the fines. He had consulted the judge and said everything could be disposed of for thirty thousand pesos.

"Fine," I said, "but I need that in writing." He complied. I was relieved. The fine equaled $2400—less than I thought it would be.

Back at the jail I updated Mr. Republican, then returned to the hotel to talk with his wife. I told her that they must pay the fines and fees to ship their car out on the same train they took to Nogales. I even estimated her hotel bill. She was okay with the total of three thousand dollars in costs. I told her I'd spent five hundred pesos at the jail for tips, outside food, a fan, and cot for her husband. I said, "This is hard on everyone, but is the best I can do at the moment."

Of course the consul's office in Hermosillo wasn't doing shit—there was "little they could do except recommend a Mexican lawyer." It was the standard, "you're out of the country and a nobody, so screw you anyway." Your government dollars at work . . .

It was Tuesday evening. I was feeling "up" when I sat down at the Colmenar and ordered my meal. Mrs. Smith had told me that she would give me a hundred dollars traveling money for Tucson. That was great. I talked to Mercedes, "I'm going to go to the *frontera;* if Max really wants anything, let me know."

She called Max, who arrived in about fifteen minutes. His house was up the hill a few blocks, where he lived with his widowed mom, doña Adelpha. Max wanted a fan, two blenders, and a big Westinghouse electric mixing bowl. I told him I'd do my best.

Then Lupita showed up in the Pasaje with her little ward, Juanito. He was a sweetheart. The poor little guy must have been a bit brain-damaged. His face was misshapen, and his speech was slurred. He was a heartbreaking little character, but plucky. And he had transformed my boots into a visual feast that attracted attention on the street.

I sent him into the men's room to wash up. Lupita did likewise. Once degrimed, the pair sat in front of the Colmenar with me, inhaling soup and tortillas.

I was looking forward to the trip, but told Lupita not to talk about the frontera on the street. Rather than follow my directive, she instructed me to take notes—she had garnered more orders for fans, blenders, and waffle irons. That's when Juanito started crying.

He was terrified that I would take Lupita from him. Gravely, he told me he could not work without her, and asked me to "swear" I'd bring her back. I did the "te lo juro (I swear it)" bit. Consoled, he gave my Red Wings another hell of a shine, gratis, so that I would "take good care of Lupita" for him.

Lupita, his protector, gave him twenty pesos of her weekly wage so he would have "money to give his mother for tortillas" while she was gone. I started to reach into my pocket to add another twenty pesos, but Lupita quickly shook her head "no."

Just as I was Lupita's patrón, she was his patrona. In turn this crippled kid was his mom's. The chain of patronage in Mexico is fragile, but sacred. It is at the core of "doing things for people." I slid my hand away from my pocket, not wanting to disrupt Lupita's role on the street. She smiled, her *palanca* (leverage) with the shoeshine boys intact.

I walked back to the Rubi about nine, as usual, and talked to Jesse. Out at the sitio, El Burro also had a list of items that people wanted. It was mostly fans, blenders, calculators, waffle irons, radios, and the like.

I went to my room early to get ready for the trip, wrote in my journal, then tried to sleep. The next day, after reading the newspaper, I went to the tourist office at one o'clock, as agreed.

On the way I stopped at the Banco de Sonora, where I had opened the account with Jesse, and drew deep into my funds for the tourist papers and purchases to fill my orders. I spent two hundred dollars of it fifteen minutes later and got the import papers from señor X. So far, so good.

That afternoon around four, I went to meet Lupita in front of La Gorda's place, in the street behind the Rubi. I had not wanted to meet her at the sitio—fear of ragging.

Since I had just paid her wages, she promised to eat a decent meal at Gorda's before I picked her up. I had also called the Colmenar and asked Mercedes to have a bag of burritos *de machaca* (shredded beef) made up for us to take on the road.

It's hard to convey how excited she was. This was "big-time adventure." I pulled up to a gorgeous, old colonial house, long past its heyday. A heavyset middle-aged woman sat in her floor-to-ceiling iron-grated corner window. I had seen her often but did not realize she was the lady who provided Lupita meals.

Lupita came scampering out with her nylon-net bag, which contained a brown paper sack. I asked her what she had—underwear and a "change of clothes." The old señora came to the car and asked Lupita to bring back some men's cotton underwear, U.S. size 44. I introduced myself.

I reckoned they were for Gorda herself. Years before I'd known a maid in Mexico City who was into wearing men's jockey shorts, because the cotton was so much more comfortable than the cheap polyester panties that women could purchase in Mexico. Gorda sized me up carefully and admonished me to take care of Lupita. She liked the kid. Good.

We took off with a wave, turning straight up the hill to drive the high road, rather than Avenida Serdán. I was not anxious to have everyone see the Rambler with Lupita in it. I told Lupita, "Keep your head down until we are out of town!" and asked her if Gorda would talk about our mission.

Lupita said "No." We were supposed to bring Gorda underpants. We were buying silence about our contraband operation for the price of several pairs of cotton underpants. Worked for me!

It was a blazing hot afternoon as we drove north. At the edge of town, we stopped at El Corsario gasoline station, as Jesse had asked. There a clerk handed me an envelope with "El Güero" written on it in pencil. Lupita grabbed several cold sodas to take with us and we took off again, nonstop to Hermosillo. I told Lupita that we wouldn't stop, except for gas and *"pipí,"* until we reached the frontera.

It was blindingly bright and hotter than hell, even with all the windows open. But we were excited and turned the radio on full blast. Lupita was bouncing up and down like a two-year-old. I lit a smoke, and she asked me for one. I hesitated. She scowled, *"¡No me chingues! ¡Fumo!* (Don't fuck with me, I smoke!)" Since she put it that way, I gave her a Raleigh.

She took a couple of puffs, scowled again, and said she wanted a filter cigarette. When we reached "El Gallo" (The Rooster), the big Pemex station on the south side of Hermosillo, I gave Lupita a few pesos for sodas and her cigarettes. She dashed into the station and returned with sodas and cheap Alas (Wings brand) filter tips.

We didn't need gas and were anxious to keep moving, so pulled out three minutes later, taking the bus bypass to the right, which circles Hermosillo and passes the state prison. On the north end of town the road branches. Straight ahead is Kino Bay. Right becomes Route 15 to Nogales. We took the right turn, then drove hard. About seven-thirty in the evening we stopped at a roadside place south of Magdalena to get more cold sodas.

Hungry, we dug into our bag of food and ate in the car. Apparently Lupita approved of the machaca burritos. They were a combo of shredded beef, chopped potato, chile sauce, tomato, and onion. It was all I could do to prevent her from simply inserting her head into the bag to vacuum up the food.

When she wasn't eating, Lupita talked nonstop. She looked out the window absolutely goggle-eyed at everything. She told me this was her first trip away from Guaymas. I asked her how far she had traveled before. She thought, then answered that she had once been to the statue at the head of Avenida Serdán, which was about a mile from the Rubi.

That surprised me, so I asked if she'd been to Empalme. She shook her head. When I tried Primaverales, she lit up. "That is where *you* are from. I have heard people talk about it and I want to see it someday." My God! Her whole world had been confined to several square miles of old Guaymas. I was having trouble processing this, but she seemed not to notice.

I said, "Look, *hijita* (little daughter, a term of endearment with kids), I'll take you to Primaverales." She was instantly bright-eyed. La Gorda had seen to it that she was sparkling clean for this trip, her khaki pants and striped top freshly washed. When I called her "hijita," she stopped gawking out the window and came to attention like a dog waiting for its treat. That surprised me.

That's when I decided, unsuccessfully, to ask again about her background. She didn't want to talk about her mom. Period. So I asked her more generally about her "family." Were they dead? All she would say is that she was alone.

Then she asked about my family, and again pressed for permission to call me "Davíd." I said, "Well, I'll think about that." Then she asked if she could call me "señor Davíd" when no one else was around. I said, "Yes." She promised she'd call me "Güero" in front of others. I said, "Fine." The señor Davíd bit lasted only two minutes. First she asked me about my family.

"Señor Davíd, what's your father like?" I answered, "Well, he's dead." She pried, "But you knew him; you actually knew him?" with genuine eagerness. I said, "Yes, I knew my father." She asked, "What was it like?"

I looked uncertain, so she clarified, "Having a father. What was it like, Davíd?" I explained, "Well, actually I did not get along very well with my father. That's the way things are sometimes."

She moved on and asked about my mother, "Is your mother alive?" "Yes, my mother is alive."

"Do you see your mother?" "Well," I said "not often, but I spoke to her on the phone once this summer, and she is well." Then she asked if my mother was married.

"No, no, she's a widow lady." She pressed, "Do you have brothers and sisters?" I told her I had one brother, John—my twin. She was amazed, then asked if he lived nearby.

"No," I answered. I told her the government had taken him to the army and I'd last seen him at my father's funeral, three years before. She looked away, patted my arm, and changed the subject.

Next it was, "What is it like in Nogales? Have you actually seen Tucson? I hear the people talk about Tucson."

"Oh yes. I've seen those places and many more."

She was warming up emotionally, much less guarded than usual. She even asked politely if she could change radio stations. I nodded.

She was not being bratty at all. She had become just a wide-eyed kid. She said she liked traveling with me. Again I asked her more questions about her family, but she remained evasive. Finally I said, "Well, you asked me about my family; why don't you tell me anything about yours?" She said, "Well, they are just secrets; secrets."

I let it go and turned back to ordinary chatter. She asked questions about things along the road. "What mountains are these?" "What is this place called?" . . . "What does that sign say?"

I pointed out things to her. She was like a sponge, soaking it all up. At one point she startled me, asking what the animals were along the highway. Then I realized that if she only knew el centro in Guaymas, she probably had never seen cattle before.

I had been doing about seventy-five or eighty the whole way, so we reached Nogales just after nine at night. I announced, "Okay, I am going to leave you here in Nogales and go to the other side." She threw a tantrum, determined to cross the border. She wanted to tell the boleadores she had been in the United States.

"I don't know how to get you past American immigration *(la migra)*. They are real hard-asses." She was aware of that. That was gospel on the street. The exasperating characters our nation hired to staff its southern border were as notorious as Mexico's federales. I told her I would leave her at the train station with a hundred pesos and return for her the next night.

I pulled into the train station in Nogales, Mexico, and ordered Lupita out. She was sullen but resigned. I parked, rolled down the window, lit up a cigarette, and zipped open the envelope I had been given at El Corsario.

Out of one eye I watched Lupita go inside, her little nylon bag with her. The envelope contained instructions about refrigerators and electrical equipment. Attached were five thousand pesos in large banknotes.

213

Relieved, I was glad it wasn't anything like drugs. All I had to do was to deliver some items to a certain address in Nogales. Enclosed was another envelope that had a person's name and address in Nogales. It was very thin. Again no drugs. Cool!

As I finished reading the instructions and smoked my cigarette, Lupita came running back to my window, still holding her little bag. She'd been crying, tears running down her face. Her eyes looked so big and sad.

"What's the matter, *mija* (kiddo)?" I asked. She pleaded, "*¡Mira Davíd! Es mi sueño* (it is my dream) to say I've been to 'the other side.' I told the shoeshine boys, the *boleadores*, that I was going to 'the other side' with you."

I felt bad but told her I wasn't going to carry her through immigration. She said, "Okay. I can cross over if you wait for me." I said, "You've got to be shitting me! (*¡Me estás vacillando!*)" She said, "No, I can cross over. Give me another hundred pesos!"

I said, "*¡Mierda!* You can't bribe an American customs official. You got to be crazy." She said, "No, no, no, no. I know what I am doing. I hear the *contrabandistas* talk about this on the Serdán. I know lots of things in the street."

I relented, telling her I'd let her out just before U.S. customs and wait for her at a restaurant called Zula's, on the right-hand side of the road about three-quarters of a mile from the frontera—about the same distance as the walk from the Rubi to the statue at the head of the Serdán. She nodded. I offered to wait one hour before going on to Tucson.

She agreed, promising that she would go back to the train station and wait for me there until eight the next night if anything went wrong. Again composed, she stepped in the car, dried off her face and said, "Well, I knew you liked me."

When we reached the area where U.S. customs forces traffic to form several different lines, I pulled to the far-right lane. Three hundred yards short of U.S. jurisdiction, and almost exactly opposite Mexican immigration, she opened the back door and bailed out.

Seconds later she was walking in the endless crowd of Mexican foot traffic, carrying her net bag, slipstreaming a Mexican family with a bunch of kids.

"*¡Ándale, Lupita!*" I thought, and grinned. My mandadera was a genuine piece of work!

I moved up the line and went through. Coming back to the States is always tougher than leaving. Worse yet, my agent was a stupid South Texas redneck with a major hard-on. The kind of guy who always wanted to be a Texas Ranger, but couldn't make it. He waved me into the area where they hand-check your gear.

There was nothing unusual about my papers or my suitcase. But he was suspicious. "Careful, Dave!" I told myself. I took deep breaths. Smiled. Made eye contact.

In the sixties these guys were suspicious of every young, single American guy crossing over. We met "The Profile"—draft dodger, drug dealer, gunrunner, or worse. Worse meaning "Mexican-lovers." They had strip-searched me a number of times.

Once you experience a rubber-gloved hunt for imaginary condoms of heroin up your own butt, you make concessions. You had to keep these guys calm. They were dangerous when either confused or aroused. I kissed his ass.

215

Fifteen minutes and no rubber gloves later I pulled out of line, then stopped to change money about three hundred yards up the road. Less than half an hour after Lupita had bailed out I pulled up to Zula's. Inside I ordered a "Zula burger" and a chocolate malt. For the second time that summer I ate American junk food. Zula's was a lot better than the bus station in Tucson, but there were other aspects of culture shock.

I sat in Zula's, dazzled by the sounds of English from the tables around me. I picked at my hamburger, nervous. I ate slowly, nursed my milkshake, then ordered a coffee. No Lupita. I began to panic, worrying about her. I got American coins from the cashier in order to buy myself a pack of Pall Mall reds—my one true American fixation. As I dropped the coins into the cigarette machine, I was struck by how small and light American money is. Compared to Mexican pesos, the American stuff felt like toy money. Pesos are big and solid.

Worse yet, it smelled like the United States again—that bland, antiseptic Pinesol smell. Even the light was different. Nearly all the lights in hotels and restaurants in Mexico are bright, uncovered bulbs. In Zula's the light was much more subdued. I looked at my watch. Still no Lupita!

Next I went to the counter and bought the Tucson evening paper. Time to check out the ads for the next day's shopping. Still no Lupita. I waited an hour and thirty-five minutes, then gave up and paid my tab. I was so worried I actually prayed that the little rat was all right. I hoped she had simply turned back to the train station in Nogales, Mexico.

Worried, I went out and stood next to the car, looking around the parking lot. Jeez! No sign of her. I unlocked the Rambler, got in, sighed, and figured, "Well, I'll go on to Tucson."

That's when I heard her voice. The backseat. She had been lying on the back floor to stay out of sight and immediately started to rag my butt. "Boy, some kind of employer you are! Here I am roasting my *nalgas* (buns) in the back of your car while you are in there drinking *malteadas!*"

Teasingly, she called me a cabrón. I told her I had been worried sick about her and pulled her to me. I even hugged her. Amazingly, she did not resist. "Lupita, how did you get over?"

She said, "Well, that's my secret." "Okay, then how *did* you get in my car?"

She filled me in, "Oh, you forget. I've lived in the street all my life. I can get in a car any time I wish. I've slept in lots of cars parked on the street, especially when it rains."

Then she asked, "Are you impressed, Güero? You didn't think I could do it, did you?" "No," I said, "I didn't think you could. How *did* you do it?"

She cackled, "That's my secret." I tried again, "No really, tell me!"

For the third time, she refused, "That's my secret . . . now can I call you Davíd?" I said, "Okay! You can call me Davíd. I'm impressed." She bragged, "I know lots of things. I will be a good employee for you. Can we go to Tucson now?"

I said, "Yes, but there might be an immigration stop between Nogales and Tucson. If there's trouble, what then? Suppose they catch you and take you back?"

She said, "Well, if they catch me, they'll only take me back to Mexico, and I left money in Nogales where I can find it. I can catch a bus back to Guaymas."

217

I approved the plan. "Okay. Do you want to sit up front?"

"No, maybe I'd better just stay in back." I continued, "Well, we ought to have some sort of story." She gave me one.

"Well, you can say that you're my godfather, *mi padrino*." I said, "Okay, good! I'm just taking you to Tucson for a shopping trip. If somebody makes a stink, I'll just say, 'Okay, I'll take you back tomorrow.'" She said that sounded fine.

We drove on and about two minutes later she said, "I never got any dinner." Denny's restaurant was coming up on the left. I said, "You're right. You sat in the car. Why didn't you come into Zula's?"

"Well, I didn't know what to expect. They told me there were migra and federales everywhere."

About three minutes after having pulled out of Zula's we pulled into Denny's, on the left-hand side of the road. She asked to go in with me. I said, "Yes, sure. But you let me do the talking. If I say something to you in English, you nod at me so people don't realize that you don't speak any English." She said, "Okay, fine."

We walked in and I ordered her a hamburger, fries, and a milkshake. Again this kid could wolf food down! In less than fifteen minutes she had packed it all away. While she ate, her head was going in every direction. She was taking in everything she could.

Finished, we got up and went to the register. As we headed out the door, she wanted to go to the restroom. I had to point to which one, because *men* and *women* didn't mean anything to her.

She was in there twelve or fifteen seconds before she came out. I asked softly, in Spanish, "What did you do, pee on the floor?" Whispering, she said, "No," and explained she wanted to see an American bathroom, because she'd heard that they had seats on the toilets.

I asked her if she was sure she didn't have to "go." She said she did, but the toilet was strange. I told her how to flip the handle—something she had never seen. Most Mexican toilets in places she would have frequented were either old-fashioned pull-chain or "toss in the bucket of water" models.

She went into the bathroom again and this time stayed so long I had to send a waitress in to get her. One of the girls there was speaking Spanish to a cook at the window, so I asked her to go.

She brought Lupita out, a big grin on her face. Lupita had been in there giggling and flushing the toilet over and over. The Chicana asked if she was my daughter. I said, "god-daughter." In Guaymas Lupita had heard on the street that there were toilet seats on American commodes. Now she also knew how they flushed.

As we walked out to the car she was bubbly and complimented me, "You were very good with the English. They understood you perfectly! I didn't know you were that good." I grinned—she didn't grasp the irony.

We arrived in Tucson just before midnight. Lupita was animated the whole way, commenting on America from her hideaway on the floor of the backseat. I stopped at a clean, decent-looking motel just south of Tucson on the main highway that passed Green Valley. I still wasn't sure how I was going to handle the business with Lupita, so I told her to stay in the car and keep out of sight.

I went in and hit the bell. A young Hispanic guy came out. I was relieved. I told him I needed a room and asked him how much. He asked, "Well, how many people?" I said, "Two. One double bed, one single. A child's bed or a rollaway would be okay for the second bed." I had asked for a room in the back corner, ground-floor if possible. No problem. I decided that Lupita should be in the same room with me. That way she wouldn't be loose on the street in the States. I didn't want to lose her anywhere.

I was sure the guy was going to ask me, "Your daughter, your son?" or something. He could have cared less. I had the distinct impression that I could have had four teen-aged girlfriends, two German shepherds, and a midget in there as long as the cops didn't show up.

He did ask to see my driver's license and wanted a deposit for the room. I filled out the register, gave him fifteen dollars for the night, and got the key.

Done at the office, I went out to the car, cranked it up,

and pulled over to the space in front of our room. It was inconspicuous and I wouldn't have to carry purchases up the stairs. I announced our arrival to the backseat, "*¡Ya llegamos!* (Well, here we are!)" She queried, "Will I see you in the morning?" I responded, "This is our room. I got a room with two beds. Come on." She was doubtful, "I don't know about that."

I told her, "Look, you know the street, *la calle*, in Mexico, but this is my country. I don't want you running around where *la migra* might grab you. We'll go a few places together, but when I'm not here I want you in this room. I'm going to write you a note to keep with you, to explain who you are. Okay?"

Once inside, she looked around awkwardly. There was a double bed, which I patted, "mine," and a single bed to one side, "hers." The room was air-conditioned—a luxury after all those hot nights in Guaymas. I left her inside while I got our belongings from the Rambler.

She'd been watching me from the window and had spotted a big, red Coca Cola machine outside. She couldn't read, but the Coke logos are the same everywhere. She wanted to go out and put money in the machine, so I gave her a quarter.

She ran out and dropped her quarter into the machine, but came back totally baffled because she'd gotten a can. These were pre-pop-top cans. She had no idea you pulled a lever to punch holes in the top.

I chuckled and took her out to show her how it worked. First she was totally amazed, then realized that she now knew something that the boleadores didn't. Ripped, she started vibrating again and asked for another quarter. Giggling, she dealt the next can a savage blow. "*¡Qué padre!* (Totally cool!)" she squealed. I got the ice bucket and filled it.

Inside I savored my coke, swirling the ice. Still jazzed, she explained that the taxistas had told her that the "*pinche gringos* are *cabrones de la tecnología* (the frigging gringos are hell on technology)."

I reminded her I was a gringo and didn't appreciate the *pinche*, adding that I wasn't thrilled with the *gringo*, either. For once she stopped moving, talking, even vibrating, and stared, incredulous, then spoke, "I'm sorry. I forgot."

That settled, I explained the next day's business and wrote a note on University of New Mexico letterhead: "To Whom It May Concern: . . ." explaining that my goddaughter did not speak English and giving the phone number of the Sitio Rubi in Guaymas, in case of emergency. I told her to keep it and show it to anyone who tried to take her anywhere.

Finished, I told her to go to bed. Then I went into the bathroom, closed the door, took a shower, and dressed for bed. When I came out, it was already 1:30 A.M., but she was still sitting erect on her bed, looking uncomfortable. She hadn't even taken her clothes off—maybe she slept in hers, too. I asked if she was okay.

221

She said she didn't remember ever sleeping on a bed before, and that she was cold. I asked her, "Lupita, do you have any pajamas?" She said, "*¿Que es? ¿Ropa de noche?* (What's that? Night clothes?)" I nodded. She went on, "Well, no. Is that bad?"

I said, "No. How about I lend you one of my big, warm field shirts?" Animated again she said, "Okay." So I dug out a worn Gokey chamois-cloth shirt and handed it to her. I turned off the light, rolled over, and told her "good night."

As I drifted off to sleep she called to me, "Davíd?" I said, "Yes. What's the matter?" She said, "You're not going to leave me are you? You wouldn't leave me, would you?" I told her "no," that I would take care of her and not leave her. Frankly I was relieved, because I had been afraid *she* might take off.

I never did see her change into my shirt, but sometime late in the night I awakened, startled to hear strange noises. At first I was disoriented because I was accustomed to my room at the Hotel Rubi. The noises were coming from her bed underneath the window. I went over to take a look.

Lupita had my big fuzzy fawn-colored shirt wrapped around her. The covers were half-down and she was lying on her side in the fetal position, sucking her thumb to beat the band. Wow! My little mandadera seemed so streetwise and so saucy, yet here she was, looking like "Dondi," the comic-strip character, with her thumb completely jammed into her mouth.

She was just a fragile kid, after all. Gently I pushed a strand of hair back from her forehead and watched her for a minute, then covered her and went back to bed.

It was cool. Heavenly! But I didn't get to sleep late the next morning. Lupita was up. She'd probably been up for a while, but couldn't wait any longer. Like a kid on Christmas morning, she pounded on me, "Get up! Get up! We have business!" It was only a quarter after eight in the morning. Reluctantly I got up.

Ready for the day, we walked across the highway to a café. I ordered pancakes, sausage, and scrambled eggs. She wanted exactly the same, telling me she wanted a "real American breakfast."

I was impressed. She couldn't have weighed seventy pounds but ate like a horse! She went through a stack of pancakes, sausage, and eggs in her regulation fifteen minutes and would've kept going, had I let her.

222

Breakfast out of the way, I left Lupita in our room to wait, while I drove to the bank to get the Smiths' money. She didn't want to stay, but I insisted, reminding her we would have to pass policemen stationed in the bank. That did it. I hung a "Do Not Disturb" sign on the door, then drove up Route 19.

At First National I picked up the Smiths' four thousand dollars. They were expecting me. I showed my passport, driver's license, and a note from Mrs. Smith. I asked for the money in American Express Traveler's checks, countersigned them, got a "proof of receipt" for four thousand dollars, and walked out.

223

ten

LA MOVIDA

As I pulled up to the motel Lupita was watching for me at the window, looking anxious. Though I had been gone just over an hour, she was obviously relieved to see me. She hugged me. I gave her a pat, "Well, kid, this is it. Now we go shopping."

I told her that after shopping I needed to make a round trip over to Nogales, Mexico. She squealed, "*¡Ándale!*" and began jumping up and down, vibrating again. The vibrating thing was fascinating—it was as if she were shivering. She shook and jiggled like a rocket ready for launch.

J. C. Penney's had a big sale, so we went there first. When I invited her to help me pick fans, she went into full-launch mode. As we walked through the front door of Penney's she exploded into low orbit, awed at the quantity and variety of stuff.

In her words it was "*un chingote de una tienda* (a frigging huge store)." Several heads turned as Lupita let it rip—local

Spanish speakers, no doubt impressed at the unusually color-ful tone of the kid's description.

We scored eight restaurant-grade fans, eight blenders, several waffle irons (for streetside sandwich shops), calcula-tors, radios, and an ordinary toaster. We even found Max's big dough mixer. Then I went to Safeway and bought several cases of soup and Carnation milk on speculation.

Lupita was having a ball, vibrating the whole time. Done power shopping, we hauled everything back to our motel room where I left Lupita to "guard" it. That worked. Then I got to work on the Corsario request.

I drove off to an electric supply house, per instructions in the envelope, and bought the items specified. Then back to the motel room, where I checked on Lupita before going over to Mexico. She insisted that I let her help me "arrange" the crossing with Mexican customs.

I was nervous about crossing over, so relented and brought her along. I had spent more than four hundred dol-lars of my own money on appliances and didn't want anything to go wrong.

I piled Lupita into the car, leaving our purchases and the Smiths' traveler's checks at the motel. An hour later we crossed over and pulled into the line of cars arriving in Mexico. It was hot and I was nervous. But Lupita was strangely calm. I was jumpy as a cat. She patted me, "*¡Cálmate! ¡Cálmate!* (Calm down!)"

We got to the Mexican customs station in Nogales. I didn't need a new tourist card, because I hadn't surrendered mine on the way out the night before, so I drove past migración, no sweat. Then it got complicated.

I was stuck in the line of cars being pulled over for *aduana* (customs) inspection. We edged right up to a *federal* directing traffic, who waved me over into customs. I thought we were ruined, but Lupita simply stuck her head out of the window, waved at him, and went "psst-psst!" He came over and she told him, "My godfather is supposed to deliver me to *calle 17, número 176*, and we're not familiar with Nogales. Which way do we go?" He hesitated.

Sounding totally pathetic, she said, "My godfather is delivering me for my mother—to stay with an aunt that I don't know." The guy looked sad for a second, then said, "Are you a Mexican national?" She nodded.

"Just go on straight," he said. "Well, do we need papers for my *padrino* to leave me here in Nogales?" Amazingly, he said, "No." So Lupita handled it. He waved us through, no problem.

226

We wound along countless streets, asking directions several times, and finally found our delivery address—a machine shop. I went in with my envelope for a "señor Alarcón." I asked at the counter, "Is señor Alarcón here?" He said, "Yes. I'm Alarcón. I've been expecting you. Are you the one they call El Güero, from Guaymas?" I said, "Yes, I am."

He asked, "What kind of car have you?" I answered, "A gray Rambler." "*¿Placas?*" he asked. "West Virginia!" He grinned, ear to ear. The Rambler was a very unusual car in Mexico. So were West Virginia plates.

My ID confirmed, we stepped out and looked over the electrical parts I'd brought. "Everything is good," he smiled. Then he whistled over his shoulder. A couple of young guys hustled out to unload the Rambler.

Alarcón asked me inside while his boys unloaded and gave me a thin, sealed envelope addressed simply to El

Corsario, in Guaymas, instructing me to "take this there." I thanked him and left, wondering if I'd get paid for all this.

This was my first experience with "contraband." Unlike my romantic notions, it had been very uneventful. A letdown. I rounded up Lupita, who had been bragging to the shop guys that she was showing me the ropes. They grinned, winked at me, and gave her candy. Obviously they thought she was a normal kid. Wrong!

As we drove back to the border again, I said, "God, I can't believe how easy it was crossing over with these three huge boxes in the back of this car! It's amazing that the federales didn't nab us. You were great!" She was pleased, but told me, "Oh, Davíd, I gave him two hundred pesos when I called him to the window." Hell, I hadn't even seen this action, and told her so. The little brat had given him his mordida after all. I told her again that I was impressed. She was thrilled, but reminded me I owed her the bribe, plus interest. "No problem," I grinned.

227

I drove back across the border, dropping her out the back door as before, then waited for her at the money changer's. She met me in twenty minutes. As I dangled over two hundred pesos in front of her face, I insisted on knowing how this was done.

"Tunnels!" she replied, grabbing the bills. "It costs fifty pesos each way. You owe me another hundred pesos." As she grabbed another bill she smiled radiantly, "¡*Muchísimas gracias!* (Thank you very much!)" This was the second time I noticed that money had a profoundly civilizing effect on Lupita.

Back at our motel we checked the room, then crossed the highway to the same café. Time for a late lunch. She wanted to stay another day. I vetoed that, reminding her the American wanted out of jail. She said, "*¡Pues, no sirve cruzar más noche!* (Well it won't work to cross later tonight)." I asked why not. She shot back, "Weeknight. Not enough traffic. We'll get stopped." So "we" decided to go immediately.

We checked out and loaded the car. I said, "Suppose we run into the same guy crossing over?" She said, "Well, I'll need more money." So I gave her five hundred-peso notes and asked, "Do you think you can get us through this time?" Fondling the bills, she glowed, "Oh, yes. We'll be fine."

An hour later we were in the line when she said, "Wait. Pull over!" So I pulled out of line and parked about a hundred feet short of the crossing. Lupita told me to wait for her. She was back in about fifteen minutes. Smiling, she announced "Okay. Now it's okay to go on."

I asked, "Well, what did you do? What's going on?" She said, "Well, I talked to somebody that I talked to the other night. I saw somebody." She had seen somebody that she recognized, one of the Mexican border agents.

We got in line again, but got stopped cold. Mr. federal asked, "What are you carrying? What have you got?" I answered, "Some household goods to take back to Guaymas." He said, "Well, you need a tourist card." I showed him my tourist card and told him I had gone over to get some of my personal effects.

That's when Lupita popped in and started chattering about "capitán Raúl," and slipped him two hundred pesos. He looked surprised, shrugged, and waved us through. I drove on.

I asked Lupita what that was all about. She told me she had to pay off the captain first—five hundred pesos. I asked, "Where did you get the other money?"

"I am making an investment with my salary," she replied, "*¡Con intereses!* (With interest!)" She told me she had to let this guy know that his captain had already been "tipped"; that there wasn't going to be any trouble if he waved us through. I asked, "Is that all there is to it? What happens when we get down the highway to the next checkpoint?" She said, "Don't stop. Just wave, honk your horn, and drive past."

"Lupita! What do you *mean*, wave, honk the horn, and drive past?" She explained, "You honk the horn twice, you wave, and you go past. That's what all the contrabandistas do who pay for special service. That's the number of horn honks that you're supposed to give today when you go past the army station. There should be one down at a place called Imuris."

I said, "Yes, well, that's where it usually is." She clarified, "Well, today the captain says it's two honks."

I said, "You're kidding me? It's just this easy?" She said, "Yeah, that's all there is to it, just the *mordida*." I said, "Well, what did you say we were carrying?" Looking angelic, she said, "The truth—just Carnation milk and fans."

229

I had thought this was going to be exotic, perhaps even dangerous. But for a total of nine hundred pesos (seventy-two dollars), we had come and gone several times. I now had about six hundred dollars invested in this trip, so I hoped our stuff sold in Guaymas. I didn't want to go back to eating every other day. And now I also had a "payroll" to maintain.

We drove south, past Nogales, on a hot July evening, my gray Rambler loaded to the roof with "contraband" goodies, my little mandadera, and enough cash to spring a country-man from jail.

That's when it hit me that we had not needed to use the documents from the tourist bureau. I mentioned this to

Lupita, who said, "I remembered. Save it! Save that paper from señor X. We can get through this without that. Then you can come back another time and no one needs to know, or you can sell the papers."

I told her that if we got past the federales at Imuris, she could have anything she wanted. Lupita vibrated, "Well, would you take me to the beach?" And I said, "Sure. Where? Primaverales?" She said, "No! I want to have dinner at San Carlos; at the Yacht Club in San Carlos." I said, "Have you been there?" She shook her head. I said, "Okay. You got it—San Carlos." She wiggled her eyebrows just like Groucho Marx and leaned back in the seat, triumphant.

At Imuris we slowed, tapped the horn twice, waved, and were motioned on with a nod and wave by a soldier at the side of the road, shouldering his Garand. That was it. We were home free.

230

I pulled out the hand-throttle, relaxed, and rolled along, keeping pace with a huge Tres Estrellas (Three Stars) bus heading south. We made it to Guaymas about eleven o'clock that night. I dropped Lupita off at the back corner of the Rubi. She said she'd see me the next day and scampered off.

I pulled up right behind the taxis parked at the Sitio Rubi and went in to the Smiths' room. It was late, but she was ecstatic to know that we'd be able to pay the fines and get her husband out the next day, Friday. It had only been five days since the ill-fated dance on the roof of the Miramar, but that already seemed like another world.

By the time I finished with Mrs. Smith and made it outside to the sitio, several customers had already gotten the word that their "orders" had arrived. Three fans and a waffle iron were already gone by midnight. Excited, the guys at the sitio had started spreading the word, but I asked them to hold off.

El Burro had a piece of the action, but was not around. Besides, I was simply exhausted from the long drives and the tension of the border crossings.

Around ten the next morning I went to town hall and finalized the paperwork for Mr. Smith's fines. As is often the case in Mexico, it was getting unexpectedly complicated, so I made only a down payment on the fine and called the consul in Hermosillo from the big mahogany booth in the Rubi.

Burro was waiting for me as I stepped out of the booth. Our customers were anxious, one might even say hysterical, to complete their transactions. Afternoon temperatures were peaking at about 110°—our fans were worth their weight in gold. The car and contents were untouched.

In those days you could leave gold bars stacked on the curb space of a Mexican sitio and, for a reasonable tip, they'd be there the next day. Even the local police didn't screw with the sitios—their curb space was as sacred as the altar of a church.

I went out with El Burro and reparked my car in the quiet street behind the hotel. It was only four blocks to the port's customs office. No need to attract unwanted attention.

El Burro had made calls to both his clients and mine from the sitio phone box. He had begged me to let him "bring clients," and treated my cargo like the grand opening of an important business enterprise. "Got to get the word out *en la calle. ¡Es mi chanza elevarme!* (It's my chance to pull myself up!)" he had confided. "Please let me bring you clients!"

Burro had gone on, "You are my good luck, Güero! Going into business with you will give me a *movida* (hustle).

The other taxistas think I will fail. This is important to me. *¡Tengo valor!* (I'm worth something!) I'm not too stupid to do my part."

Jesus! I thought about his situation. Late twenties, short, plain, no girlfriend, and no family that I knew of, he rented a beat-up taxi and a sleeping room. Then I thought about begging for the same kind of chance from my father when I was eighteen. I had lost that one, so I cut Burro in for a 6-percent commission on my profit. It was a good move.

Thus began my formal introduction to the concept of *movida*, or "the moves." The concept is similar to the Stateside notion of "action."

Burro had come through. As our clients lined up, fans, blenders, radios, and waffle irons quickly found their new homes.

Lupita had assured me that if I merely doubled my state-side purchase price it would be a bargain, since the usual traffickers tripled theirs. As usual Lupita was right. Burro had become my promoter and charged his clients a "finder's fee" on top, to get their orders placed with me.

It was a beautiful day, hot but breezy. Puffy clouds were rolling in with the Pacific breeze, carrying the scent of taco carts, saltwater, and limes from nearby gardens. The taxistas, impressed, had bought one of my radios for the sitio at a preferred price and were playing rancheras full blast a hundred feet away.

Burro had worn his only white guayabera and black pants, telling me we had to "give our clients a good impression." He sure looked different without his signature plaid shirt! I put on a dress shirt and dark pants.

Little Lupita came and went, bringing Cokes and selling

candy to those waiting at the curb to complete their transactions under the magnificent, dense corazón de la india (Indian girl's heart) tree, where we had parked the Rambler.

One of the taco carts from the malecón had come round the corner at her invitation to serve our clients. Several nearby householders came out to make impulse purchases, chattering in the street. Fans were hot! The soup and canned milk were gone and folks were placing new orders. By three in the afternoon, I had only two radios, a blender, and a calculator, plus Max's Colmenar purchase. I told Max I'd deliver when I came for lunch.

This was my introduction to a free market in operation. We had assessed demand, invested our own money, taken risks, and set a competitive price. I aced our business model by offering a thirty-day replacement on any of the appliances that failed.

233

By three both Lupita and El Burro were vibrating in unison. I had nearly sixteen thousand pesos (fourteen hundred dollars) stuffed into my pockets, and it was time to divide the spoils. Burro got four hundred pesos plus his "finder's fees" (over thirteen hundred pesos, in all). The night shift at the sitio got a nice tip.

Lupita's cut was six hundred pesos, including the money she had "invested" in mordidas at the border. Security issues momentarily forgotten, she ran off to La Gorda's, waving her arms and screaming about her "*pinche rollote de lana* (frigging huge roll of cash)." She was upset only in that we had completely forgotten underpants for La Gorda.

As I got ready to go to the Colmenar, Burro was basking in the moment with several of the sitio taxistas who had come over to buy tacos and check out the proceedings. He was pumping his arm in the air to the beat of the radio and waving a fistful of bills at me. "¡Ya, estamos en la MOVIDA, 'mano! (We're in the action, 'bro'!)"

Damned if we weren't! Everyone was laughing and slapping our shoulders. I passed out cigarettes, shook hands all around, and stepped into the Rambler, feeling eighteen again. As I pulled away Burro was smack-dab in the middle of the street, doing a lively two-step to the sitio's new radio and still waving the bills in one joyously upraised fist.

It was one of the most memorable afternoons of my life. Two young men known on the street only by their nicknames and an orphan mandadera scoring food and rent money in the real world. It's a shame that most big-shot businessmen in the States who talk "free market" have never actually experienced the real thing. It *is* exhilarating.

I drove to the Colmenar, interrupted by a quick stop at the Banco de Sonora. I had more than enough money in my pockets to cover a year's rent, meals, cigarettes, and occasional parties. A deposit seemed wise.

Max was happy with his purchases. The cost had been less than he expected. Dinner was on the house. I had camarones borrachos at a table out in front of the Pasaje, enjoying the breeze from Max's new fan. Mercedes wasn't around so Max chatted and kept me company.

As we talked, one of the local businessmen came over to sit with us. Of Middle Eastern descent, his name was Santiago, "Jimmy," Kiami. He owned El Capricho clothing shop, on the opposite corner. Smart, affable, and gregarious, he was a mover and shaker among the area's small businessmen. I raised the "Smith problem" with him. He said I needed some *palanca* (political leverage) to get that done.

I left the Colmenar and headed to the Rubi about six, glowing from the effects of a nearly perfect day. My only remaining problem was getting Mr. Smith out of jail. It looked like I might have to call in the cavalry on that one. Jesse was tied up at the time, so I did early evening rounds of the sitios, serdaneando until nearly eight, when I walked back to the Rubi.

As I passed the Rubi's desk the patrón said, "Jesse would like to see you in the bar." I answered, "Okay," and turned down the long hallway to the rear, paneled bar. Jesse was just setting up in back, while Enrique finished cleaning the front bar, which closed early. As soon as he saw me Jesse jerked his head, motioning me to none other than don Francisco, who wanted to buy me a drink. Uncertain, I didn't move very fast.

That is when don Francisco stood up and motioned me over. He was effusive. "Well, Davíd, I understand you had a nice trip to Nogales and are getting to know our country." That's when I reckoned the Corsario transaction originated with him—but nothing about it was ever mentioned overtly.

Still cautious, I answered simply, "Oh, yes. It was very enjoyable." He asked if it was an eventful trip, and I said, "No, not at all. I had some personal business to take care of."

Then I told him I'd been quite concerned about an American couple, the Smiths. He said, "Yes, I heard. She was hurt." I said, "Yes, they wrecked their car up on Route 15, but didn't have the proper insurance. I went and paid a deposit on his fine with the *teniente's* office and was hoping to get him out of jail quickly, but it has become unnecessarily complicated."

I continued, telling him I just wanted to see them pay their fines and return to *el otro lado* quickly. He asked, "Well,

235

was anyone else hurt?" I said, "No. Only his wife with a sprain. They just ran their car off the road." He smiled, "Well, perhaps something can be done. How much are the fines?" I said, "Thirty thousand pesos." He said, "Oh, gee. That's quite a sum of money. Are these very wealthy people?"

"No, I don't think so. But they have agreed to pay it." He said, "Well, I know people around town. Let's see what happens." I said, "Great. If anyone can get that guy out of jail, I'd be very grateful. I think it's time to send them home."

He bought me another drink, then said lightly, "I hear you met several of my daughters at the Miramar last Saturday." Defensive, I corrected him. "I believe I only met one, don Francisco—she was lovely, gracious, and granted me a dance." He grinned like the Cheshire cat. "To be precise, you met *two* of them, Davíd."

He paused for effect, enjoying the moment. I figured it out. But before I could tender an apology, he laughed heartily, told me I was an "astronaut," slapped me on the back, and walked out, cackling the whole way. I stood there stunned as Jesse winked at me. When the door shut behind don Francisco, Jesse said, "He likes you. He told me you were trustworthy."

I went out, walking the malecón. It was a Friday evening. Hot, but lively. At the statue to the fisherman, near the Copa de Leche, a small, grassy curve of the malecón was filled with amusement rides and food stalls. Kids everywhere. The rich scents of charcoaled beef and onions wafted across the Serdán from Doney's, the large sandwich shop on the corner.

Near the carnival a *churro* cart sold the cinnamon-sugared pastries that looked like pipe cactus. I bought one to eat on the way back to the Rubi. While passing the Casa Blanca, the strange mulatto couple lounging in the front door nodded. I smiled and returned the greeting in kind, reflecting on just how lucky I was not to be staying there.

I reached the Rubi about nine and went down to the bar. Jesse announced, "Well, we have miracles here!" I asked, "Of what kind?" He said, "Well, the *señor norteamericano* is here." Old Francisco had apparently had the sucker sprung in just over an hour. He said, "They're leaving tonight. You should go see them." I said, "Jesse, you're kidding me! The fines aren't even fully paid."

Jesse laughed, "They are going on the train at midnight. The car is now on a *plataforma* (flatbed) on its way to Empalme. It is all arranged, *está arreglado*." Wow! I was amazed. Don Francisco had obviously supplied the needed palanca. Even the president of Mexico would have been in awe of how quickly this had happened. don Francisco was far more powerful than I had imagined.

I hustled down the corridor, knocked on the Smiths' door, and was invited in. They were waiting for me, ecstatic. Señor X from the tourism office was already on his way over, with a special permission for them to exit the country. He knocked about ten minutes later and presented them their documents and train tickets. He had a bill for the car and tickets. I signed some traveler's checks and we settled that on the spot (the bill had been calculated in pesos to equal exactly four hundred dollars).

Then señor X escorted me to town hall, where I signed enough additional traveler's checks to clear the fine, which had actually been reduced a bit. I was back in the hotel by ten. Everything was in order. There was only one catch—Mr. Smith now had the charge of driving without insurance entered on a list sent to Mexico City. No more tourist cards for Mr. Smith, until and unless he successfully petitioned in a Mexican court.

The Smiths could have cared less. They were already packing as I explained. I began to sign the rest of their traveler's checks so they could cash them in Nogales or Tucson. They reminded me that four of the hundred-dollar checks were for my services, since they had already "advanced" me a hundred dollars for travel to Tucson.

I didn't argue, but cautioned them to guard their signed checks and offered to drive them to the train when they were ready. I went back to the bar and ordered an Orange Crush, telling Jesse that I just couldn't believe that everything seemed to be working. He said, "Well, you know. You did people favors. That's the way things work around here."

A few minutes later I went back to the American couple's room and asked if they were ready. Talk about ready to go! These folks were hysterical to get the hell out of Mexico. I packed them and their suitcases into the Rambler. They were amazed that no policemen were along for the trip. I assured them not, but was soon proved wrong. At the Empalme station's platform a Guaymas policeman waited discreetly. I guessed that he had been sent to make certain these folks left, as promised.

There I stood in late July, on the same platform where I had stood with Iliana and Lisa more than six weeks earlier, waiting for another midnight train to the border. I nodded at the cop standing there on the platform. He nodded back.

I again reminded the Smiths to make certain their exit papers were stamped on the way out, advising them to simply leave their car in the wrecking yard in Nogales and let their stateside insurance company worry about retrieving it later. Then I showed them to their seats. Once they were settled, I walked to the rear of the car and stepped out, nodding to the cop. He tipped his cap. Then I drove back to the Rubi.

By that hour the bar had already closed. It was a Friday night, and there was dancing at Chapúltepec. I walked over to the Pavilion and had a Coca Cola. I watched the dancing, took in the music, and nodded at a couple of the girls, but I was edgy over the events of the last few days and decided to walk the malecón.

I had only gone about five hundred feet before I spotted Lupita again, standing under her favorite streetlight, staring intently across the harbor. I was on the harbor side of the Serdán. She was landward. I walked by but she didn't notice. So I kept going. Whatever had caught her attention, I couldn't spot it. There was nothing at all moving out in the harbor.

239

Not far from the Casa Blanca, Lupita came scampering out of the dark, her reverie past. I exclaimed, "You don't sleep there, do you?" She said, "No, no. I have to talk to you." We continued up the Serdán to the town hall, before turning toward the Almita. I was getting hungry again.

She asked me if I'd enjoyed the trip. I told her it had been very exciting and profitable. I let her know that the American couple was on the train and now headed for the border. She said, "Yes, I heard. That was good work. You'll make good money on this." Then I invited her to eat with me at the Almita. She said, "No, I won't. You eat. But you promised to take *me* to San Carlos!" I told her I'd take her there soon, as promised.

She said, "By the way, I told La Flaca (Marta) that you had returned. I saw her *en la calle* and told her you were back."

Lupita was pleased with herself—undoubtedly she had rubbed the trip in Marta's face. Jeez! Before I could snarl, she scampered off.

I wandered into the Almita and said "hello" to Ana María López, and my regular meal materialized like magic. About two in the morning I walked back to the Rubi and checked in with the taxistas to make certain they had gotten their tip money from our movida.

They had and, at the prices I offered, new orders were trickling in. I referred them to Burro, since I didn't want to make another trip to the border too soon.

It would have been stupid to attract unwanted attention or imply that my first trip had been more than modestly profitable. I went inside, showered, and dressed. Thinking about Burro, Lupita, movida, and long-term survival in Guaymas, I drifted off to sleep.

The next morning I got up, put three of my hundred-dollar traveler's checks into the hotel safe, then went to the bar for my usual Orange Crushes. It was slow, so I wandered back to my room and wrote halfheartedly in my journal, then ambled back to the bar for a short newspaper session. The heat was driving everybody crazy—it was relentless. Not a cloud in the sky. It was too hot even to smoke!

Next I went serdaneando, hitting the sitios. I loved the routine: greetings, shake every hand in sight, make small talk or tell jokes and pass out a few cigarettes, shake hands again, and move on. As I'd walk away it was, *"Ándale, Güero,"* or similar goodbyes.

By the time I reached the Medrano, on Calle 19, I was soaked in sweat. So were the taxistas. Bathed in blinding sunlight, the Serdán was drenched in the scents of sweat, hot concrete, and gasoline from the idle taxis.

A tallish Japanese-Mexican taxista known simply as "Japón" had just won a bet of twenty pesos by frying an egg on the black sedan parked irreverently in the sitio's curb space. The egg was actually sizzling on the dark sheet metal as if in a frying pan on low heat. We all watched, laughing, until one of the shoeshine boys said it smelled good and asked if he could have it when we were through.

Without missing a beat in the joke he was telling, Japón nodded quickly at the sitio's errand boy, while jerking his eyes toward the *lonchería* (lunchroom) three doors up the street. The Medrano's mandadero returned in less than five minutes with a fried-egg torta (sandwich) wrapped in newspaper. He handed it subtly to the skinny little guy, who was still sitting on his shoeshine box, staring intently at the puffy white egg stuck to the sedan's black hood.

As the scrawny boleador stuffed the torta into his face, looking surprised, one of the older taxistas asked for a quick shine when he was finished eating. The kid smiled and nodded. This was typical of the smooth, quiet solutions to problems that arose every day en la calle.

No stateside-style heroics. Just get the kid a meal without humiliating him and move on. On the Serdán this was as natural as breathing. I said my goodbyes and headed to the Colmenar.

There I ordered café con leche and a bowl of soup. Local theory held that the hot food would bring out the sweat and cool you down. Bullshit!

I wanted Lupita, but her ward, Juanito, showed up alone. Looking nervous, the little guy stood and fidgeted while he formally thanked me for "bringing Lupita back to me." I told him he was welcome and asked him to find her for me. I dangled a five-peso note and he shuffled off, all lopsided, leaving his shoeshine box for me to watch.

About ten minutes later Lupita came hustling into the passage, her panting ward about three minutes behind her. I told her that much of my business was settled and asked if she wanted to go with me that afternoon to San Carlos for our victory dinner.

She began to vibrate, asking me to pick her up at the Sitio Rubi in an hour. As she took off running, she shouted over her shoulder that she had to change clothes, a woman's prerogative. I chatted with Mercedes and Max for another ten minutes. Then I walked back to the Rubi, using Avenida 15, one street back from the Serdán, to eliminate the obligatory sitio stops.

At the Rubi bar I had an Orange Crush and played a quick game of *chingona*. I was doing poorly with the dice when Edward Meyers walked in at a critical juncture, saving me from losing more money. He had asked to marry Epifania and wanted me to go with him to her house—they needed to work out family matters.

Edward was so animated that it was hard to believe he was the same fellow who had moped around the trailer camp at Primaverales. He'd lost five to ten pounds, was wearing a white guayabera, and had the start of a tan. His transformation from dramatic gray tones to subtle brown ones was progressing nicely.

He didn't yet look local, but then again he didn't look like he had just risen from a stainless-steel tray in the cold room at the county morgue. As we left the bar, he even said, *"Adios y buenas tardes"* to Jesse, in Spanish.

Finishing our conversation, we walked down the long corridor to the lobby, passing the big mahogany phone booth. Once Edward was on his way I stepped into my room to freshen up and change shirts. Ready to meet Lupita, I walked out to the sitio.

She was waiting, the taxistas studiously ignoring her. Her hair was freshly brushed and she wore a bright blue shirt I'd not seen before. I commented. Pleased, she reminded me that she *liked blue*. I didn't bite on her reference to her old dress, but she was undaunted, constantly trying to shame me into buying her a new one.

As we walked to the rear corner she announced that she intended to have lobster for dinner, asked if she were going to get a bonus, reminded me that she hadn't gotten under-pants for La Gorda and didn't know what to tell her. Whew!

She did that all in one breath. No small trick for a smoker. I told her I'd meet her at Gorda's in the back street and have a word with her about the underpants. She looked relieved. We parted. This served my purpose, because I didn't want to be obvious about taking her around with me and suffer more ragging from the taxistas and boleadores.

I walked down to the street fronting the stone ware-houses, cranked up the Rambler, and drove it along the back street toward La Gorda's, passing señor Morales's Victorian wooden house on the rear corner of his hotel's grounds. At Gorda's I was again struck by the colonial architecture of her house. There must have been at least a dozen families living in it, but it was easy to imagine it in 1900 as a prosperous merchant's family compound.

Gorda came shuffling out with Lupita, cackling and scolding that we had forgotten her underpants. I apologized profusely. Then it occurred to me I still had two unsold radios. I asked if she'd accept a radio, so that Lupita would be back in good graces. She was delighted. I told her I'd bring her a radio later and wanted her to take extra good care of Lupita's meals. I stuffed a fifty-peso note into her hand and suggested that Lupita should have an egg on her rice now and again. She nodded and grinned.

Her missing front teeth marring an otherwise warm, grandmotherly smile, she gave Lupita a tender pat on the head. True to form, the kid pulled away and made a dive for the Rambler, vibrating in anticipation.

We drove out to San Carlos Yacht Basin, north of town, Lupita hanging out of the window and trying to see everything at once. I acted as tour guide.

I decided to pass on the main hotel, the Posada de San Carlos, since the seafood there was indifferently prepared. Nearby a better seafood restaurant with a lovely, awninged roof terrace offered us a fabulous view of San Carlos Bay and its yacht basin. Rocky hills, saguaros, and a few red-tiled condominium houses filled out the view. We walked up a steep outside staircase to the roof and took a table on the terrace overlooking the water. It was hot, but simply gorgeous.

We started with tall, iced limeades, then ordered two *langosta* dinners. Our waiter, a tall, slim guy wearing black pants, a white shirt, and black tuxedo vest, figured out who I was. "*Perdóneme señor, ¿tal vez sea usted El Güero?* (Excuse me, sir, might you be El Güero?)"

"Yes, thank you," I answered. He explained that his cousin was a waiter at the Hotel Playa de Cortés and had spoken well of me. I asked how he had recognized me. "The boots," he replied. I grinned and thanked him again. Thanks to Juanito, my beautifully polished Red Wings had gained local fame.

The dinners were fabulous. Large lobsters with lime-cilantro butter, potato salad, and frijoles. Realizing the gravity of the occasion, Lupita actually sat up straight and tried to eat with her utensils. Still, she became frustrated with the lobster at one point, threw a fit, and began to attack it forcefully. Fortunately, our waiter hustled over, grinning, and deftly pulled the meat out for her. Lupita was in heaven at the service, vibrating as she requested a second limeade.

She loved being waited on and became expansive, telling me that she wanted to be a great lady when she grew up. That way she could have lobster and real shoes and dresses and all those things. We spent about an hour and a half eating. Then she wanted me to show her Algodones (Cotton Plant) beach, since she had heard the contrabandistas talk about it on the street.

As we stood up from the table I presented her with a 100-peso bonus for the work she had done and told her to keep it in a safe place. She was pleased, rolling the bill into a tight tube to stick in her hair. I asked what she had done with the money I gave her the day before. She told me she had paid Gorda 250 pesos for four months' meals and had given Juanito another 50. The rest was in a "safe place."

I put Lupita back into the Rambler and drove out one of the unpaved roads toward Algodones beach, where local smugglers off-loaded their goods. On the way we passed through an exquisite little canyon, several miles beyond San Carlos Yacht Basin.

High rocky cliffs on either side of the road formed the canyon, through which trickled a spring-fed stream. There were ancient pictographs, quantities of broken prehistoric pottery, and a grove of palm trees clustered next to the spring.

At the far end of the little canyon, the cliffs fell away and we emerged onto a rocky shelf above a compact, half-moon-shaped estuary. A wide sand spit separated it from the outer bay. The spit was dotted with small, three-sided, palm-leafed shelters, where mullet fishermen spent the cooler fishing season.

We walked along this exquisite spit of sand, high cliffs in the background, and hunted shells. Lupita insisted that I explain everything to her. I named all the shells I could in Spanish. She repeated them after me, memorizing everything.

246   Next we picked up some colorful green-banded stones and I showed her how to skip them on the water. She was ecstatic. It was a gorgeous place—like a picture out of the South Seas, the water a crystalline blue.

We could actually see fish swimming around in the estuary. Except for a few scraps of tarpaper on several of the fishermen's shacks, it probably looked just as it had for the last thousand years. We were only about three miles from the Yacht Basin at San Carlos, but ecologically we were in another world, hidden behind a crack in the cliffs.

As we drove back through the narrow, watered canyon I stopped to look under a large rock overhang. It was heavily smoke-stained from ancient cooking fires. The narrow talus slope at the mouth of the overhang was littered with broken pottery fragments from ancient storage jars. Chert flakes discarded in the process of making stone tools were mixed with the broken pottery.

Lupita was happy and effusive. She seemed to relax. The vibrating subsided and she started chattering about how she was going to bring in more business so we could go to the border again. I was noncommittal.

I didn't want to stir up local envy. Lupita never understood that as a foreigner I was automatically conspicuous, just as she was all but invisible to many Mexicans, in denial over the existence of street children.

Then she asked, "When are you going to the Río Rita tonight?" I asked, "How do you know about that?" She said, "Oh, I know where you go. Everybody knows where you go." I said, "*¡Por Dios!* That's not your business!" She cackled. It was Saturday night. I had a date with Jesse and Negro to go clubbing and was in the mood to have a good time.

We drove back toward Guaymas. I turned into Primaverales on the way, stopped and said hello to Manuel, and bought Lupita an Orange Crush. I showed her my palapa and acted as tour guide again. Next we stopped at the Miramar Hotel.

247

Business was slow—the tourists leave when it gets too hot. I left Lupita by the car. Negro asked me how my trip had gone. I told him it was good and that I'd made enough money to cover expenses, plus some rent money for my room at the Rubi.

He asked if I'd seen Marta recently and I said "no." Again Negro advised me to be careful and not get hurt again—that Marta was no señorita.

The advice given, he reminded me that it was Saturday and I was to join Jesse and him for the floor show at the Río Rita. Negro said he'd come to the Rubi after work, so we could all go together. He told me Chang had promised us a good table up front. I laughed, "Thanks, Negro!" and left.

I had parked the car on the cobblestone lane in front of the hotel, and stopped to look at the sea twenty yards away. It was so beautiful. I never quite took for granted how pretty it was around Guaymas.

Lupita had gotten out of the car and was standing nearby, looking out at the bay. A fishing trawler five hundred yards out was letting out its nets. I asked, "Do you like the boat?" She answered, "*No mucho* (not much)." I confided, "I once wanted to be a sailor." She looked at me oddly and hissed, "I don't like sailors!" Then she clammed up, scowling. I left her to her mood as we drove back to the Hotel Rubi.

I had only been in my room about twenty minutes when I was called out to take a telephone call at the desk. It was Marta, wanting to find out if I might be interested in seeing her again. I was.

She was waiting for me on the plaza by the time I had managed a quick, lukewarm shower, changed shirts for the third time that day, and walked up to meet her. She'd been there ten minutes when I arrived. In Mexico ten minutes is not late, so she was in a good mood.

She ate a *carne asada* (grilled beef) taco in the sandwich shop on the corner, while I sipped an Orange Crush. Then we walked up the Serdán. Marta asked how my trip to the border had gone. I brushed it off as just a "diversion." She gave me the worldwide sisterhood's smile that says, "Right! Tell me another one, fella."

I conceded that there were some business deals as well. She was still wearing her gray-striped blouse and black skirt. As we walked past the window of Jimmy Kiami's El Capricho boutique, I offered to buy her something there, as I'd had a good week.

At first she declined, saying she didn't want anything from me, especially if it "obligated" her. I assured her it would not. After some coaxing, she went in with me and looked through several racks of clothes. Ironically, a nice blue dress finally caught her eye, so I bought it for her. She wore it out of the shop, her old outfit in a paper sack. I hoped Lupita wouldn't get wind of the gift.

She wanted to eat dinner at the Paradise seafood house, so we walked the five blocks. I was still full from my meal with Lupita, so ordered a shrimp cocktail and picked at it. Marta ordered their specialty—grilled shrimp with garlic, *camarón al moje de ajo*.

Dinner over, we walked and talked. About two blocks from the malecón, she asked, "Do you want to dance?" I said, "Sure. Do you want to go down to the Chapúltepec Pavilion?" She said, "Yes. Fine. It's a pretty dress and I want to dance, but I don't want to carry my other clothes with me everywhere." I said, "Well, I've got the car up on the other side of the Rubi. We'll put your clothes in the car. After a few dances we can get your clothes and I'll take you home." She smiled.

249

We walked past the Hotel Rubi, dumped her clothes into the Rambler, and went to Chapúltepec, which was already filling with the Saturday-night dance crowd. We ordered Cokes and danced a few tunes. Then she wanted me to order her a Cuba libre.

Eva at the Rubi had warned me several times not to drink with Marta and to "let her know exactly how I expected her to behave." She had been very pointed about it, and I trusted Eva.

So I demurred, "Well I am only drinking Cokes. Why don't you just have a Coke?" I ordered more Cokes, but she wasn't happy and said, "I'd still like a drink." I replied, "Oh, I'm not in a drinking mood." She said, "Well, I am!"

We danced to several more tunes, but she was irritated—stiff and avoiding body contact. Apparently she didn't like her drinking curtailed.

Later she again insisted, "I'd like to order drinks for us." Again I declined to drink with her. Smoldering, she said she was ready to go home. I told her I was sorry she was irritated but didn't do much drinking. She said, "I understand, but I am ready to go home."

We walked to the Rambler, where she retrieved her clothes. Things were strained. I offered her a ride home. She declined and called a taxi. She thanked me again for the dress and repeated that she didn't want to be obligated. I told her for the third time that she wasn't. Then she left.

250

I watched her go, caught myself staring at her legs again, stopped, and turned back into the Rubi's paneled bar, feeling disgruntled. Jesse said, "Oh, we saw you go past with La Flaca. How'd it go? Isn't this early for a Saturday night?"

Shrugging, I explained, "I didn't want to drink." Eva was there and asked, "What happened?" I said, "We had a nice dinner, then we walked and danced, but she got pissed off, *enfadada*, because I wouldn't buy drinks." Eva said, "Don't worry. You did the right thing. She drinks too much. You've got to be *macho* (assertively male). You've got to be *hombre* (a man)—let her know how you expect her to behave."

A typically male Mexican attitude, in this case it had come from a Mexican woman. I said, "Well, I took your advice, Eva." Jesse said we'd head out to the Río Rita and take in the floor show when he closed the bar.

I had a beer and danced a cumbia with Eva until another

gentleman came in who was interested in her. She smiled, winked, and slid off to another table with her businessman "date." Negro walked in just as Eva was leaving. He said he was going to drive to the Río Rita separately and would meet us there.

About 11:15 we began our "closing down the bar" ritual, with Jesse goosing around in the old kitchen area as he switched off the main circuits in preparation for the mad dash down the long, dark hallway to the lobby. As the three of us ran into the long corridor, Jesse screamed that he'd heard a ghost behind him. Negro snickered uncontrollably as we ran. The front desk staff was waiting for us "bug-eyed," just in case Jesse was right for once.

When it became obvious that no spooks were actually pursuing us, everyone broke out in laughter. Still shaking as he lit his cigarette, Jesse waited on the curb, touching up his James Dean and trying to regain his cool while I brought the Rambler around front.

We hit the Río Rita about 11:30, a dozen girls screaming "*¡Desgraciado!*" at my Rambler as we pulled up. Jesse was ecstatic! The desgraciado bit was the girls' most cherished double entendre that summer, reserved for their favorite visitors. It was the first time they'd used it on us.

It meant, variously, "a guy who hadn't the sense to be grateful for their services," a "fallen" guy who really should be at home with his family, and a "pathetic unfortunate."

As Jesse and I made our entrance, the girls still making a fuss, Chang greeted us like royalty and showed us to the front table, where Negro was already seated. Saturday night at the Río Rita was the big night. I ordered a Coke with lime.

Some of the girls began teasing me about my trip to the

border—ragging me that I had an old lady on "the other side" and asking if the local girls weren't good enough for me. I teased back and Elsa, La Chuleta, flipped up the back of her dress to prove the Mexican chicks were cuter. Point well taken!

As she wiggled, about twenty guys clapped and whistled. She took a bow! My mood was lifting. As they set up for the show, I stuck my head out front for a breath of cooler air, bull-shitting with Burro and the other taxistas.

As the band struck up a damn good rendition of "Night Train" Jesse came running out to get me, stuttering. He didn't want me to miss anything, since I had paid a hundred-peso *cubierta* (cover charge) for the table. That was because this "Mariquita" was going to dance. Jesse and Negro were describing her to me as the lights went down and the announcer took the stage.

"*Bienvenidos caballeros y . . . viejas* (Welcome gentlemen and, uh, hookers)." Laughter all around. Then came a lovely young torch singer from Hermosillo in a slinky sequined dress. The next act were two gay guys *(maricones)* dressed up as friars, doing a send-up on the Catholic Church in falsetto voices.

After "the boys" exited a nice-looking dark-haired "artist" did a half-strip, down to her pasties. About 250 men were beginning to show the effects of increased testosterone flow, screaming "*¡Mucha ropa!* (take it off!)" in near unison. The torch singer returned. As she finished her second song the lights dimmed and a spotlight came on behind her.

Standing in the light was Mariquita, dressed in a little Catholic girl's school uniform. White shirt and tie, pigtails, short plaid skirt, and socks to her knees. She was slow and coy. It got quiet—reverently so.

She stood about five feet four, had a lovely oval face, very even features, huge eyes, and honey-blonde hair. She looked to be about eighteen, perhaps a year younger. The blood pressure of several hundred men was rising rapidly.

After about five minutes of near quiet, someone again screamed *"¡Mucha ropa!"* The tone was one of true desperation. Mariquita smiled blissfully in his direction, swiveled her hips, and picked up the pace. She pulled off the tie and undid several buttons.

Unlike every other stripper I'd ever seen, she wasn't doing a rehearsed, set routine, detached from the audience. She was actually stripping for each one of us, and absolutely glowed from the attention.

She adored the crowd. The coarser they got, the more they screamed *"¡mucha ropa!"*, the farther their tongues hung out, the more she loved it. As the men went nuts, she transformed—her face came alive and she radiated sex. The crowd began to scream and go nuts when her shirt hit the floor.

Sweet heavens above! She had about a twenty-inch waist and her belly was beautifully muscled. She rippled those muscles and blew each of us a kiss as her little skirt hit the boards. You could have cut the testosterone with a knife. In fact you could actually smell it, mixed with the scents of sweat, tobacco, and warm beer.

The average pulse rate was now about a hundred and ten. Another moment of involuntary reverence came over the crowd. Even the guys in the band laid off a couple of bars. As one of the horn men later explained it's very hard to concentrate with that much of a hard-on.

Jesse punched my shoulder as I gaped at her in bra, G-string, and kneesocks. *"¡Te dije!* (I told you!)." Yes, he had—

and at that moment she *was* as good as the World Series. With her honey-blonde hair, knockout figure, and fresh, angelic face, she was the finest-looking girl I had ever laid eyes on.

Someone in the crowd yelled hoarsely, "Help me, God!" It sounded as if he really meant it. Three hundred people, including the viejas, laughed at once. That's when her bra hit the deck. No pasties! All natural! Erect, hard nipples and lovely breasts. Someone threw a "Cuauhtémoc" at the stage— a five-hundred-peso note. Wow!

As she caressed each of us at the front tables with her eyes, it rained money for two full minutes. Jesus, her pupils were actually dilating! She was physically getting off on this attention. She undulated, broke into a sweat, closed her eyes, and threw her head back, sighing.

254

As the spotlight dimmed, the G-string shot out of the darkness, landing at my place. She turned just as the spotlight gave us a one-second "encore" glimpse of her bare ass. Then she bounded off the stage into the darkness. If there was any man in the place without a raging hard-on, the poor bastard was already clinically dead.

When the lights came up, a suspicious number of the viejas were nowhere to be found. I watched, fascinated, as more than two hundred desperate men tried to arrange assignations with about fifty girls. The standard hundred-peso price for thirty minutes was now two hundred pesos, and a couple of the knockouts, like La Chuleta, were at three hundred. It was the law of supply and demand, right out of Economics 101.

The slow, poor, and unlucky guys had to settle for ordering fresh drinks and waiting for new, or slightly used, girls to come back into the nightclub. Meanwhile Jesse told me that it could not be an accident that Mariquita's G-string landed at my place.

He confided that she had set her salida (exit fee) at ten thousand pesos (eight hundred dollars!) and was refusing all customers until someone put that sum on the bar in front of Chang. I told Jesse I wished I had the money. He laughed, "There is no one in the house who doesn't wish he had the money. Even a couple of the *tortilleras* (lesbians) wished they had her price."

About fifteen minutes later Mariquita, again fully dressed, went over to the table that had thrown her the Cuauhtémoc, but stayed only a courteous five minutes. Then she came over to us, was introduced by Chang, and sat down. Jesse was elbowing me under the table like a high-school boy. Negro was a bit more urbane—at least he didn't drool and stutter like Jesse. I did a pretty good imitation of a schoolboy and actually blushed.

But she was no longer Aphrodite-on-the-stage. Without the crowd she was just a gorgeous teenager, sweet and a touch silly. Mariquita drank limeades at full cocktail price, of course. Like her natural boobs, she apparently couldn't be bothered with pretense. She wanted to talk and had heard the girls chatter about us.

I interested her—first she checked out my boots, actually ducking under the table for a look. That created instant pandemonium at the Cuauhtémoc table. I loved those Red Wing Wellingtons!

Giggling about the reaction of the other table, she asked me all the standard questions: Married? Children? Livelihood? Sisters? Hmm! There was a trend here—all were standard except "Do you have sisters?" She asked, as had

Francisca. Interesting! I filed this away as meriting future research. I gave back her G-string. She giggled again.

I was really enjoying the conversation, when Francisca came over and sat down. She reminded me in front of everyone that I "should marry a nice girl and settle down." Thanks, Francisca! That pretty much ended the festivities, just as intended.

Jesse and I said goodbye to Negro and drove to the Almita. Ana María was her usual competent, lively, sexy self. I ate my milanesa the way Lupita usually ate her food. María noticed. Jesse wisecracked "*Rebuena* (super-good) floor show; Davíd enjoyed the *chica* (girl) in pigtails." Ana María grinned and, without asking, brought me a second milanesa, which I ate.

When Jesse started the parrot jokes, I left and drove back to the Rubi. I wrote in my journal, noting that it had been one heck of a week since the fiasco on the roof of the Miramar. I chain-smoked and took a cool shower. That helped.

About 3 A.M. I drifted off, my little fan blowing puffs of towel-moistened air across my face. I dreamed of sensual eyes, plaid skirts, cute buns, and pigtails. Sometime in my dream night I ravished Mariquita. She was great . . . and so was I.

When I awoke in the morning I was relieved that my testosterone levels had returned to near normal. I was pretty sure they hadn't been so high since my sophomore year in high school.

eleven

THE BEST MANDADERA IN MEXICO

Though my testosterone levels seemed near normal, my fluid levels definitely were not. I had awakened bathed in sweat and dehydrated again. My head hurt and my throat was a blast furnace. No Orange Crushes for relief. On Sunday mornings the Rubi bar was closed. I had to settle for ice water from the cooler out front.

Sweating like a pig, clothes already limp and sticking to me, I opened my door and started toward the shaded archway at the front of the conservatory. Shit! Two steps and I tripped over a large sack standing in front of the door. It popped open. Like a bad penny returned, it contained Marta's blue dress.

Screw her, anyway, I decided—viciously kicking the damn thing halfway down the tiled walkway. Maybe my testosterone levels weren't quite back to normal after all.

I walked past the wreckage and jerked a paper cup from the metal holder above the cooler. By the time I'd finished four cups of water I had carefully imagined Mariquita's legs juxtaposed to Marta's. Testosterone-driven comparison shopping.

Mariquita was now looking pretty good in my imaginary comparison test—younger, much sweeter, and far less complicated. The only negative was the cost-benefit calculation. Mariquita's entry price was ten thousand pesos. A high-maintenance model and way out of my league. Bummer!

A college friend of mine once told me he'd "rather fuck than eat." That had sounded like a serious world observation when I was eighteen and had never slept with a woman. But I knew better now. A good meal lasted all day. Sex lasted about thirty minutes. Obviously the stupid jerk had never actually been hungry.

As I passed the ruptured sack with the disheveled blue dress on the way back to my room, I scooped them up and slammed the door behind me. A shower and fresh clothes helped. I even read the little note Marta had left in the sack— she was "sorry, but didn't want to be obligated." In a petulant mood I walked up the Serdán to the Morales market, intent on a tall, iced limeade and some solitude at the old-fashioned soda counter.

The market was picturesque—think large, 1940s state-side market in a farm town. Food, dry goods, pharmacy, sundries, soda counter, and a large, but not fully refrigerated, meat section—nothing wrapped. It was already about a hundred degrees out and it wasn't even noon. The meat was dark, aromatic, and flyblown. Somehow that didn't seem to hurt business. The place was packed.

I grabbed a stool and got the "xtra-grande" limeade. As the first ice-cold blast gushed through the straw I sighed in relief. If you drink ice-cold stuff too fast, you lose the pleasure—it's far better to pace things so your throat heats up between each sip. That way you get the icy waterfall sensation on the back of your throat again and again.

If you were careful you could get twenty full minutes of intermittent ecstasy from a Morales "xtra-grande." I was deep into the rhythm and concentrating intently on the rear of my throat, when a hard tug on my sleeve broke my concentration.

Lupita was perched on the stool next to me, pulling on my sleeve. Irritated, I scolded, "I was enjoying the swallows!. Couldn't you wait?" She was contrite. Kids understand this stuff.

My pique had attracted a young waitress, who hurried over to shoo Lupita out—shooing Lupita away was obviously an integral part of the daily routine of many employees in el centro. Triumphantly Lupita refused and slapped a five-peso note onto the counter, ordering a small limeade.

259

For a moment the scene was almost like a bad Western movie—clean-cut stranger slaps a silver dollar on the bar, "Sarsaparilla, bartender, and no lip, thank you!" Startled, the waitress warned, "Okay, but don't bother *el señor turista* (Mr. tourist)."

I interrupted in Spanish, "It's all right, Miss, Lupita works for me. She is my *mandadera*, we'll talk business." Completely bewildered, the poor thing left, then came back with an "xtra-grande" for just five pesos. Advantage four pesos. Score! Lupita vibrated. She even said, *"Muchas gracias, señorita,"* batted her eyes, and smiled radiantly. On the street you've got to savor your victories as they are granted. Lupita knew the drill.

In fact she was all bright-eyed and bushy-tailed. I'd rarely seen her so animated. It had to be more than the petty win of four pesos for her drink. I leaned to her conspiratorially and whispered, "What's with you? *¿Que le hace?*" She looked up at me, angelic, and said, "La Marta."

Like a dope I smiled and said, "Yes?" With a wicked grin on her face, she asked if I'd screwed Marta the night before. I barked, "You're *una traviesa* (a pain)." Just out of reach, she grinned. I came back at her, "It's *not* your business."

Undeterred she said, "Well, I have to keep my employer's mind on his business," and cackled. She was outrageous. I was pissed, so told her, "Look, I'm going to spank you. Knock it off."

She squeaked and jumped back off the stool, still holding her big limeade glass. She watched me, sucking on the limeade, her eyes intense and glassy. Then she demanded, "When are you going to buy *me* a blue dress?"

I blew up, my outrage fueled by my guilt, "*¡Mierda!* Isn't there anything I can do in this town that you don't know?" Still keeping enough distance from me that I couldn't grab her, she said, "I'm here to remind you that you have a twelve-o'clock appointment with señor Meyers."

I said, "That's it? Damn you! I'm going to get you for minding my business." My tone was hard, so she slammed the limeade glass onto the counter and hightailed it out the front door before I could collar her. The counter girl was taking in the whole scene, her head cocked in a smirking "I told you so" look.

I finished my "xtra-grande" in silence, then worked my way to the door. I was always amazed at what Lupita knew about events on the street in Guaymas. It was even more disconcerting that she was able to draw such an accurate bead on my personal movements.

My male friends in Guaymas had openly envied me

because I had no females or family to answer to. I could go to the zona and no pissed-off mom would be at the door, arms crossed, waiting for me when I came home. They simply didn't realize I had Lupita shadowing me like a miniature Sam Spade.

It was obvious that Lupita was obsessed with my relationships—real and imagined. It unnerved me, because I couldn't understand it. No matter what I did, this was a side of her that I was not going to squelch easily.

I walked out of the Morales market, turned right, and headed back down the Serdán toward El Pollito and the Rubi. As I passed El Capricho, where I had bought Marta the blue dress, Lupita popped out of the doorway and hollered, pointing, "Hey, Güero. They've got pretty *blue* dresses in this store!" I answered, "I'm going to give you a *nalgada* (spanking)." Unrepentant, she taunted, "When will you buy me a blue dress?"

I answered, "When you stay out of my personal life for a couple of months, I'll buy you a blue dress." She said, "With shoes, too?" I said, "Yes." She asked, "You promise?" I said, "Yes, okay. I promise, *if* you stay out of my personal life. Until then I don't want to hear anything more about a blue dress."

I kept going until she called again. "Güero . . ." I turned and looked over my shoulder. She was standing there, suddenly shy and tentative, "You're not teasing me? You're telling the truth?" I said, "Yes, but you stay out of my business."

Then she smiled and ran back into the store. I walked on a few paces, then turned and saw her in there looking through racks of dresses while trying to evade the store clerks intent on shooing her out. She'd been shooed out of every place in Guaymas.

I shook my head and picked up the pace. Time to see Edward Meyers at El Pollito. He showed up at the appointed hour, then we went to see Epifania and her family, to discuss details of their proposed marriage. When Edward and I parted ways it must have been three o'clock in the afternoon.

I walked downhill to the Rubi and changed clothes. I was just soaked. Up at Epifania's place on the hill above town it had been so damn hot that I felt like a dishrag. I guessed it was 107° or 108° that afternoon. The sun was relentless.

At the hotel I showered, dug into Dad's field chest, and pulled out a pair of light khaki pants and an old short-sleeved Madras shirt, the coolest piece of clothing I owned. I was not up to the Sunday finery of dark pants and starched guayabera. Dressed like a tourist for once, I went out to Primaverales. Whenever things were complex for me it always cheered me up to go out to the beach and just watch people. It was about four o'clock when I got there. But the beach was nearly deserted.

It was so bloody hot that it had even driven the locals away from the beaches. It was impossible to walk barefoot in the sand. The only way you could handle the sand, barefoot, was at the tide line itself. The electric sign fronting the Serdán on the Banco de Comercio had read 46°C (115°F!) as I passed.

Manuel wasn't around so I said hello to some of the regulars and drank an Orange Crush at the bar. It was far too hot to endure the pavilion for long. I went next door to the little restaurant and sat right under a ceiling fan. They brought me a soda with a hand-chiseled chunk of ice in it—fresh off a big block. Most of the ice in Guaymas was delivered in forty-kilo (eighty-eight-pound) blocks every day and worked down with an ice pick. Ice cubes were rare at the time.

I sipped my cool soda and surveyed the action. Iliana's "aunt" didn't materialize and the other women there largely ignored me. That had become the pattern since my return to Primaverales after Iliana took off for San Luis Río Colorado. Silly cows! They acted as if they were the only ones in town who didn't know I'd defended Iliana.

I was reflecting on the odds for and against any of them having spoken to their husbands about Iliana and me—a tough call in compartmentalized, working-class Mexico.

I reckoned that virtually all the women working on the beach had known Iliana was pregnant since, oh, an hour or two after the final downstroke that created the situation. All the men knew I'd defended her on the roof of the Miramar within a couple of hours.

Hell, maybe they *didn't* talk to each other—a local Maginot Line between women's and men's business. Given the secrets, hidden compartments, and layers of complexity, I wondered if I'd ever fully understand life on the street in Guaymas.

While indulging in these riddles, I spotted a familiar gray-striped blouse at the restaurant's screened door. Uh oh!

Marta entered, walked straight to me, said *"Buenas tardes,"* and asked if I would invite her to a soda. I stood up and seated her. She ordered a Coke—lots of ice—and began talking pleasantly, as if nothing had happened. I pretended to listen, going into cordial autopilot mode. As she chattered I resisted a powerful urge to snarl, "I got the dress back," stand up, and walk out.

That's the least any of the taxistas would have done. Most would have kicked her ass! It was the leftover American side of me that made me sit there and take it.

Ironically, in Mexico my calm demeanor, given the circumstances, would generally have been considered *muy caballero* (gentlemanly) and culto (educated upper-class). Equally ironically, since my behavior was expected in the States, it was known at home simply as "pussy-whipped." I didn't like that thought and began to rationalize. I told myself that she was a time bomb with a short fuse. No sense in striking the match right here in the restaurant. It's complicated to be stuck between two worlds.

Then she got to the point. "I saw La Gatita (Lupita)." I said, "Oh, was she bothering you again?" She said, "No, I saw her in the street and asked where you were. She said she had seen your car go up the Serdán past the statue and you either had to be at Miramar seeing Negro Jacinto or at Primaverales."

Marta paused. . . . "So I took the bus to see if you were here." Still on autopilot I said, "Well, here I am." She said, "Well, I wasn't sure I'd find you. I didn't know whether La Gatita was telling me the truth or not." I said, "I already told you her name is Lupita. She irritates you, doesn't she?" She said, "Yes, *no me gusta* (I don't care for her)."

I decided not to push it. Their dislike for each other clearly made sense to them, and it came up again and again. She asked me to take her for a ride. No harm there, I supposed. My mistake.

We took off, driving dirt roads, but her side of the conversation quickly turned intense. Questions. Many of them. She was trying to figure out what made me tick. What I "wanted." If I'd known I would have told her. Frustrated at my ambivalence, she said, "Well, you should find a nice girl and get married!" This line was becoming seriously overused!

I shook my head. I was actually enjoying my post-Iliana

life, and had never before been so free from the oppressive, judgmental behavior that dominates every facet of American existence.

She demanded, "Well, what do you want, then?" I answered, "I don't know. Do I have to?" No good. She wanted ANSWERS. NOW! Her voice had taken on that ripsaw tone again. I told her I didn't want to argue. In silence we drove back toward Guaymas.

After a long while she turned to me, her voice gentle, "I'd still like to have the dress back." I said, "Sure, but I don't want to argue about it." She was quiet again for a minute and then she said, "You're just not like other men I know. There's so much you don't understand."

I conceded, "You're probably right," then lit up a cigarette. No more talk. We drove to the Rubi. She smiled at me several times and touched my arm once. Again another side of her.

I parked out front by the malecón, left her in the car, went inside, and retrieved the bag with the blue dress in it. I came out and handed it to her, then drove her home. She thanked me for the dress and said she was accepting it as a token of friendship. I answered, casually, "*¡Está bien!* (That's fine.)" Satisfied, and relieved, that this "relationship" was going nowhere, I waved goodbye and drove to the Colmenar.

My boots echoed in the passage to the restaurant and alerted Juanito, who materialized, looking hopeful. I plunked down at an outside table, pleased to see my favorite waitress's beaming face, freckles, and pretty eyes. Mercedes was always cheerful, upbeat.

A light meal in front of the fan and another superb shine from Juanito picked me up. I hung around for a couple of hours that evening, drinking café con leche and BS-ing with Mercedes and the cook. They were trying to fix me up with a cute, little nurse's assistant who worked in the medical office down the passage. But I really didn't want to go the Iliana route again.

The cook, named María—a big, pleasingly raunchy woman—started telling dirty jokes while Juanito plied his trade and a few regulars stopped by for coffee. Around eight I drove back down to the Rubi.

That night there was virtually no activity at Chapúltepec pavilion. Odd. So I sat on the seawall, a hundred feet from the Rubi, dangled my legs, and smoked, enjoying the rippling lights that played across the harbor.

Lupita popped up behind me. I didn't notice her at first. She had apparently been standing next to me patiently for a couple of minutes. Softly she said, "Davíd, *vamos a cenar* (Let's eat dinner)." I replied, "Oh I'm not hungry, Lupita."

She said, "You are thoughtful, *pensativo*, have you been fighting with La Marta?" I grinned, but did not answer. Then Lupita informed me, "I don't care for her." I said, "Well, at least you are equal. She doesn't like you, either." There! It was right out in the open.

She said, "Yes, I know. She's jealous of me." I looked over my shoulder at her, surprised, and said, "Well, let's go eat. I think you're right, perhaps I should eat. But let me tell you again, you will never earn a blue dress if you don't stay out of my business." She nodded.

I asked, "Where do you want to eat?" She said, "Well, let's go to the *cárcel* (jail)." We drove the Rambler to the open-air kiosk where they sold tortas (sandwiches) next to the city jail—the same place Mr. Smith had recently been a guest.

I went there several times a week. It was a wooden concession stand, about ten feet square, just like you would see at a state fair. A row of bright light bulbs lined its roof. A beacon for prisoners aching for something other than the standard ration of beans and rice once a day. The regular clientele consisted of prosperous prisoners (takeout, of course), taxistas, and families of the unfortunates housed next door.

Lupita was the first to notice that one of our new blenders and a waffle iron graced the premises. On that basis she hustled the proprietor's son into a two-peso discount on four toasted ham-and-cheese tortas. Tomato, avocado, onion, cilantro, and chile sauce topped them off. These were delicious. I noticed that the hinge of our waffle iron had already been lengthened and rewelded to accommodate the pudgy little sandwiches. Nice work!

They also specialized in malted milks made with blended banana. For an extra two pesos they would add a raw egg before blending. In those days no one was concerned about cholesterol, and these malts were considered "health food." I loved the banana ones. They used a variety of tiny, red banana you never see in the States. These added a sweet, nutty flavor.

A big Tres Estrellas double-decker bus had just pulled in at the station a half-block away, so we passed on the malts and took our sack of tortas "to go," before fifty local passengers hit the stand on their way home from a long ride.

We cranked up the Rambler, took off, and ate our sandwiches on the fly as I drove Lupita out to the Miramar Hotel on a lark. A hot night, but a pretty one. At the Miramar I got two cold sodas from the bar and we walked up and down the little bayside promenade, just chatting.

Lupita asked how business with Edward Meyers had gone

that day—the negotiations with the woman he was going to marry. I told her that had all gone right. It was pretty well worked out. That they were going to get married in two weeks. She asked, "Well, is he going to pay you?" I said, "Yes, he is."

She said, "Good! Are we going to go to the border again?" I hesitated, telling her I didn't know. That I wasn't certain when I might do that again. She pressed, "Well, you have your papers?" I said, "Yes, but I don't want to rent a trailer and bring down furniture that local people don't want to buy."

Trying a different tack, she said that she knew of a man who would buy the papers. I asked, "Are you serious?" She said, "Oh, yes," that there was a foreigner living in one of the fancy cliffside houses in town who wanted to bring things but had already used his household permit. I pried to find out where she'd come by her information. She said, "Oh, just hanging about the restaurants." This kid had spent her whole life being everywhere, just within earshot. So I asked her to check it out for me. That satisfied her for the moment.

About then Negro shouted out at me from the restaurant. So I left Lupita out front and went inside to see Jacinto, who was still on shift. He asked how things were going. I said, "Well, things with Edward Meyers are going pretty well and all, but I haven't hit it off well with Marta." He waved it off, "Oh don't worry about that too much. Whatever will be, will be."

Negro pursued his theme, "You know, the other thing that I notice about you—you are fascinated with children. You put up with all the little shoeshine boys, you give *centavos* to the kids on the street. I see you along the *malecón* talking to the children on Sundays and out here in front of the hotel sometimes. Why are you fascinated so with children?"

I said, "Oh, I don't know, really—they make me happy."

He nodded gently and said, "You know, you should settle down, Davíd. There would be worse things than you opening a school in Guaymas. You could make money teaching English, buy a little house. You could always have little ones around you. You could have your own children, a wife. You are free to start again.

"You are enough like us to get along here in Guaymas; but in some ways not like us at all. We have so few choices, you know? But you have many. You have all the choices in the world before you. That in itself is a problem—too many choices. You have to decide what you want."

Coming from him, the "wife, children, settle down" argument sounded different. And the "you need to decide what you want" actually began to seem sensible. He paused. "I wouldn't want to be *norteamericano*—too complicated. Too many choices."

269

If only he knew how much I agreed with him. In Mexico "kids make me happy" was both a complete answer and a universally accepted explanation. In the States you are expected to analyze the hell out of everything first, then have reasons—"kids make me happy BECAUSE . . ." But I said nothing—in Mexico one does not dump on one's own country—but simply thanked my friend and confessor and took my leave.

Lupita was standing outside by the Rambler, waiting for me. I looked down at her intently for a minute. She looked up, quizzically, wide-eyed. I smiled and said, "Well, *hijita*, let's get in. We've got things to do." She came to attention again. But I let the moment pass.

What I really wanted to say was, "I want you for my

daughter," but I never did. I have wished so many times since that I'd had the courage to say that to her as she stared at me, expectant. I didn't know it then, but I look back on that moment now as a serious sin of omission.

We drove on back to town and I dropped her off on the main street in front of the Morales market, as I had so many times before. As she rounded the corner toward the Almita, she turned and hollered over her shoulder, "I'll sell your papers for you! You'll see. You'll see."

After dropping Lupita off, I drove back to the Rubi, parked by the stone bodegas, and walked back along the Serdán to the lobby. I headed for my room to get a pack of smokes and write in my journal, then planned to go out with the taxistas. It had been a tough day emotionally, and I wanted some peace and quiet. No such luck!

As I entered the lobby fat Ramón was sprawled out on the large green couch that sat right in the middle of the room, facing the main desk. Ramón was not only my least-favorite deskman, but also perfectly defined the epithet *huevón*. A huevón is a guy so lazy and disgusting that even his balls *(huevos)* have grown huge and soft from sloth and disuse. In fact a true huevón's lazy balls are so huge that it's hard for him even to move around. This accurately defined my main man Ramón.

At the moment he was sprawled out with his feet up on one of the lobby's expensive end tables. It was a characteristic pose—arms spread wide, head thrown back against the couch, mouth hanging open, feet straight out, his huge belly protruding six disgusting inches below his shirt. Like most huevones, he never wore an undershirt or socks—too much work to put them on. I prayed that he wore underpants, but would not have bet on it.

Miraculously he looked up, nodded at me, then jerked his head toward my room at the rear of the hotel and announced, "You have company, Güero!" That took a lot of energy for a huevón, so I walked into the conservatory both curious and cautious.

As I reached for my doorknob I realized it was unlocked. Uh oh! I had no idea what to expect, so froze.

After listening for thirty seconds or so I opened the door carefully with one hand, swung it wide, and looked in. I was prepared to turn and run if circumstances warranted it. False alarm! My antics proved irritatingly stupid. It was only Marta, sitting on my bed smoking a cigarette and looking smugly amused.

271

Embarrassed, I turned bright red. She noticed—and loved it. I stepped in and closed the door. She laughed. Then without a word, turned off the light, closed the window on the side by the taxi stand, and undressed, hidden in the bathroom foyer. Wow!

By the time she came to the bed, I was shaking like Lupita, testosterone and adrenaline coursing through every fiber of my body. "*¿Listo?* (Ready?)" she asked softly. "*¡Sí!*" I croaked. She laughed again, then, in spite of the stifling heat, got on top of me. I reached for her legs. Finally! Paradise. She was profiled in dim light from the bathroom, her distinctive vanilla scent filling the room.

For years afterward when I thought of her, it brought back the image of her dim silhouette, diffused light in the background, the sensation of dense, hot night air in Guaymas, and the scent of vanilla.

She had very soft skin and muscular legs. Once on top of me she made full body contact from knees to breasts. Lying down, with her head propped up on one elbow, she stared right into my eyes and made love to me. She never said a word—just stared at me intently the whole time, her eyes wide open. Checking my reactions?

Considering all the buildup there had been and how sexy she seemed, it was surprising how quietly and peacefully, almost effortlessly, she made love. Glued to me for twenty minutes, the room temperature about ninety-five, we gener-ated an impressive pool of sweat.

Afterward she wanted me to hold her. That's when she came to life. I remember her lighting a cigarette and laugh-ing as I ran my finger around her breasts, making designs, then down her belly to those wonderful legs. She left after about an hour and a half, reminding me that hookers never work on Sundays. Off the clock. Ironically, she came every Sunday night thereafter—just like clockwork.

After the blue dress she rarely accepted anything else tan-gible from me. Once I successfully stuffed a small strand of hematites into her purse while she showered. The next week I saw her wearing them on the Serdán with the blue dress, her little son in tow.

That's when I figured it out. She had kept the blue dress to change her identity—her persona—from "La Flaca, the vieja," to just "Mom." She never wore it when she visited me—off the clock. The dress was reserved for her son. I didn't see the hematites again until several years later. But that's another story.

THE BEST MANDADERA IN MEXICO

We occasionally did go out for a walk or a meal, but never on Sunday afternoons. Thereafter she spent Sundays almost exclusively with her little boy.

And my Sunday nights with her were peaceful—the hard tones never crept back into her voice. She never drank, or had been drinking, when she came around, though she did elsewhere. At other times our relationship was pretty stormy, but not on Sundays.

In many respects our relationship became a metaphor of life in working-class Mexico—compartmentalized. Beyond the confines of Sunday night's boundaries, she drank, cursed, snarled, and—I discovered later—whored when I wasn't around.

After Marta left I took a cool shower, got the windows open, dressed, and walked out to the lobby. Ramón, El Huevón, was asleep on the couch. I had fully expected him, fat hand extended, to demand forty pesos, but he never again did. Apparently Marta was now considered my novia.

I walked quietly past Ramón and went for a long walk up the Serdán to the Almita. It was the twenty-sixth of July. I ambled along the malecón, hoping I might spot Lupita, but she had gone to ground. Like me, the kid was a hard-core insomniac. I walked into the Almita and blew Ana María a kiss. My milanesa appeared like magic, as always.

This became my set routine on Sunday nights—to be with Marta, to shower, to go out and *matar un rato* with the taxistas, walk the malecón, move on to the Almita for a late meal, tease Ana María, then walk until exhausted. Only then could I sleep.

That night, as usual, talking to Ana María was great. She was lively and full of chatter. Her wonderful slanted, almond-shaped eyes always crinkled at the corners, along with her nose, when she grinned or laughed. She was generous with both. About three that morning I left the Almita. It was still blazing hot.

I half expected to see Lupita pop out from the tortilla factory behind the Morales market as I walked past, but she didn't. I'd been thinking about her since my conversation with Negro. I wanted both a closer relationship and to find a way to keep her out of my business with Marta. Wishful thinking, perhaps.

Back at the Rubi, I nosed around the corner behind the shrimp-packing plant in case she was hanging around. Still no sign of her, so I shot some craps with the taxistas on the street corner, then went to bed.

The next morning, like most days at that season, I did my imitation of racewalking down the long corridor of the Rubi to get an ice-cold Orange Crush from the bottom of the cooler and break the heavy, burning thirst that came from waking up bathed in sweat every morning. As July ended, afternoon temperatures hovered between 108° and 111°. In August it got even hotter.

As I chugged my first Orange Crush in the front bar, Lupita began banging on the huge front window's glass and pointing emphatically down the block. This meant "meet me at the barbershop. *¡Pronto!*" I grabbed a second soda from the bottom of the cooler and walked down the long corridor to the hotel door of the Rubi barbershop.

She was waiting in the streetside doorway, vibrating. She was not allowed inside without adult, read Güero's, supervision. I let her into the old-fashioned barbershop and she went immediately into launch mode. Her first question, in front of everyone, was "Did you enjoy your date with La Flaca last night?" Bad move, Lupita!

Her verbal jets were on full blast as I got into the barber's chair to get my hair trimmed, a straight-razor shave, and my boots shined. This pissed Lupita off, since she refused to discuss our movida openly at the barbershop. Security issues, you know.

After chattering hysterically about nothing for several minutes she got to her coded message. "Güero, do you have things to buy at the Morales market today?" Of course this meant, "I need to meet you at the soda counter at the north end of Morales market."

I answered a muffled "Oh, yes," as the barber's steamed towel went over my face. "I think I'll probably be going up there around two o'clock, before I go to the Colmenar." Then I leaned back for my shave and relaxed.

275

She stormed out, frustrated, and I thought I heard a squeaky "*¡cabrón!*" as the street door slammed. The barber and a couple of the regulars chuckled.

She was still at the window, doing a twist-and-shout, when the towel came off. Once she knew she had my attention, she again pointed frantically up the street to let me know that she really did need to meet me later. She looked mighty frustrated.

I smiled and waved the tips of my fingers at her. Then she exploded —her twist-and-shout transformed into a simply stunning "James Brown." Juanito, who was doing my boots, began to panic. "Why are you angry with Lupita?" "She messed with my personal business again." The little peace-maker thought for a moment. "If she promises not to do it *ever* again, will everything be all right?" "Yes, Juanito." He dashed outside and explained the situation.

I finished my shave and went back down to the public bar to do the sacred newspaper reading and drink another Orange Crush. I was in no hurry. It would do Lupita good to stew for a while.

I met her at the Morales market's soda counter at two. I didn't know what to expect from her. The "James Brown" had been so spectacular that I had to ask the barbershop crowd not to laugh at her.

She was waiting, looking resigned. I took a stool and ordered an "xtra-grande." She grabbed onto me to swing up to the next stool and also ordered a limeade. She even let me have my first two swallows, unmolested, before she spoke.

"*¡Lo siento!* (I'm sorry!) I have my secrets, which you permit me. I won't talk about Marta in front of others again. I swear it!"

Nodding, I reached out to touch her shoulder and said softly, "Thank you! And your news?" She smiled radiantly, vibrated subtly, and told me that we had a firm buyer for my import papers. "How much?" I asked. Vibrating harder, she said, "Five thousand pesos. Four hundred dollars." Now I understood why she had been pounding on the hotel window.

I asked, "Well, who, when, and where?" She said she'd asked around and had been contacted. An attorney was going to meet us in the city graveyard the next day.

I asked, "Well, why there?" She said, "Well, that's just the way they want to do it." I thought this odd, but I'd been past the city graveyard a number of times—there was nothing ominous about it. If anything it was a rather public place during the daytime.

Dozens of people came and went daily, tending graves,

arranging flowers, or picnicking on the graves of their loved ones. Like serdaneando, it takes work to maintain important relationships in Mexico. Simply being dead doesn't erase one from the family.

I decided I liked the idea and told Lupita she had done a great job. She beamed, "And my bonus?" I answered, "Ten percent of the *gananza* (profit) and a raise of twenty pesos (a dollar sixty) a week . . . and when are we supposed to meet?"

She beamed, "Two P.M., and we should take the bus. I'll meet you at the Pemex near Copa de Leche tomorrow at one-thirty." I asked, uncertain, "Are you sure?" She said, "Yes, I think we should just take the bus and go up there to see what happens—see if everything works out. I'm pretty sure it will. I feel good about this deal."

My natural inclination was to go with her "plan"—it would be pretty hard to rob or mug us in such a public place, and if no one showed we'd just take the bus back to the Serdán. So I said, "Okay, I'll meet you tomorrow."

She actually touched my arm and smiled again before she took off. I went across the street to the Colmenar, had my soup and coffee. Jimmy Kiami joined me. He was in a "they ought to open the border to new business" mode, arguing that the Mexican government should liberalize the laws limiting foreign investment in factories. He envisioned American-run factories on Mexican soil, using local Mexican labor. He thought both nations would benefit.

I don't know whether he originated the idea, or had elaborated on conversations started by others, but he was describing NAFTA and *maquiladoras* a generation before they became realities. What I do know is that if the big shots in Mexico City had put Kiami in charge of that vision, it would have happened sooner and been far better managed than it has been.

I enjoyed an ordinary afternoon at the Colmenar. I wasn't worried about Lupita's deal the next day—I had enough money to go for more than a year in Guaymas.

Sitting there in the passage in front of the Colmenar, savoring my café con leche, talking to señor Kiami and Juanito, my shoeshine boy, Mercedes, and the raunchy cook, María, was emotionally comfortable for me. I liked my life, centered on the street. The States were beginning to seem as foreign to me as they did to the locals.

That Monday night was like any other. I spent the early part of the evening in the Rubi and the rest serdaneando.

We closed the Rubi about eleven and went out to the Río Rita. This Monday night ended with an early morning meal at the Almita with Chang, Jesse, and some of the other late-nighters.

Tuesday I got up, sprinted for the life-saving Orange Crushes, then returned to my room to retrieve señor X's import papers from the very bottom of my dad's footlocker. I didn't want to get ripped off at the graveyard, so I folded them into a Hotel Rubi envelope, then folded that into a Guaymas newspaper lining the bottom of my net shopping bag. Locals often folded newspapers into the bottom of their net bags to hold junk in.

Then I stuffed in a bunch of my dirty clothes as if I were going to the laundry and walked out, ready to grab the bag and hit the street after my newspaper reading. About one o'clock I walked out of the Rubi with my bag of soiled clothes.

No one paid any attention at all. Tourists don't carry net bags. I'd even ditched the Red Wings and wore a pair of my dad's old dress shoes. Worn black pants and a slightly frayed dress shirt with blue bandana, my mustache trimmed, and I was as close to invisible as a gringo can get.

I walked uptown past the Pemex and waited for Lupita. She was a no-show, so I let the first bus go and smoked a cigarette, Alas brand—no dead giveaway Pall Malls. The corner was packed with people. Neat, awninged shops extended in three directions. Clothing, new and used, hardware stores, shoe-repair shops, pharmacy, opticians, laundromat—the works.

These looked so lively by day that I was always amazed at how somber they seemed at night, padlocked, chain-link grates pulled down to protect the stores from robbery, and virtually no lights on. Too expensive.

There were about forty of us jammed into a stingy three-foot-wide scrap of shade, waiting for the next bus. The heat was unbearable. So when the bus came, I took it, irritated at Lupita. Shit! The damn thing was packed. Standing room only on a 110° afternoon. It was probably 130° at head level under the metal roof. I paid my fifty centavos on the way in, jammed into the aisle with my nylon bag between my legs.

About eight bouncing and swaying blocks later we came to the major cross street that went through the heart of the old San Vicente neighborhood. Mercifully a large number of locals got off to change buses. I turned to see if there were any empty seats. No. But Lupita was wedged into the big rear seat, enjoying herself. She waved the tips of her fingers at me in a very nice imitation of my stunt at the barbershop the day before. I rolled my eyes.

Looking angelic, she curled her fingers and hooked her two hands together in her lap. Lupita sign language for *esta-*

mos a mano (even Steven). She loved paybacks and was radiant. Anyone might have confused her with a sweet, innocent ten-year-old kid instead of a card-carrying agent of evil.

Grudgingly I admired her. She didn't take shit off anyone, even if they kicked her ass for it. Sometimes she reminded me of Paul Newman's character in "Cool Hand Luke." Perhaps it was her dreamy grin. More likely it was the steely will that had allowed her to make it on the street since she was five.

As we wound our way through the barrio I realized with satisfaction that I was not drawing any real attention. I had very dark, wavy hair, a narrow mustache, a deep tan, and worn clothes. The net bag was my "ace."

Lost in my own little world, I wasn't aware that Lupita was preparing to get off until the bus began jerking to a stop. She was hanging onto the emergency cord like a monkey, infuriating the driver, but it got the job done. She slipped out the middle door. I stepped off the front. Fortunately other folks got off with us.

280

We were half a block from the graveyard, opposite the *rastro*, the slaughterhouse. Once outside, Lupita came scampering up. I asked, "Why did we stop here? I thought we were going to the graveyard." She said, "I didn't want to attract attention." I shook my head in disbelief, ". . . and hanging on the cord?"

Undaunted, she filled me in. "I thought this was a good spot. We'll just walk the rest of the way. What have you got in the bag?" I said, "Well, I've got the papers. You're going to carry the bag, because I don't want to get ripped off. If there are a bunch of guys here to kick my butt and steal the papers, you can just take off with the bag." She said, "Okay, that's a good idea; but nothing bad will happen."

She looked me over carefully and said, "I was waiting to get on the bus with you but didn't know you in those clothes. I didn't know it was you getting on till I saw you reach for the door with your left hand. You aren't even wearing your glasses. The bus almost left without me. I like you much better with your boots and usual clothes." Mission accomplished.

So we trudged uphill about two or three hundred yards. Man, it was hot. I was soaked. I asked who we were looking for. Lupita said, "Well, a man. I'll know him." We kept walking along the perimeter of the graveyard, but didn't see anybody, so walked up into the barrio that had grown up along the cemetery wall.

At the top of the hill there were several little *refresco* (refreshment) stands that sold iced fruit punches, candy, and cigarettes. These are ubiquitous in Mexican barrios. We stopped and had fruit punches under the shade of a large wooden awning. Lupita was into watermelon punch. I went for the mango. It was just after two o'clock, so we started walking back down the hill.

A hundred yards more and Lupita became agitated. She had spotted her man wearing a white guayabera and a pair of gray slacks. He was at one of the graves near the top of the hill, leaving flowers. The guy did not look ominous at all; he looked just like a middle-class Mexican lawyer. I guessed that he actually was visiting a family member's grave. Perhaps he had chosen this meeting place because he came on occasion and it wouldn't look out of the ordinary.

We headed up the dirt road toward him as he started in our direction. As he neared, I asked Lupita what was arranged. She said, "We are to ask directions to the baseball park. That is all." As we came abreast of him I hesitated and asked, "*Señor,* can you tell me how to reach the ballpark?" He looked surprised, giving me a quick head-to-toe inspection. I wasn't what he expected, but my accent was right.

He smiled, pulled out an envelope, and said, "Let me write it down for you. Do you have a city map or something that I can write your directions on?" Lupita tugged at me; the cue for us to pull our papers out. His envelope was fat with cash.

I pulled out my newspapers, opened them up for him, and he began pointing directions. I did likewise. During our little pantomime we traded envelopes. The gentleman stood there another minute giving me a chance to check my new envelope. There were ten five-hundred-peso Cuauhtémocs in it. Lovely!

He took his papers, smiled, and walked on down the road, tipping his hat as he left. Culto. I tucked the envelope back in my net bag as if it had been my own. No one took particular notice.

Weeks later I was formally introduced to the same gentleman. He was an attorney and respected as a stand-up guy. This was simply the way a certain type of business was transacted. My papers were legal. They weren't twice-used or forged. They were simply more valuable to his client than to me.

We do exactly the same thing in the States, but we think of it differently. Businessman A buys a liquor license from the state, never intending to build a bar, and later sells his license for a profit to businessman B, who owns a restaurant with no liquor license. In both cases the document, or permission, is a commodity.

Lupita and I walked back up the hill and decided to buy tacos and cold sodas. This had been a good day's work!

Lupita was in an "up" mood, the transaction having been made, and told me that she wanted her two-hundred-peso bonus that afternoon, if she could get it. For a kid who had never been to school, her command of percentages was impressive. I nodded, pointing toward the barrio. Food first. Payday for dessert.

As we walked Lupita fished for approval. "Did I do good? Is it what you hoped? You see, I can do things!" I gave her a little squeeze and told her that apart from giving me grief over Marta, "She was the best mandadera in Mexico." She vibrated, then actually started skipping, just like a happy little girl.

Lupita and I walked back uphill in the blinding sun. We headed for the settlement of tin-roofed houses sprawling along one wall of the graveyard and the small cluster of stores and refresco stands that announced the center of activity. There were still a number of people, dogs, and kids milling around—as there always are in the poorer barrios.

We went to a little slump-block restaurant that had two tables and chairs perched under the shady side of its metal roof. A red-and-white-checkered counter opened to the street next to the tables. Their sign advertised *tacos al carbón*, charcoal-broiled beef tacos. Lupita had wanted their tacos. Worked for me.

I leaned against the counter and "oinked" as they passed our tacos out the window. Lupita laughed, her chin about even with the counter. They smelled great. Even better, they had ice-cold sodas. Orange Crush for me; strawberry for my little Sam Spade.

We stuffed ourselves with tacos—they kept passing them out until we begged them to quit. These tacos were rolled in small corn tortillas, a couple of pesos each—charcoaled beef, onion, salsa, tomato, and lettuce. We ate eight or ten between us. It was a typical *al fresco* meal.

As we ate Lupita went through an animated "I'm hot shit" recounting of our exploits. I tossed her hair. She didn't pull away. Instead she giggled and told me she was going to keep on eating tacos. I stopped at three or four; she probably stopped at five or six.

Our bellies filled, she wanted to get paid. I said, "Well, okay. But do you think you should be carrying around money? Do you want to open a bank account?" She said no, she dealt only in cash, *en efectivo*, on the street. Fair enough.

I dug into the leather tobacco pouch I carried inside my shirt at the back of my belt and whipped out two one-hundred-peso notes. Immediately she turned away from the taco stand, walked a few feet, and rolled up the bills into tight little tubes. Then she unfastened one of her blue plastic butterfly barrettes and shoved a rolled-up note deep into her mop of hair, with just the blue butterfly sticking out. Next she hid the other bill in the same fashion.

Her stash now invisible, she turned back to the counter and asked for a *dulce* (sweet) for dessert. The vendor held out a selection. Unable to decide, she chose two and motioned for me to pay, smiling angelically.

I asked what she wanted to do next. Pleased with herself—a bonus and a meal—she said, "Well, let's take a walk." I asked, "Well, where to?" She pointed up the hill toward a row of big, nearly impassable sandstone hills. We started out, but heard music drifting our way from somewhere below us. I said, "Well, let's follow the music and see what that is." She nodded animatedly—action, adventure.

THE BEST MANDADERA IN MEXICO

We walked down a rutted dirt side street, following the music. As we got closer it sounded like a little band somewhere. In five minutes or so we had reached the wide, dirt street that followed the wall along the graveyard. The street was red clay, dusty, and loaded with small rocks—a hot walk. As we rounded a curve we spotted the music's source. There was a small brass band proceeding slowly upward from the very base of the hill, two hundred yards from us. We stopped and stared—our view from above, panoramic.

An old green, round-top pickup truck, 1940s vintage, slowly ground up the hill, its engine straining. Initially we couldn't quite make out what was happening, but the little band led a procession of people behind the battered truck. As the pickup came up the hill, it turned off into the graveyard. Lupita got it first. "*Fúnebre* (funeral)," she whispered, wide-eyed. She turned to me for an explanation, but I had never seen anything quite like it. I shrugged and stared.

Below us a five- or six-piece brass band played, its members a bunch of poor guys wearing their hallmark dark pants, patched and mended, and threadbare white shirts. The band was probably made up of the members of a local *cofradía*, a brotherhood association.

Such associations were old in Mexico. Members paid a few pesos each month for life to share in the benefits—burial expenses, weddings, and other similar things. The cofradías I had heard of in Mexico City were organized by trade or guild membership, and sometimes by neighborhood. This was probably a local barrio cofradía.

There was a plain, pine casket nestled in the back of the beat-up pickup and twenty or thirty people walking behind, the men with their hats in hand. All very poor people.

After the initial jolt, we walked down the hill a bit farther, the band still playing. Then six men stepped up, pulled the plank casket from the back of the pickup, and carried it on their shoulders. These guys carried the casket up the steep hill in 110° heat.

A hundred yards above, several gravediggers stood by a fresh grave, a young *padre* waiting to finish this funeral in the barrio. The little brass band marched ahead very solemnly, playing slow versions of John Philip Sousa marches.

I was struck dumb. This scene seemed inexpressibly sad, even pathetic. The end of some tragic soul here in Guaymas, with six poor guys in front playing them to the grave and six others sweating with the casket in the dusty heat. They did not even own proper shoes and pants.

286

Imagine being brought to the local graveyard in a beat-up pickup truck, in a homemade coffin, with these people, obviously the bereaved family, walking behind in the hot sun, dazed. Gradually they worked their way up to the graveside and rested the casket on the dusty, red soil opposite the pile of dirt cut out of the grave. "My Lord," I thought to myself, "what a painful and humble way to end a lifetime."

About then Lupita tugged at me and looked up. Obviously awed by this, she said, "That must be someone very important, don't you think?" Stunned at her observation, I gaped at her for a minute, almost popping out with something like, "Don't be ridiculous!"

Fortunately I said nothing and she went on, her tone one of suppressed excitement, "You see they have a band and a *padre*. Look at all the people. It must be someone very grand, don't you think?"

Gently I said, "Oh, I suppose it must be. I don't know a

lot about these things." Then she added, "I hope I am important enough someday to have a band play for me when I die, when they bury me." Unnerved I said, "Oh Lupita, you've got fifty or sixty years to wait. You shouldn't be thinking about those kinds of things."

She comforted me, "Oh it doesn't bother me. I think it's quite grand. It would be nice to be so important." We shuffled on down the road. I couldn't keep watching. But Lupita kept looking back over her shoulder, fascinated. I felt uncomfortable. I saw this as pathetic. She saw it as grand—two different worlds.

As we walked down the hill, she asked, "When your father died . . . you told me your father had died." I said, "Yes." She continued, "When he was buried, *enterrado*, was there a band for him? Did he have a band?" I looked at her and said, "No."

287

Contrite, she looked away and said gently, "Well, I shouldn't have asked. I didn't mean it. Not everyone would have a band. Even I know that."

I thought to myself, how odd, because I was, at that moment, remembering my dad's funeral; and it was his funeral and the contrast with this one that had given me my sense of just how humble this one was. When my dad died they flew the state flags in West Virginia at half-mast for the day and closed the university. He had run the University Medical Center, then the second-largest in the nation. That was a big deal.

The motorcade to his grave stretched the entire length of the main street in Morgantown, West Virginia. There were state police everywhere, the main street closed to traffic. I bet there were a thousand people at his funeral, perhaps more.

Yet little Lupita was embarrassed for me—she had asked too pointed a question and made an unfortunate comparison. First she made a big deal about having a funeral band, then discovered my father hadn't had one. This, like the incident on the roof of the Miramar, had the potential to humiliate. In Mexico such pointed comparisons were rarely made.

Lupita was quiet as we walked on, but she kept turning her head to look back. She was obviously impressed. She didn't' seem frightened—just bug-eyed over the whole affair. Looking back on it now, her conclusion was, I am certain, "Well, not even every gringo gets to have a band." It probably even further reinforced in her own mind what a big deal this funeral was.

This funeral scene was indelibly burned into my memory. That day Lupita and I walked side by side, obviously sharing the same tangible world—but we were from radically different emotional planets. Lupita and I shared space, food, adventure, and our little business ventures. But we were truly worlds apart in where we had come from.

Now I am a middle-aged man and I am asking myself, "Well, do I have twenty or thirty friends who, even if dead broke, would still chip in to get me buried as properly as was this poor soul in Guaymas? Would they carry me on their shoulders up a hill in 110° temperatures to see me off?" I don't know. But I doubt it.

In the States both poverty and death are equivalent. Either way one simply ceases to exist. Viewed in these terms, Lupita was probably more on target than was I at the time.

twelve

TO KINO BAY

Lupita was still unable to make eye contact as we parted, so I shoved my dirty clothes at her and told her to get them cleaned. That's what mandaderas do. Relieved, and no longer afraid that she'd lost her job over my dad's funeral arrangements, she said she'd have them the next day and offered me the second candy bar. One doesn't refuse peace offerings.

She said she had business, so she took off on the first bus that stopped. Flush, I hailed a cab and paid the fifteen pesos for a ride to the Banco de Sonora. Another deposit seemed wise. At the counter I pulled the deposit book out of my pouch and shoved five of the bills into the cage. The cashier smiled, took my book, entered the deposit, then remarked that some *baboso* (idiot) had forgotten to enter my previous deposit.

He handed it back. Nervous, I checked it out. Nice! Someone had apparently deposited fifteen hundred pesos ($120) on my behalf. I asked if there were a mistake. He shook his head and smiled. The El Corsario job offered the only likely explanation. Well, thank you, don Francisco!

I dropped by the Colmenar and was deep in conversation with señor Kiami when Lupita popped up from the Sánchez Clinic's end of the passage, gyrating and pointing frantically. More Lupita sign language that translated, "I'm going to pee myself if you don't get over here and listen to what I have to say."

She had a new business alert. "There is another American woman in Clínica Sánchez. Car wreck on Route 15 early this morning. She's hurt BAD and her husband was killed!" I said that was a shame and thanked her, turning to go. "Güero—its our BUSINESS to help foreigners! You ought to go see her. She's BLONDE!" I promised I would and asked her to get me more details. Detective work excited her. Ripped and vibrating, she put her finger to her eye, sign language for "I'll be careful," and disappeared stealthily around the corner.

290

I went back to my table. Kiami was curious. I told him, "My *mandadera*—she told me some Americans got in a car wreck." Jimmy nodded, "I heard the same thing. It should be in the papers." He snapped his fingers at the next shoeshine boy who passed and told him to bring us an afternoon paper, "*pronto*". Under two minutes for the delivery. Not bad. A two-peso tip. Zoom, gone again. Kiami commented, "I wonder why he didn't stick around to give us a shine."

I explained, "Mortal fear—the Pasaje Marví is Lupita and Juanito's territory." Kiami laughed and commented that I knew the kids on the street better than the locals did.

Little Lupita had been known to grab Juanito's glass jars of shoeblack and beat the snot out of trespassers if they weren't too big for her. She feared cops, taxistas, and boleadores in packs. But a nine-year-old alone on Juanito's turf—bam! A glass jar upside his little head. I had already pulled her off offenders several times. She knew I objected to the violence.

To accommodate me and still accomplish her goals, I later found out that she had simply told several of the older boleadores that I would have them killed if they messed with her or Juanito. Let me stipulate that although I really loved—and trusted—Lupita, she didn't suffer much torment over moral niceties. Territory had always meant "eat." Loss of territory meant "no eat." Case closed.

Sure enough the newspaper had our car-wreck story below the fold, front page. As usual Lupita had the scoop. I took off, serdaneando, passing out cigarettes and bitching about the heat. Several of the taxistas at Sitio Centenario asked if I'd bring them fans on my next trip, at the same price that Burro and I had sold the first batch. I said *seguro* (certainly) and ambled on. Two hours later I discovered I had tempted fate.

When I reached the Rubi, Mateo whispered that Jesse wanted to see me in the bar. I went down the corridor past the big mahogany phone booth and stuck my head in—it was about 7 PM and lots of regulars had gathered.

I asked for my Orange Crush and Jesse served it, stuttering that I needed to "buy gasoline." Obviously I didn't get it, so Jesse repeated, "You asked me this morning to remind you to buy gasoline at El Corsario before dinner, TONIGHT!" ending with a wink. Jesse was so subtle.

As I drank my Orange Crush, Jesse kept jerking his head and raising his eyebrows, to make sure I'd gotten the message. I gave him five minutes but couldn't bear watching him lose his cool any longer and said, "Thanks, Jesse, I'd better fill my tank. Got to go." As I took the last swallow and plunked the bottle on the bar, he looked as relieved as a guy who'd just gotten over a weeklong episode of constipation.

His stutter gone, he bid me goodbye, "*Ándale*, Davíd. See you in a while." As I walked out, he reached for the pocket comb to touch up his James Dean. As a friend Jesse was a rock. As a spook he was iffy.

I took the Rambler up the high road to the Pemex and tanked up. Uneventful. I pulled out money to pay but the attendant told me to pay inside. Ah! Unusual. Inside the clerk gave me change and an envelope with "Güero" penciled on it. I thanked him and walked out. They were topping off the oil and radiator and checking the tires when I went out. Hmmm . . . unusually thorough.

Back at the Rubi, I headed straight to my room, turned on the fan, lit a smoke, and fluffed up the pillows to read my mail. Now the attention to my oil and tires made sense. It looked like I needed to go to "the other side" again. A bank deposit. No sweat.

It was just as well, since Mr. Smith's lawyer had called a few days before. Having gotten home in one piece after his unfortunate guest appearance at the Guaymas jail, he was now pissed off at the world and wanted his money back—not just my fee, but more.

"Ah! Lean on the very people who helped your pathetic ass," I thought to myself. Then I realized how very American this was. It simply would not happen in Mexico, where favors were repaid in kind and friendship was not a casual concept.

The world I had been raised in seemed stranger—and colder—by the day. No wonder the locals sometimes referred to us norteamericanos as *lobos,* wolves. Americans are competitive because they want to be successful. In contrast, Mexicans want to be happy. I had experienced a shitty childhood and wanted to be happy. Advantage Mexico.

Perched on the bed, I realized this had been a big factor in my attraction to Iliana. As a Mexican woman she had brought the promise of happiness in marriage as part of her cultural dowry. That had blown up for me, but I was happy on the street in Guaymas. The happiest I'd ever been.

Negro, Jesse, Enrique, Mercedes, Max, Mateo, El Burro, Chang, Eva, Ana María, and my very own mandadera made up the best, and least judgmental, family I'd ever had. As I stubbed out my cigarette, I felt that fortune had finally smiled on me. I was in the right place at the right time. "Grazing in the tall grass," as they say in West Texas. Life in Guaymas was like living in Technicolor—on a big screen. I actually got a chill as I pulled on the Red Wings.

As I turned through the lobby to head toward the bar, Lupita's urgent "psst, psst" echoed from the doorway. I was thrilled to see her. "Want to go to the other side again, *hijita?*" Oh yeah! She vibrated right on cue, "Tonight, Davíd?" I shook my head, "Early tomorrow. Nine sharp—gringo time. La Gorda's. Be ready."

I pulled off my Timex, showed her where the hands would be, and shoved it into her fist, "*¡Ándale! Hasta la mañana* (Move it! Until morning)." As she gaped I turned and headed for the bar.

The front bar had closed, so I turned left into the paneled one, took my favorite stool, and hollered to Jesse for an Orange Crush. When he brought it I leaned forward and told him I had business on "the other side" and would be leaving early in the morning. He nodded, "Be careful on the highway." I thanked him, drank the soda, and went up to the Colmenar.

Lupita rocketed past not long after I got seated in the passage next to the fan. She needed another hundred pesos "advance" on her salary. I asked what she had done with the money from the graveyard job. "Spent it!" I told her I'd give her money in the morning. She asked me to get the machaca burritos again for the trip and promised to pick them up for me before I got to Gorda's.

As she took off I spotted my watch buckled through her little belt. I also noticed that her pants were now too short. Had they shrunk, or was she growing? I reminded myself to check that out in the morning. Finished eating, I asked the cook to have a bag ready to pick up in the morning. No problem. I signed for the check and walked out.

It was a routine night in paradise. Per instructions, the deskman pounded insistently on my door at eight sharp. I tipped him, dressed, and headed for the bank to withdraw money for purchases. I always split my money between the bank and the hotel safe, so that my total net worth was obscure. Same on withdrawals. Half the money I carried that day was from the safe. Half from the bank. Burro had asked to put worn tires on my car and for me to bring back a new set from "a friend" in Nogales, Arizona. Changing the tires ate up twenty minutes more than I'd figured. He gave me instructions and the money for new tires. Then to Gorda's.

Running behind schedule, I reached Gorda's close to 9:10. This wasn't late in Mexican time. Lupita was ready both with her little bag and my nylon bag containing freshly cleaned and pressed clothes. Gorda was happy with the radio but still wanted underpants.

As Lupita passed under my arm, I was pretty certain she had sprouted an inch or so. She was now just over four feet tall, and there was less room to spare as her head passed under my armpit.

She had forgotten the burritos, so we went past the Almita and she ran in to grab the sack. Then we headed for the border. We made only one stop, at a roadside tile-and-glass-front restaurant to get sodas, scrambled eggs, and ice for the burritos. Fifteen minutes—record time.

I told Lupita that I wanted to make time in order to reach the bank in Tucson by three o'clock, and that when she got too hot she could take one of my bandanas and mop her face from the melting ice in my nylon bag, then do the same for me. I told her I wouldn't wait for her at the border—I'd just dump her before crossing and go right on through to the bank, then double back and meet her at Zula's. She started laughing and became animated.

295

As I broke speed limits, cruising at eighty, Lupita was having a ball watching for federales. She got up on the front seat facing backward, playing lookout, and even refused to let me play the radio, in case she heard a siren. Of course most federal police cars in those days didn't even have sirens, but she laughed and giggled as she stood her watch.

Being on watch didn't stop her from chattering a mile a minute, though. She informed me that this time she intended to make purchases in the United States. She wanted to actually select and pay for things herself. I said "Sure." She reminded me that she needed money and that I had promised to advance her some. I nodded.

Then she gave me Spanish lessons—teaching me names of different fish and shrimp—*camarón azul* (blue shrimp), and *camarón de luna* (moon shrimp), and others that she knew from the shrimp-packing plant. I already knew a fair amount about the shrimp business, but played along. Teaching me pleased her. That's when she told me she'd always wanted to go to school. I told her I'd take her in the fall. Instantly she forgot about the federales and vibrated.

That's when I asked again about her *tiritando* (shivering). She was quiet for a moment then told me she didn't' know why she did it or why it started. She had never done it till recently, and she couldn't control it. It happened when she "felt things."

I asked if she also "felt things" when she was younger. She thought, then said, *no mucho* (not much). She complained that the boleadores teased her about it, then looked away. The subject was apparently too close for comfort, so I let it drop. She asked once again if I would take her to school. I said, "Certainly." She shivered self-consciously, then went back to watching for federales.

At the border I handed 150 pesos to her as she bailed out the back door. It was 1:45. We'd made amazing time. I pulled into the U.S. Customs station and was through in five minutes. Also amazing. It was so hot there was almost no tourist traffic coming back into the States. I made it to the bank in Tucson just after three. Pounding on the door got me in, saving one whole day of trip time.

Fortunately, I caught the same assistant manager who had helped me before. He had heard from the Smiths and was glad to see me. The bank had screwed up on their wired money and had made a five-hundred-dollar refund. I tossed in another hundred to get them out of my life, then got a deposit slip for the contents of the Corsario envelope. It was just over a grand, but I asked them to seal the receipt in a bank envelope and sign on the flap. No problem.

I reckoned that someone in Guaymas had a U.S. dollar account that skirted Mexico's currency laws. The folks in Mexico City liked to scoop up all the actual American bank notes and traveler's checks to cover their foreign debt. I'm told Mexican banks still gather up the greenbacks for the same purpose.

Burning up, I drove across the parking lot to a McDonald's and got myself a milkshake. It was hotter than hell. Southern Arizona in July/August is miserable. If Tucsonites had to live in non-air-conditioned houses like those in Sonora, there would be mass suicides before Labor Day each summer.

Milkshake in one hand, steering wheel in the other, I headed south to Nogales, passing the mission at San Javier del Bac. I spotted Burro's tire emporium on my side of the four-lane and pulled in, a thousand yards north of Zula's. They were expecting me. I told them I was in a hurry. Seventeen minutes and $74.20 later, I rolled out on a set of kick-ass tires for Burro's taxi. Nice price.

Next I drove down to Zula's and pulled in, doing a slow cruise around the lot so Lupita could jump aboard. No sign of the kid. Uh oh! I parked and looked around—there was a big drop-off into the creek behind the restaurant, and I thought she might be waiting there. No soap. Perhaps she was hiding again, like the last trip.

I went inside and ordered a Zula burger and a huge iced tea. As I ate I checked out an afternoon paper in English to see what was happening in the States. The Vietnam thing was eating the country alive. Both the control freaks and the antiestablishment types were still acting out in the streets.

I sat there reading my paper, but no Lupita. After about forty minutes I decided to go out to the Rambler and have another look around. Nothing.

As I started back inside, a Mexican taxi that had been sitting across the street pulled over. The driver stuck his head out the window and went "psst-psst" as he came past. I walked over—he had a message for me if I was the one they called "Güero." I said, "Yes, I am." He double-checked, "Well, are you the one with the gray Rambler?" I said, "Yes. What's the problem?"

He answered, "I have a message from a *chamaca*, a girl named Lupita; says she's your goddaughter." I said, "Oh, yes, she is. What's the trouble? Is she okay?" He said, "Well, she had trouble with la migra (U.S. Immigration) and is at the train station on our side, waiting for you there. She said you were to pay me a hundred pesos to bring a message back."

I paid him the hundred pesos and sent a message for her to wait inside the train station, that I would come and get her in an hour and a half. I asked again if she was okay. He nodded, grabbed his hundred pesos, and pulled out. The whole exchange took about a minute.

I went back inside, paid, and asked the cashier where, at 5:45 P.M., might be a good place to buy a fan. She directed me to a little discount store a few blocks up and one block over. I got four table fans and four blenders for less than a hundred bucks. Not as good as Tucson, but I figured I'd pay for the trip and make back part of the money refunded to Mr. Smith.

Shopping done, I turned around and headed for the border. A "tip" for the extra fans and fifteen minutes at the Mexican customs, and I was once again in old Mexico, anxious to retrieve my mandadera.

It didn't take me long to spot Lupita at the train station. She was standing next to one of the big cast-iron and wood columns near the main platform. Oddly, she didn't come right over, so I walked up to her. She was in a funk—her image had been dented. She had lost face. It made no difference that I was genuinely relieved to see her.

I asked how she was. As I reached out to touch her, she didn't answer. Instead she squealed and pulled away. Angry and frightened. I again asked if she was "okay." Again she didn't answer. Then she looked up at me, defiant. "*Me chingaron* (they screwed me over)."

I asked "Did you pay a *mordida?*" She said, "*¡Sí, pero me chingaron!* (Yes, but they screwed me)." It turned out she had paid someone on the Mexican side to guide her through. They sent her through a hole in the fence, straight into the arms of la migra. She barely got away before they nabbed her, then raced back through the fence, narrowly making it.

299

A couple of guys on the Mexican side had been laughing at her the whole time. They set her up, made a couple hundred pesos, and had a joke on her. To compound the pain, she'd paid the taxi driver to bring a message over with a fare, then bring mine back to her. He took my money and vanished—never telling her I was coming. She'd waited for me at the train station anyway, because that had been our agreement all along.

I asked why she didn't use the tunnels again. "Reserved for *mulos* (drug mules) today." Wow! At the time it was still early days in the cocaine trade, but the traffickers who occasionally came to the Río Rita were already a cold, scary bunch. That meant nothing to Lupita—she was out three hundred pesos and had been humiliated. And it was a huge amount of money for her. She was one seriously pissed-off kid.

So I said, "*Mira, trataste* (Look, you tried)," and patted her. She didn't pull away as I reached out again, pulled her to me, and squeezed. This time she wrapped her arms around my waist and hung on, glued to me. That was the most physical contact that I had with her. It gave me a warm feeling. Like being a dad? After about twenty seconds of hanging on, she asked, without looking up, "Are you angry with me?"

I answered, "No, I am glad you are okay, Lupita." Trying to keep her voice from cracking, she asked, "And what about the money?" I answered, "*Ni modo* (No big deal)." After hesitating a second or two, she whispered, "*¿De veras?* (Really?)" I said, "Yes. Come on, let's go. Let's go."

300

This incident made me realize how much she wanted my approval. Since the beginning Lupita had gotten it largely by surprising and impressing me. Doing things I didn't think were doable. Now she had a failure on her hands and hadn't known how I would take it.

Frankly I was glad for the incident, because until then, our relationship had yo-yoed. After brief moments of warmth and emotional intimacy she would draw back or disappear. From this point on my relationship with her became richer and deeper. She didn't try as hard to impress me, and I quit trying to keep her in line. We both loosened up and enjoyed it more.

As we walked across the train station, she let go of me. Forty-five seconds of clinging to me was, for her, a mountain of intimacy. She was not like Lisa, Iliana's little sister, who had followed me everywhere. Lupita was different. She had been on the street most of her life, her family God knows where, and she wasn't used to this kind of stuff.

Next, we got lucky. As we walked past the ticket windows, two American couples were shouting in English at a clerk. They wanted to leave immediately on the southbound train. But there wasn't another till morning.

So I walked up to the jerk who was doing most of the shouting (this is how you get an "Ugly American" tag) and said, "Hey, excuse me, but the agent is telling you that the afternoon train has already gone. There won't be another until eight o'clock in the morning."

One of the women looked like she was going to faint, "Oh, my God, what are we going to do? We have friends who are supposed to meet us in Hermosillo tonight." I said, "Well, you've got several other choices of transportation. You can fly, take a bus, or you can take a taxi. They've got buses that run every half hour." No good—these Americans were not about to get on a Mexican bus.

Actually, the first-class buses and the extra-fancy "Pullmans" were fast and comfortable. Some even had stewardesses!

But they weren't having any of it. I said, "Sorry. Those are your options." Then one of the men asked, "Can you help us rent a car or get a taxi to Hermosillo?" The nervous, older woman said, "Well, my God, I don't want to get in some taxi. They could take us anywhere."

The other woman with them was younger, about thirty, and pretty. Much softer in tone, she asked if I had a car. "Yes," I answered, "but I was planning on going over to 'the other side' on business." Confused, she asked, "What do you mean, 'the other side'?" I said, "The United States."

She asked, "You don't live in Mexico, do you?" I said, "Yes—Guaymas. I'm an anthropologist." Calmer and smarter than the rest, she asked if I could drive them straightaway to Hermosillo. I said I had to confer with Lupita and needed a few minutes to think it over.

I walked over to Lupita, who had posted herself twenty feet away, and explained, "Look, these people want to go to Hermosillo. How do you feel about going tonight? I am asking because you wanted to go shopping." She said, "Yes, but now I don't know." Then she brightened, "Well, let's take these people to Hermosillo. Will they pay?" I said, "Yes! But what do we do about Gorda's underpants?" She shrugged.

So I walked back over to my countrymen. They offered seventy dollars and gas. I agreed, on the condition that they mail us a pack of men's cotton underpants, size 44. The younger woman smiled and agreed, checking out my waist. Obviously they weren't for either me or Lupita. Lupita went about eighteen inches. I went thirty-three.

302

We collected their luggage. Jeez! They were prepared for a world tour. Fortunately the old Rambler had a really immense trunk. But it was a tight fit with the fans, blenders, and luggage. The trunk wouldn't close all the way, so I tied it down. Then we headed south through Nogales.

I had Lupita beside me, next to the gearshift lever. I told her to look out for the nearest refresco stand and pulled into one, so she could stock up on cold sodas. She took my net bag, lined it with fresh newspaper, purchased a chunk of ice with the sodas, and set them to chill on the back floor. The pretty woman had her feet up over it. I opened the wing windows for air and took off down the highway for Hermosillo.

The Rambler was crowded, but our passengers tamed down once we got going. Then they started asking questions. I explained I was an anthropologist—a doctoral student at the

University of New Mexico. That satisfied them and they began chattering among themselves until we stopped at kilometer 21, to show passports and get tourist cards. That drove them nuts, but only took fifteen minutes.

The next stop was Imuris. On the off chance that Lupita had gotten the latest, I asked her how many honks today. "Two short, one long." Redeemed and in control again, she beamed. It worked like a charm.

The pretty woman asked if Lupita was my daughter. I answered, "No, she works for me." She freaked, "My God, what does she do?" I told her, "Well, she runs errands for me and stuff like that. She's an orphan and I keep her employed, but she's not my daughter." That ended the conversation.

We got into Hermosillo around nine-thirty that night and took our charges to a fancy hotel on the north side of town. I showed them to the lobby while Lupita helped with their gear. Inside, I wrote out my address at the Hotel Rubi and again asked the pretty one to mail the underpants. She nodded, smiling, and tipped Lupita a ten-spot for helping with the luggage and getting the bellboys out in record time.

Loudmouth gave me eighty bucks, including gas, so the trip hadn't been a total loss. I still had a half a tank of gas and eighty bucks.

Lupita was starving—the burritos hadn't survived the afternoon heat. We decided on milanesas at an unpretentious little steakhouse on Hermosillo's main drag.

Lupita inhaled her food, elbows on the table, head almost in the plate. I thought about how many meals she'd missed in her young life. Then I thought about how many times she had likely fought off boleadores for scraps of food on the street—and said nothing.

Finally she came up for air and smiled, announcing that she was "inviting" me to the meal. I accepted, reaching over to her, my fingers curled. She curled hers and joined hands, our fingers hooked. Lupita sign language for "we're even." She nodded her head in approval and went back to her food. I listened to the restaurant's ranchera music until she came up for air again.

When I had her attention, I suggested that "we really ought to do something different and not go straight home." Enthusiastic, she agreed.

Then I had a flash, "Look, why don't we go to Kino Bay? A vacation!" Kino Bay was on the coast, about eighty miles off to the west. The idea positively thrilled Lupita, because, number one, she'd never been there; number two, taxistas, shrimpers, and tourists around Guaymas talked about Kino; and number three, because this would be the first vacation in her life.

304

She vibrated, then got up and paid the tab with her ten-dollar luggage tip. I heard her telling the young cashier that she was treating her patrón to dinner with money she had made *en negocios* (in business). The kid was back to normal.

Dinner over, we piled into the Rambler and turned it toward the traffic circle at one end of town, which leads to Kino. I gassed at the Pemex while Lupita did a soda run. She came back with sodas, ice, and a big sack of oranges—a local specialty—that she'd paid for. I again curled my fingers to receive hers and offered her a smoke. She shook her head.

We pulled out of the gas station and took the long, two-lane road that headed to Kino Bay, crossing the coastal plain that was once part of the Seri Indian homeland. The Pedro Domecq brandy folks had "acquired" rights to farm huge, irrigated plots of virgin desert to produce brandy grapes. Ecologically and culturally, it was very costly booze. Lupita curled up on the front seat. Hot and full of food, she drifted off to sleep.

I turned the radio to ranchera music to keep me awake, enjoying the occasional acid-crystalline smells from the desert ironwood and *palo duro*. From time to time jagged flashes of dry lightning over the Sierra Madre lit up the rear window. I hoped the rains would come soon and break this heat.

Startled by an unexpected sharp turn to the right and a cluster of brightly lit sandwich and cigarette shops barely ten feet from the pavement, I stood on the brakes and coasted into Kino Bay around midnight.

After miles of nothing but darkness and desert smells, Kino's narrow lane and cluster of brightly lit buildings were a shocking contrast. I pulled off to a sandwich stand and woke Lupita. She was hungry again and wanted café con leche and some *panes dulces* (sweet rolls). So I said, "Fine. I'll order. You find us a place to stay!" The people nearby watched us—no one expected to see a gringo and a little Mexican girl pop into Kino Bay at midnight.

305

Lupita reappeared as the coffee was served. She had settled on a small, commercial hotel, three hundred feet away. After coffee we pulled the Rambler over to the little two-story brick and concrete hotel and got our room.

The hotel catered to Mexican businessmen, not tourists. One night, seventy-five pesos; two nights, a hundred. I plunked down the hundred pesos and we climbed the outside concrete staircase to our second-story room—sea breezes were desirable. So were the southeast-facing windows. West windows meant slow death by heat in August.

The room was modest, but clean. Two single beds, a minimalist bathroom, and red tile floor. It was the kind of distinctly Mexican hotel room that made voices sound harsh and tinny due to the hard tiled surfaces and few furnishings to soak up sound. At that hour the only sounds we heard were from the Honda generator downstairs, providing electricity. There were no power lines to the building.

I sent Lupita back down to the Rambler to get one of the new fans, then pulled the beds close together so the fan would hit both of us as it swiveled back and forth. A wet towel over the fan, my suitcase against the door, boots next to the bed, and I was dead to the world.

It was broad daylight when I awoke, bathed in sweat. The fan was not going—they had cut the generator off. Lupita got up before me and had already been out exploring.

I got up, took a tepid shower, dressed, then stepped out to the staircase. The view was lovely. Old Kino village was to my left, consisting of several dirt streets and a jumble of modest houses. Off to the right, the road passed a prominent headland. New Kino Bay was to the right, on the headland.

Local fishing boats were drawn up right out front. It looked like they had a decent little fishing fleet there—thirty or forty boats, mostly small eighteen- to twenty-foot skiffs. One paved street went north to the headland—tourist central. The norteamericano tourists, as they did nearly everywhere, had gravitated to the north side of the settlement.

I went downstairs to the lobby and asked for Lupita. They hadn't seen her. I ambled outside to look around, then heard Lupita hollering. She was coming from the tourist district to the north, on a dead run. She was breathless, wide-eyed, and babbling when she reached me. Business first! She had already negotiated the sale of three fans, and a restaurant called El Pingüino ("The Penguin") needed a waffle iron. She had gotten offers in excess of four hundred pesos for each.

My little mandadera was on a hot streak, so I authorized the deals. She wanted me to drive up there and do business right away. I told her I'd drive, but the transactions were hers. Ripped, she wanted a bonus. I assumed the ordinary 10 percent as we piled into the Rambler. But when the transactions were completed, she firmly refused her hundred pesos.

Instead she wanted a rather remarkable bonus—to go fishing on one of the boats. She was holding out for "a real vacation." I thought about the cost, then remembered my twenty-first birthday in Vera Cruz, when my twin brother, John, and I went barracuda fishing. It was a great memory, so I proposed that we eat in the old village, then check out the boats.

We returned to the same open-air restaurant where we'd had late-night coffee and enjoyed a nice breakfast—broiled fish for me, huevos rancheros (scrambled eggs with tomato, onion, and chile sauce) for my business agent.

Lupita already had plans, urging me to eat quickly. She'd run into a local guy earlier who had a nice boat moored in the old village. I complained, "Lupita, this is going to cost big money!" She said, "But we sold the fans. We made money for taking the Americans to Hermosillo. Will you talk to this guy?" I said, "Okay." Right then and there she jumped up and was gone.

In ten minutes she returned with her prospect in tow— a pleasant, well-spoken local Mexican man. Slightly silvering at the temples and leather-skinned, he wore the obligatory captain's cap. He made us a great price on an overnight trip to legendary Tiburón Island, returning the next day. Cool! We walked down to see his boat. It was nice, seaworthy-looking, and well kept.

After dickering over the details, I was still undecided. But Lupita was already vibrating so hard in anticipation that I asked if she was okay. She told me she thought the vibrating might be what "happy" felt like and asked if it bothered me. I shook my head. So she started checking out the boat, shivering and chattering.

The captain looked at me, perplexed. "Orphan," I said. "My errand girl. We're from Guaymas. I'm her godfather." He nodded. Mexicans instantly understand relationships. If you claim a kid as your own and act like the father, then you're Dad. Period. Ditto, padrino, or godfather. Lupita heard part of this and started calling me "Nino" (short for Padrino).

Let me explain why we were so excited. Tiburón (shark) Island is an immense jagged shadow—a four-hundred-square-mile mystery that rises over three thousand feet from the Sea of Cortés. You could see it from Kino Bay. It looms on the horizon—one of the last strongholds of the Seri Indians before they were "pacified."

According to the locals, it was littered with abandoned nineteenth-century whaling camps and was still home to pirates, wild goats, pigs, and wolves. On the south side of the island a deep ocean trench allegedly sheltered three-hundred-and four-hundred-pound groupers. Even in Mexico, Tiburón was a legend.

So I asked Lupita, "Well Lupita. What do you want—a hundred dollars? Do you want to go to Tiburón?" She said, her eyes popping, "Oh, ¡*por Dios!* If I could tell the boleadores that I had been to Tiburón, they would kiss my *culo* (ass)." I didn't jump on her for the crude language, but responded, "Damn if they wouldn't!" The Captain laughed, "*¡Hecho!* (Done deal!)." He suggested we leave at twelve-thirty. Two hours to get ready.

Lupita and I went to the room and made a list—suntan lotion, sodas, smokes, flashlight and blankets from the trunk, a hat and long-sleeved shirt for Lupita, some snack food. We checked out of the hotel, got a partial refund, and went shopping.

We parked the Rambler by the captain's place and put our gear together in the back of his pickup. He dug up a small baseball cap and shirt for Lupita, and then we drove four hundred yards to his boat.

I helped him and his mate carry a drum of fresh water and a full block of ice on board. We had bought Lupita heavy truck-tire huaraches (sandals) in the village and were all set. I even brought one of my green journals to write in. Lupita waved to everyone on shore as we pulled out—just like we were on a big cruise liner.

309

We had purchased an entire case of tinned Mexican fruit juices—mango, papaya, pineapple—and I was putting them on ice. But Lupita was bouncing around so much the captain asked me to trap her and get a life jacket on her. Fortunately she thought the vest was *muy padre* (cool!).

For good measure I attached a light, nylon mooring stringer to the D ring on her vest. The captain gave me a thumbs-up. My little swashbuckler tethered to her pirate ship, we slipped out of Old Kino, bound for Cape Johnson, near the north end of Tiburón.

As I finished putting the juices on ice the captain told us he had stowed a large sack of oranges and another of limes, along with tortillas, beans, rice, and cooking oil. He said we'd catch our own fish. I nodded in approval, then started rubbing suntan lotion all over Lupita's exposed parts—including her feet.

It was a very comfortable ride. And beautiful—sparkling blue water and blazing sun. It was also beastly hot, but with the boat thumping along in the spray, it was bearable. Facing aft, we watched Kino Bay disappear in the background. The captain indicated that it wasn't going to be productive fishing in that heat, so we headed straight for a "camp" on Tiburón. It was a surprisingly long trip.

We made Tiburón around three-thirty and tied up to an old stone pier. We carried our supplies for the night onto the beach—a camp-out. The mountains rose straight up behind us, providing afternoon shade. Nice choice.

310

Judging from the layout and what appeared to be discarded whale ribs, I thought it might be an old whaling camp. I turned to the Captain and asked, "*¿Ballena?* (whale?)" He nodded, "This is a whaling camp." Wow! We were standing smack in the middle of a late-nineteenth-century whaling camp. I asked "Why here?"

Pointing to the dramatic skyline he explained, "Well, the mountain behind us breaks storms, and it's only about forty kilometers [about twenty-five miles] across to the Whale Strait." That's a famous stretch of the Sea of Cortés where ecotourists go to see the whales migrate each year. We were camping in the lee of a huge stone-and-timber skidway where they had once pulled the whales up to strip off the blubber.

At the base of the mountain, dark grottos beckoned. There we found rock overhangs, their roofs blackened from ancient cooking fires. A small spring bubbled out of the ground nearby. On one of the talus slopes near the spring I found a perfect, triangular Archaic Period (4000 B.C.) dart point of the type called Pinto Basin. Now I got to teach Lupita. As I showed her the point, she vibrated. I gave it to her as a gift. She had me tell her again what it was called and how old it was.

"¿*Los boleadores?*" I suggested. She nodded—a potential "one up" on the shoeshine boys.

Exploring this area was fascinating, but the captain had asked us to return about six. The program was to go fishing in deep water nearby while his mate started beans and rice for dinner. Lupita and I returned on schedule and boarded the boat with the old man.

The first thing the two of us did was soak up about four cans apiece of iced fruit juice. We timed our swallows simultaneously—nudging each other and enjoying our secret hot-weather ritual. The captain had also taken some empty quart liquor bottles and filled them with water and lime, then put them on ice. We were set.

We took off around a nearby cape at a nice, slow pace and dropped anchor after about twenty minutes. The water was pale green on one side of the boat; on the other it was emerald. We were hanging right over the edge of a steep shelf—a grouper hole. The captain hauled out his fishing gear—a couple of stout sea rods fitted with heavy Penn reels.

As I palmed my reel, a wave of nostalgia washed over me. These had been made in Philadelphia—not two miles from my grandfather's brownstone row house. He had suffered a heart attack at a Phillies game in '56 and died a week later. A working man's working man, he'd have been proud as hell to see those big Penn reels in service three thousand miles from where some of his buddies had made them.

The huge reels, heavy line, and the biggest damn hooks I had ever seen on anything had Lupita goggling. The captain stripped some mullet onto the hooks and put both Lupita and me into side-by-side backed chairs, fitted with strap harnesses.

We reeled up and down, up and down. At intervals the captain changed bait but nothing happened. After an hour we moved just a bit, maybe another hundred and fifty yards. Lupita was wearing thin on this. She had expected something spectacular to happen, pronto! So we tried a third spot, again moving just a hundred yards.

This time I took my rod down and put more weight on it. Unlike before, when I had let out a hundred and twenty feet of line before hitting bottom, it went to the end of the reel—a very deep hole. In a few minutes, I hooked onto something. Frustrated, I was sure I had become snagged. I pulled on the rod but simply couldn't budge it—and was embarrassed.

I called the Captain aft and said, "Look, I'm sorry I got this thing hung up; that's all there is to it." He pulled on the rod for a minute, held onto it, feeling the tension with his fingertips. Then announced, "No, you got a grouper!"

He buckled my harness. Following his direction, I started hauling on the reel until the rod had bent so far that my eyes were about to pop out from the exertion. Little Lupita became excited, bouncing around in her seat. So the captain reeled her in to keep her, and his gear, safe.

Still, I believed the hook was merely hung on a rock. Finally I felt something start to give. Pulling as hard as I could, I kept warning the captain, "This thing's got to break; it's got to be on a rock."

He answered, "No. Got a grouper. Keep pulling. Keep pulling." After about ten minutes of gut-busting effort I was about to give up, when suddenly the line started to give and the rod tip came up. He told me to keep cranking, keep the tension on. So I did.

It took me another fifteen minutes to reel in, sweat pouring down me, requiring Lupita to come over and wipe my face. By God, I had hoisted a huge grouper to the surface. For the Sea of Cortés it was nothing special, even though it weighed fifty pounds or so. No matter—I thought it was a pretty spectacular fish.

I had to bring the fish in with a gaffing hook. Lupita was helping. Once aboard, it looked just like a huge bass. The captain began to dress it right away and asked Lupita if she wanted to fish while he worked. But Lupita was ready to go. She was hungry and hadn't caught a fish.

So we hauled up and headed back to the stone pier, where we moored. There were still pearly streaks of light and one patch of gorgeous steel-blue sky overhead as we walked across the beach to camp. Twilight was majestic.

The mate met us, dinner well along. It turned out that he was the captain's son. The old man took a nice strip of grouper—about three or four pounds—for dinner and carefully stowed the rest in an iced well on board.

The mate had set up a little camp for us right on the seaside wall of an old stone shed. The beach in front of us was sandy and air temperatures were dropping rapidly as the sun set. It was only about ninety. They brought cushions off the boat to make surprisingly comfortable beds for Lupita and me. The smell of hot coffee blended nicely with the simmering rice. They even had a small folding table from the boat, which they pushed into the sand to steady it. Nice little spread.

As camp-outs go it was a sumptuous meal—frijoles, rice with onion and spices, and pan-fried grouper in corn oil. Oh my God, the grouper was so good! It was the best fish I'd ever tasted—sweet and flaky. We ate succulent strips of the delicate, white fish splashed with lime.

Lupita ate while leaning back lazily against one of the cushions, sucking in strips of grouper like they were fat strands of licorice. "*¡Rebuena!* (Super good!)" she pronounced dreamily. As darkness descended, the last rays of sunlight glinted off the ridge of the Sierra Madre a hundred miles east of us on the mainland. It was a peaceful and enchanting place.

Our guides regaled us with every Tiburón story one could imagine—ghosts of Seri Indians, whalers' ships, smugglers, and pirates. Lupita was having a great time. She now had fresh tales of adventure to stuff up the shoeshine boys' noses. Still, she told me she wanted a fish—badly.

314

The captain and his son were really nice guys. They had brought some beer. I didn't really want any, but Lupita insisted that I have a beer after catching a fish like that. So Lupita and I shared a cold Tecate that night. I don't know whether she'd ever drunk beer before, but she finished her third, no problem.

When the captain and I went down to the water to pee at one point, I told him, "We've got to get a fish for the girl." He agreed. "Well, look. We'll go out early in the morning. We have a Coleman lantern on board. We'll put the lantern over the back of the boat and fish with live bait from a small rod." That strategy sounded good.

Back at camp Lupita and I got our beds made up. I had a flashlight and gave her a roll of toilet paper, telling her not to go far. After the ghost stories that was easy. I curled up, rolled the blanket behind my head, lit a cigarette, and stared up at that beautiful Sea of Cortés sky, a touch of breeze coming off the water.

I reached over and patted Lupita, snuggled two feet from me, telling her to go to sleep, that we were going to go fishing early in the morning. I watched the stars and began to drift off, as Lupita's tiny voice asked, "Davíd are you *contento?* (pleased)." I said, "Yes. I feel very good." She said, "Me too." We drifted off to sleep.

Gosh, it seemed like we'd only been asleep twenty minutes until it was time to rise and shine. We had a quick breakfast and were into the boat by about a quarter after five. The son had done his stuff, all right. He had a netted a dozen big minnows, which were swimming in the live well on board. We cast off and headed out to deeper water, off an immense, jagged rock outcropping.

This time we did a very slow troll with lighter rods, a lantern aft. We'd only been at it about twenty minutes when little Lupita nailed a monster. I'll never in my life forget the look in her eyes when that thing broke the surface and went down again with her line, the big Penn reel singing, as her fish sounded. She began squealing and screeching—then vibrated.

We strapped her in quickly, as I questioned the captain. "My God, that can't be a yellowtail—too late in the season." He said, "The old ones sometimes hang around, and this one is *estupendo* (a dandy)."

He and his son were highly experienced. They maneuvered the boat deftly, to prevent her breaking the line, while I held on to Lupita. I took the pressure off her arms several times, but the kid was a fighter—she wanted to do it herself. And she never let go. It took about thirty minutes from the time she hooked that fish until she had it to the edge of the boat, groaning and cussing like a sailor.

Our guides were impressed with Lupita—both her language and her courage were extraordinary. It was about a three-and-a-half-foot yellowtail. They're muscular, torpedo-shaped fish with a bright yellow tail, and real fighters when hooked. As game fish they're highly prized. Once they'd gaffed and brought it on board, they estimated it weighed twenty-seven or twenty-eight pounds. Huge!

Lupita finally got her fish—and a half-hour fight for it—with the three of us cheering her on. But she'd paid a price—her hands were burned from the reel, even though she'd wrapped one of my bandanas around them for protection. So my mandadera was not about to have them fillet this creature. She wanted it saved, unscathed. It was a gorgeous fish.

We stayed on another hour, but nothing else bit. This had been our one unlikely stroke of luck. We hauled anchor and headed back to the whaling camp.

We collected our gear from the beach and broke camp. The stone walls of this old whaling camp were bathed in morning sunlight. It was quite a spot. We didn't' stay long—fifteen or twenty minutes to pack the gear and get the boat going again. Lupita and I had a couple of cans of juice each and some tortillas.

Before heading home we motored along the east side of the island, where we fished off a long finger of rocks that jutted out of the water. We fished for triggerfish there for about an hour and a half. This was the captain's surefire spot. He and his son both fished, bringing in nearly two dozen fish weighing a pound or so each. Lupita and I brought in a dozen between us. Her hands hurt and her muscles were shaky, so she lost interest long before we left.

They filleted them, filling the ice compartment. It was amazing to see them do this in three deft cuts, just like the Aleuts in Alaska had done when I worked up there a few years before.

Lupita was the first to quit fishing—she kept sticking her head in the ice bin to look at her yellowtail. She was upset because it was changing color. Fish do fade once they're out of the sea. In fact she acted like she was going to climb right in there and hug the damn thing.

Then we explored another cove after the triggerfish quit biting. It was an archeological treasure trove—harpoons of whale's bone set with shark teeth, flint tools, shell fish hooks, sinkers. These all could've been left by early historic Seri Indians, or they might've been three thousand years old. I wasn't an expert on that area, so I wasn't certain.

An hour there and Lupita was getting anxious to go back. She was freaking out about the potential condition of her fish and began asking to go back to Kino. She wanted people to see it. I nodded to the captain. Then we waded out to the boat and turned southeast.

Every time we turned our backs on Lupita she opened the lid of that big ice bunker and checked on her fish. She was in love with it.

We were about twenty minutes out of Kino when the captain came back and whispered to me, "You know, I really think that might be a trophy fish. Shall I fly the *bandera de trofeo* (the trophy flag)?" I said, "Sure!" But he was concerned about flying the trophy flag for the little girl and not for me.

I said, "Fly it!" He grinned. Lupita watched as they ran up the black-and-white flag to honor her catch.

As Lupita watched her trophy flag go up, she vibrated, then went into launch mode. She shivered and started recounting how she had pulled in the fish, done this, and done that. We were all enjoying it. The kid was getting a sense of triumph. Once the captain and his son realized that my feelings weren't threatened they started making a big fuss over her "trophy" fish and what a great little fisherman she was. She ate it up. We sped in to Kino Bay, her trophy flag flying on top of the radio mast.

As we pulled into the wharf I was amazed that a crowd had gathered. The captain turned to Lupita, "They are here for you!" Lupita's blistered hands went to her mouth. For once she was speechless. I'd never seen her do that before.

They hung the fish on the pier and some tourists with cameras started snapping away. Lupita was completely absorbed, making sure that everyone knew that she was the center of attention, that this was her trophy fish.

One American couple made a big fuss, so I translated for her, telling her how impressed they were. They took a couple of Polaroid shots, and she pinched one. So there was a picture of Lupita in her striped top, her little hat, her mop of hair sticking out, and the yellowtail hanging next to her, nearly as tall as she was.

As Lupita gloated I loaded our gear into the Rambler and paid the captain. When I got back to the pier to retrieve Lupita several of the local businessmen were trying to buy Lupita's fish. They wanted to mount it. Local advertising for summer sportfishing, I guess. At first Lupita was not for this at all. She was as much in love with that fish as any ten-year-old girl had ever been in love with her horse.

But Lupita was nothing if not a woman of commerce. They wanted to negotiate with me for the fish, but I said, "Nope," and pointed to Lupita. "It's her fish."

Finally, they got her fish away from her, but it cost them three hundred pesos. You should've seen this kid take on the local "chamber of commerce." By the time they got up to three hundred pesos, Lupita was content with memories of the fish and her photograph.

She wanted to give a dinner, which wasn't that unusual. Years before in Vera Cruz, when I had been sportfishing and we had a successful day, it was customary for the captain and the fisherman to gather for drinks and a meal, usually on the lucky sport fisherman. I said "sure" to this part of the deal. So Lupita gave up her fish, and it was whisked away.

We agreed to meet at the open-air tent restaurant around five-thirty. The two of us borrowed a bathroom to wash up and change. By the time we got to the restaurant there were kids from Kino Bay running all over the place—free meal. Meat for dinner consisted of my grouper and our dozen triggerfish.

We had a wonderful meal. There were fried grouper strips, fillets of triggerfish, huge pots of *frijoles de olla*, and plates of *sopa seca de arroz*. The fish was garnished with lime slices, chiles, and sliced onion arranged on top. There were stacks of tortillas, along with oranges and mangos. There were also big, five-gallon glass jars of mango fruit drink. Someone graciously donated a large jug of Bacardi rum, so there was also a huge pickle jar of low-octane planter's punch.

Initially about two dozen tourists, the captain and his family, and a few of the restaurant and hotel people showed up. We fed everybody. Then more local folks came and made tacos from the scraps. After an hour, some of the poor kids from the village began hanging around outside, so I gave the guy at the restaurant two hundred pesos in advance and told him to get stacks of tortillas, more rice, beans, and fish to at least give the kids tacos. We fed between fifty and sixty people, including kids.

The American tourists apparently thought this dinner was the closest they were ever going to get to the real Mexico. For a while Old Kino had let them become part of Mexico's big extended family! They were having a ball, actually trying to speak Spanish. I encouraged the other half of the table to try a little English. It was working. The atmosphere was friendly and upbeat.

320

Lupita and I were seated side by side at the head of the table, she to my right. Some of the locals brought their own cups and glasses to share the punch, as word spread that it was okay to join the crazy gringo and his little goddaughter, who had wrestled one hell of a fish into submission. People in Mexico love a party, and these folks were lively and gracious.

Lupita had wanted to cohost the dinner. This was very important to her. When we first made arrangements for the dinner, she shelled out a hundred and fifty pesos of the three hundred she had made from her fish. I told her, "Lupita, you don't have to pay anything. I'll take care of this. We'll have a good time." No deal! She wanted to pay for some of the food and be cohost. This was a huge event for her.

So I called for a toast. She remained seated. In Mexico the toasts can be very elaborate and formal. I had to ask the Americans to stand up, that this was going to be a formal toast. I gave a short speech that the dinner was in honor of

Lupita, her courage, and the trophy yellowtail. Then explained that Lupita was cohosting the dinner with proceeds from the fish, so that she could "invite" the village children to share her joy and eat with her. I ended, encouraging all to eat, enjoy themselves, and not be bashful.

Everyone clinked their glasses and dedicated a round to Lupita. Then the fishing captain made a toast to the two of us, "the *señor norteamericano* and his goddaughter." Everyone clapped. Lupita was glassy-eyed. Thankfully she hadn't once used her colorful street language.

Our dinner had become the kind of agreeable ritual that working folks the world over, whether farmers in West Virginia or fishermen in Kino Bay, love dearly. Forget your stereotypes—working-class Mexicans are sweet and sentimental. Several proposed nice toasts back to Lupita, who had captured their imaginations. We had a grand time. Lupita was in pig heaven. She proposed a toast to me—señor Davíd Stuart, her *padrino y patrón* (godfather and patron). She then thanked the "captain, the mayor, and other dignitaries," as she hoisted a planter's punch. Even though no dignitaries were actually present, it was great.

Around eight, more beer and rum appeared. The locals were going to make a night of it. Once these fiestas get going they can last several days. But we made our excuses, said our goodbyes, shared elaborate handshakes all around, and prepared to leave. I squared up with the guy who owned the restaurant. My total costs were about fifty bucks for the rice, beans, and tortillas, on top of the donated fish. They sure didn't gouge us.

We pulled out in the old Rambler, which had been parked nearby, and passed slowly by the open side of the canvas-roofed restaurant, the party in full swing. The crowd cheered and waved us out of town. Lupita waved, then stood looking out over the backseat of the car, savoring the last sight of all those people waving and cheering her as we rolled down the lane.

I beeped the horn a bunch of times to the beat of "La Cucaracha," as Lupita hooted, "¡*Toque!* ¡*Toque más!* (Beep! Beep some more!)"

It was a rich, waning sunset. Long red streaks painted the sky, and deep shadows already hid parts of Old Kino as we drove away. The Coleman lanterns hanging from the tent flickered in the evening breeze as we wound our way across the ironwood desert. Lupita was very quiet.

I drove on, but Lupita didn't turn to face me for a long while—she had been crying quietly as we left. After ten minutes or so, I asked, "Do you want to go back?" "No. No. ¡*Fue perfecto!* (It was perfect!)" Then she turned and sat quietly while we drove across the long desert road to Hermosillo.

That night I experienced a different Lupita. She wasn't the little chicle girl in Guaymas. They didn't know her from Adam in Kino Bay. In his toast the boat captain had referred to her very kindly as the *patroncita* (the little patron) of our *cena* (formal dinner) and fiesta. For once Lupita had been treated as a peer among her own kind, not as "La Gatita"—the irritating little street kid.

This interlude was one of the happiest of my life, and I am glad we had it. It pleased me to see her be happy and get some recognition. It must have pleased her, too. She later commented that it was the best two thousand pesos ($160) that "we" ever spent. Indeed it was.

We drove through the night, making a quick stop for gas and Cokes somewhere near Hermosillo. Finally she stopped recounting her glory and looked up, then thanked me, "Thank you Davíd, for the fishing trip and the fiesta." I answered, "Oh, Lupita, I had a grand time. I enjoy being with you. I liked it." She asked, "Davíd, did you like being with me more than with La Marta?" I said, "Yes, but you must understand that it's a very different thing." She nodded, knowingly. "Well, have you ever gone fishing or on vacation with La Marta?" I replied, "Oh, no!" I never again heard anything contentious about Marta. It didn't seem to trouble her anymore.

We reached Guaymas after midnight. It had been a long day—I was beat. I dropped Lupita off near La Gorda's, behind the hotel, then went to my room and showered, wondering if the American couples would actually send the promised underpants. After showering I was starved, so walked out to the car, waved at the taxistas, and drove to the Almita. I passed little Lupita, once again stationed under her favorite streetlight, watching the harbor. She didn't see me.

Over the next few days Lupita tormented every shoeshine boy in town with the Polaroid of her and her fish. She must have been insufferable. Several came up and asked if I'd like to hire them as assistants. This was impressively close to the butt-kissing she had hoped for. I told them that Lupita handled my daily affairs on the street. One bully whined that she was just a little GIRL. He didn't like that. I countered—"a very smart little girl with *corazón* (heart)."

I was soon to discover just how smart. Seated in the passage at the Colmenar about two days later, Juanito was doing my boots as Lupita came by to needle me. Again she urged me to check on the blonde in the Sánchez Clinic from the latest car wreck.

I needled back, "Well, I've not checked on her, but I bet that none of the *boleadores* have actually kissed your butt, either." Juanito, snot running down his chin, erupted in his unique version of a hysterical laugh, "*¡Uno, sí!* (One did!)"

"*¿De veras? ¿Quién?* (Really? Who?)" I asked. Juanito hollered, "El Chingón (Hot Shit)." El Chingón was the biggest, meanest boleador on the Serdán—he even took on taxistas. At about age thirteen and oversized, he was a social problem waiting to mature into a stone-cold animal.

324

Lupita looked triumphant, but shooed Juanito away, as I demanded an explanation. "He did kiss my bare ass, but it wasn't violence," she protested, knowing I abhorred the rough stuff. "Then what actually happened?"

"You sent him a letter saying he could be your assistant if he kissed my bare butt to make up for stealing from me on the street." "I DID?"

"Yes—a friend writes letters from you—I tell her what to write. You are the one who told me that people respect writing—and they know you can write. So I take your *mandas* (orders) and my friend makes letters from you for me to deliver. That is why señor X met us in the graveyard—YOU wrote him." I interrupted, "But I did **not** write him!" "Yes, you did—through me! You said to sell the papers."

That's when I said aloud in English, "Well I'll be screwed!" She asked, "*¿Qué?* (What?)" Lying, I said in Spanish, "You really are clever." "Thank you," Lupita smiled.

"And El Chingón?" I asked. She answered, "I made him kiss my butt while Juanito watched. I told him if anything happened to me, Juanito would tell the other boleadores. I told him if anything happened to Juanito, I'd tell."

"And if anything happened to you both?" "My friend already wrote a letter to you to tell on Chingón." "And would just telling on him work?" "Oh yes! He'd lose his *macho* (maleness, but "be deballed" is closer in this context) and his power on the street."

I tried not to laugh, but couldn't help myself. Lupita ran off, shouting over her shoulder, "I knew you'd understand!"

thirteen

THE LAST SUNDAY

After the trip to Kino Bay, my biggest problem was with anxious customers. Burro had retrieved his new tires and other taxistas began to line up for the same service. Even more wanted fans. It was already August but the rains still had not come. When they did start, the demand for fans would taper off. A quick trip to the border made sense.

Just four days after our return from Kino Lupita and I slipped out of town after a midnight meal at the Almita, and headed for the border on another set of borrowed tires. I checked this set as they went on, just in case some clown decided to hide drugs in the casings. Clean. Good to go.

Lupita liked the nighttime run. It was only about eighty out in the desert, a cool relief. She was calmer, and I took the opportunity to pump her for more information on the "letter writing." But my secret agent was only good for name, rank, and serial number. Finally she assured me they had only written "a few" letters, then clammed up. I never found out more.

Our plan was to cross over about 6 A.M., go shopping, then rent a sleeping room at "our" motel before crossing to Mexico again in the heavy, evening border traffic.

It was a great business trip. The tunnels were open and Lupita met me for breakfast at Zula's. I stuck to table fans, blenders, and pocket calculators. We changed tires about six in the evening, after almost eight hours of air-conditioned rack time, then crossed both the border and several officials' palms without problems.

It was tat-tat, pause, tat-tat on the horn at Imuris, then on to Guaymas. There was no Corsario business this trip, since I had told the taxistas that I would no longer publicly "take orders" and asked for a security blackout on my activities. No sweat. Within hours of my request at the sitios, the street was as silent on our movida as it had been on the "Francisca incident."

In order to keep my finances private, I quietly opened a second bank account—my money now divided into three places. I had told Lupita that there would be no more trips for her if she uttered even one word about this one. That did it. The veil of secrecy was nearly complete.

We arrived in Guaymas about one in the morning. I dropped Lupita near the Casa Blanca, assuming she would stand watch at her lamppost, and went to the Almita—I hadn't even missed a meal there. About an hour later Burro met me behind the Rubi and took on my cargo. He handled sales for his 6 percent so that I couldn't be identified as the supplier. I had another ten months' rent and food money from the profit when he was done. Financially I was good for the next eighteen months if I was careful.

The next several weeks were punctuated by fleeting cloud banks. Several dropped a quick sprinkle of rain, offering an hour or so of relief before drifting east toward the Sierra Madre. They were a mixed blessing. On several occasions those sprinkles knocked out the electricity—no fans. The humid air made the heat even more oppressive than in June and July. "Miserable" sums it up.

My days were consumed by the ordinary rhythm of life on the street. Newspaper readings, Orange Crushes, serdaneando, clubbing, and late night meals at the Almita. It was during this time that I began to teach Lupita about the history of Mexico. That started one evening in front of the Chapúltepec when I pulled out a box of Guerrero (warrior) brand matches to light a smoke, Lupita at my side.

328

The Guerrero matchboxes featured pictures of famous warriors and included short historical sketches of each. The box in my hand featured Cortés. Lupita was into her "I want to go to school" phase, as she had been since it came up on the Kino trip. So I read her the Cortés biography on the box and gave her a thumbnail sketch of the conquest of Mexico, 1519–21.

She was like a sponge and wanted more, asking me to repeat key events—Cortés's march from Vera Cruz to Tenochtitlán (which the Spanish renamed "México"), the *Noche Triste* (sad night), when the Spanish were forced to flee the Aztec capital, and the later battle of Otumba, where Cortés and his Tlaxcalan Indian allies broke the Aztec war machine.

She wanted all the details of the heroic Aztec retreat from Otumba to the outer causeways that protected Tenochtitlán, their capital. Then came the tragic demise of the Indian army as thousands died from smallpox, still at their battle stations. Little Lupita was hungry for knowledge and an eager student.

She was particularly transfixed by my accounts of La Malinche, the high-born, strong-willed Aztec Indian woman who had been given away by her father as an unwilling teenaged concubine to a Mayan chieftain on the gulf coast.

Malinche accompanied Cortés on his campaign to topple the Aztec nobility and take their capital. So powerful was she in the events that unfolded—translating for Cortés and briefing him on Aztec politics, war, and organization—that Indian Mexico simply called Cortés "El Malinche," or roughly, "Malinche's man." She later bore him children.

Indian Mexico has long considered her a traitor to indigenous society, giving rise to the epithet, *malinchista*, which is still used daily to describe cultural turncoats. It is not a compliment.

Lupita was ripped. The image of a brilliant, powerful woman done wrong by her parents struck compelling chords deep within the private melodies of her soul. She immediately drew parallels between Malinche's relationship to Cortés and hers to me. I agreed, in part, but pointed out that she was neither betraying her people nor her culture, since she was helping me understand Guaymas society. She paused, thoughtful, then asked, "Well, does that make you a *malinchista?*"

I told her "no," but that she had just earned a *diez* (ten—a perfect score in Mexican classrooms) for the use of analogy. She asked, "What is analogy?" I explained . . . and on it went, almost daily.

It was during this period that Max, at the Colmenar, decided he needed to put together a formal dinner, a cena, for his closest male friends. In Mexico male friends and colleagues often went out to eat together, absent the company of females. A man's public life was unabashedly male-centered.

As a young student in Mexico City I had often seen groups of five to ten men dining in the upscale restaurants along the Reforma, the city's main thoroughfare. Such dinners were as integral to creating and maintaining relationships among the salaried classes as was serdaneando among those whose pay came daily.

When Max invited me to dinner in mid-August, it was a real honor. At that stage I had not been in the houses of many of my male acquaintances. A young, single guy is not ordinarily invited "home" in working-class Mexico, unless he's a kinsman or godparent to one of the household children. Married Mexican men are generally protective, even jealous, of their wives and daughters with single fellows.

330

In contrast, I had been invited into many working-class female-headed households. I had been to Eva's place to meet her mom, sister, and the passel of kids that I could never quite pair up with a "mom." Ditto, Mercedes at the Colmenar and several other waitresses. Even a few of the girls at the Río Rita had invited me to eat with their extended families on a Sunday or Monday afternoon.

In this context Max's invitation was great. Male-centered dinners avoided the problems of sexual territory and differences in wealth and social position. For Max the choice of location was easy. On a Wednesday night in mid-August, just about ordinary closing time, we gathered at his Colmenar for our cena.

Max hosted, sitting at the head of the table. Jesse (Canelo) sat on one side of me, Negro Jacinto on the other. Enrique Velarde, Manuel Saldívar (owner of the Ladies Bar on the Serdán) and "Jimmy" Santiago Kiami sat across from us. Jimmy represented the elevated social and economic stratum to which many in Guaymas aspired, so he sat on Max's right hand. Saldívar sat next to Kiami, directly across from me, Enrique Velarde next, directly across from Negro Jacinto. Obviously Max had considered seating arrangements as carefully as any Washington socialite hosting stateside political doyens.

We began to arrive about eight-thirty—dressed. This invitation called for black pants, polished shoes, and sparkling white guayaberas for a formal dinner with the guys. Max's restaurant did not ordinarily serve liquor but he'd stocked beer, rum, brandy, and tequila for the evening.

Max greeted us at the door while his waitresses attended to finishing touches on the banquet table set up in the center of the restaurant. Mercedes and the cook, María, and a third waitress, Leovarda, were setting out the first course as we stood, chatting, Cuba libres in hand.

Max had hired a male waiter to serve us for the evening. The women had undertaken the preparation and setup, but it was a young man who attended us. It was a candlelight dinner. The table, with our name cards, nice china, and flowers was a sight to behold. Even Martha Stewart would have approved. The full array of silverware was set out in proper order.

Kiami arrived last, and then the doors were locked. We could be seen by anyone passing through Pasaje Marví, but our cena would have required no explanation for anyone going by. The patrón of the restaurant was hosting his close men friends. Being seen was a plus—not a negative.

331

Negro noticed immediately that several of the assembled were panicking over the formidable array of silverware at each setting. In classic Negro style, he took charge gently, complimenting Max and imparting critical information in one stroke, "Max, how elegant of you to have set the table in international style, where one starts with the utensils on the outside, then moves to the next for the following course. You honor us! May I propose a toast to our host . . ."

We lifted our glasses, several of the assembled quite grateful. Jacinto had deftly met every tenet of Mexican social culture—gently, obliquely, guide your friends without making pointed comparisons. Never criticize and always compliment.

Even Kiami was surprised and impressed with Negro. Had he known him better, he would have been less surprised but even more impressed. The younger waiters around Guaymas regularly sought out Jacinto on fine points of restaurant service. Negro could have served at Simpson's-on-the-Strand in London without a hiccup. His diners would have noted only that he was less officious and more efficient than the average twit serving tables there.

The first toast over, we sat and started our cena. Max toasted us next and we returned the toast to him. Then he invited us to begin our multicourse meal. The hired waiter—black pants, cummerbund, white shirt, and white towel over his arm—attended us nicely.

In the company of men here there was a great deal of joking and touching. Men friends touch each other in Mexico. They walk down the street, arms around each other's shoulders, looking one another in the eye as they talk.

Stateside, the thought of such behavior scares the shit out of most men. But it is coin of the realm in Mexico. The closer your friends are to you, the more intimate the contact, the stronger and closer the hug during an abrazo. Usually these formal hugs, where one makes no real body contact but simply pats the other on the back two or three times, are perfunctory, as are handshakes.

But the abrazo morphs into the real thing among those who are very close to one another. To give you a rough sense of how these things were done, Negro Jacinto was closest to me. So during our meal I would lean over and give him a hug now and again, and he would respond. Jesse was next closest to me—I would shake his hand and squeeze his shoulder at the same time. He did likewise in return.

With Max, who was not as close, I would shake his hand with both of mine or squeeze his forearm while I shook his hand. These gradations also tell people how close you are to your friends.

333

Similar gradations in social distance were clearly conveyed by the use of names and styles of address in face-to-face speech. Hundreds of folks on the street knew me only as "El Güero." A much smaller circle, perhaps two dozen, knew me as "Davíd," and a half-dozen knew I was Davíd Stuart. A thousand or more knew Canelo as "Canelo." Perhaps a hundred knew him as "Jesse," or Jesús—his given name. A dozen or so knew his full name.

When little Lupita had first asked to call me "Davíd," she was actually asking for an immediate acknowledgment of "closeness" to me that the young never demand of their seniors in Mexico. At that stage she had no right to my name. I addressed her in the familiar *tu* form of speech, known as *tuteando*, which is used for kids, dogs, and anyone much younger or less powerful than the speaker. Initially she addressed me with the formal *usted*—not because I cared, but because that was proper.

I used the "tu" form of address with little children, the boleadores, Lupita, Negro, Jesse, Enrique, Marta, and Iliana. Everyone else in Mexico I addressed in the formal—even Jimmy Kiami. That is until we were halfway through the delicious shrimp soup and I asked him to pass the limes. Responding in the familiar to me for the first time, he invited me to "tutear" him. I did thereafter—and was delighted at the privilege.

I was the most educated man at the table and had been the son of a prominent medical educator—a prestige occupation in the States. But I wasn't in the States. I was in Mexico—and Kiami, by virtue of age, economic status, and connections was "Big Dog" at our table. The acknowledgment of closeness was his to grant. Not mine to assume.

As the first course of shrimp soup with limes and bolillos was whisked away, the fish course was served. On small plates, it consisted of broiled shrimp, grouper fingers, and abalone, quite a delicacy. Negro reached for the fish knife and four other sets of hands did likewise.

Then the main course was brought on. Wow! It was *cabrito*, roasted baby goat, a very festive delicacy. I always loved cabrito. Then came huge serving plates of frijoles with goat cheese sprinkled on top, the traditional rice with veggies, and several exotic foods that went with Max's "international" theme.

Max had even found a source for cottage cheese in Hermosillo. At the time cottage cheese was, like peanut butter, a little-known food in Mexico.

To round out the feast we were served several other kinds

of imported cheeses and black olives—all expensive delicacies. Guaymas's pride dictated a bowl of spiced, steamed shrimp along with the delicacy course.

At the end of the meal there was flan, a caramel custard, baked in peach halves, each one in its own separate cup. How this was done, I can't tell you, but it was exquisite. A fruit bowl—mangos, papaya, oranges, and melon—was put out just in case.

The meal itself lasted from nine until about quarter of eleven. Then we moved on to small snifters of brandy and cigarettes from the generous bowls of them set out on the table. As we savored the aged brandy, we told jokes and anecdotes in turn. Jesse told his best parrot jokes. I told several anecdotes. One involved my recent crossing to the States with old tires, then returning with new ones—both U.S. and Mexican Customs unable to figure it out.

Max had done himself proud. I will remember this dinner to the end of my days—just as our host intended. Max had spent lavishly, another characteristic of such occasions. Even poor men would occasionally put on a dinner and go into hock to do it right. Their sense of pride sometimes tempted them into overextending themselves.

At such affairs it was proper to bring gifts. These were not required, but it was proper to do so. I had brought a very fine, and pricey, bottle of Chilean white wine that had been shipped down from Hermosillo. My bottle was served around the table in small glasses, as part of the fish course. Jesse had brought rum. Saldívar brought some of the high-class Bohemia beer.

Whenever I visited someone's household, I took fruit, Cokes, cigarettes, or candy for the kids. This was never a mistake so long as I kept in mind not to overdo it, lest it inadvertently humiliate another guest who might not be able to afford to bring anything.

On about one in the morning we broke up, light-headed from rounds of liquor, and bid our elaborate farewells with a "goodbye" toast, then handshakes all around. Max actually had the waiter take a couple of snapshots with the camera I'd sold him.

In Mexico such events did more than merely entertain men friends. They formally conferred a sense of peerage, or equality, on the men at the table. They enhanced closeness. After this dinner none there addressed me again as "Güero" on the street. It was always "Davíd."

It didn't matter thereafter that we were of somewhat different classes and backgrounds. The men gathered at Max's table subsequently treated one another as peers, as *socios*, even *compadres* when they met on the street. Male bonding of this sort is quite uncommon, stateside.

After this meal I added the Ladies Bar to my serdaneando, and stopped in for an Orange Crush and quick chat with Manuel Saldívar several times a week. My relationship with Jimmy Kiami became closer and much less formal. I even visited Max's house and met his mom, doña Adelpha.

In Mexico relationships fell into several broad categories. *Conocidos* ("knowns," acquaintances) were the most distant—as in "Oh, I know him." *Socios* (associates) were closer—as in "Oh yes, he is a close associate." *Amigos* (friends) were even closer—an active relationship in which much was invested, as in "Oh, he's a very close friend." Finally there were *compadres* (coparents) and *hermanos* (brothers), usually contracted to *'mano* for nonkinsmen, as in "Oh, yes, he and I are like family—very tight."

In short Max's dinner was a smashing success—each of us extended his network of socios or compadres in meaningful ways. Had I died in Guaymas that summer, these are the men who would have carried my casket in the heat.

August had been a busy month for me—the fayuca (contraband fans), Edward Meyers, and a Canadian girl. Lupita's urging notwithstanding, I never did visit the "blonde American girl" in the Sánchez Clinic. But I did run into her mom, looking lost and trying to figure out the menu at the Colmenar. Mom and her daughter turned out to be Canadian. She even had a name, Sharyn, and Mom was having big trouble negotiating the Mexican legal and medical systems.

Sharyn's mom, Mrs. K., was about as lovely a person as I've ever met. Her daughter's fiancé had, indeed, been killed, and it took lots of effort to get the daughter clear of the Mexican judicial system and out of that clinic. As I've already mentioned, getting into a private Mexican clinic was easy. Getting out presented the challenge.

The behind-the-scenes arrangements to assist in the young Canadian's repatriation were rich, complicated, outrageous, even scandalous. Young Sharyn unknowingly became a brief morality play in the life of local Guaymas society. The story behind it is worth a book in its own right. For now, however, it is only important to know that in late August the young Canadian and her mom were transported to the Hermosillo airport in Burro's taxi, him at the wheel, me riding shotgun and translating.

This panicked little Lupita beyond reason. She was

certain that I would leave for parts unknown with "La Rubia" (The Blonde). Blondes have an even greater reputation for irresistibility in Mexico than in the States. So when I returned in Burro's taxi from Hermosillo, I found Lupita waiting for me at the Sitio Rubi, in the throes of an epic panic attack.

She had been certain I would leave and not return. Lupita had heard en la calle that this girl was petite, stacked *(bien formadita)*, and had the face of an angel—all true, it turned out.

According to the taxistas, Lupita stood watch for nearly four hours at the sitio and refused to leave. She shook, sobbed, and clung to me as I stepped out of Burro's taxi. It was sad. If Lupita had known how deep a pull Guaymas had on me and just how deep a hold she had on me, she would never have panicked. But she did. How could Lupita have known that I had already asked Jimmy Kiami to recommend a lawyer, confiding in him that I wanted to adopt her?

Poor kid! I was the closest thing to a reliable adult she had ever known. She had learned to trust me enough that she no longer checked on my whereabouts every few minutes, as she had when I first hired her. By mid-August she was down to about three or four "Güero roll calls" a day. But "The Blonde" had simply been too much for her.

To compensate, I promised her Sunday together—the beach, a ballgame, and other diversions. Mollified, she stopped freaking out and let me go inside.

That Sunday with Lupita was marvelous. I got going early, collected her, and drove out to the Miramar. Negro Jacinto had a late breakfast rush—tourists were beginning to trickle back for the Labor Day season! He told me he would be late getting off work. So Lupita and I walked out to the little promenade along the hotels' seafront. She was still wearing her khaki pants, now obviously too short, and her striped top.

Chattering as we waited, she spotted the pony corral in the big, open lot that separated the Hotel Miramar from the Miramar beach colony. That Sunday the ponies had returned—apparently to provide end-of-summer diversion for the Americans who were coming down, heat and all, for one last shot before their kids started school again.

Once Lupita spotted the ponies she wanted to ride. But she wouldn't ride alone—insisting that I rent one and go with her. I detested riding horses—there was nothing I hated more than getting on a damn horse. A mule, fine. A mule won't kill you, because a mule won't kill itself. But a horse? Shades of Ecuador!

It didn't matter. Lupita was determined to ride and was as excited as could be. She had never been on a pony. Another experience to "one-up" the boleadores.

339

So I walked across to the blazing-hot open lot with her and we rented two ponies. I got a big one. She got a small one. Both were docile.

We mounted and Lupita immediately took off, clippity-clopping up the beach, right in the edge of the surf. She screamed and giggled the entire time, alternating between sliding off one side of the pony, then the other, completely unafraid.

Undaunted by the fact that she was not doing a great job of staying on her pony, she took him out even farther into the surf, to make big splashes. Her pony spraying water in every direction, she screamed her head off in delight. I followed.

Just halfway up the beach I fell off my goddamn mount. A big wave came in and spooked my pony. It shied and I went off, right into the surf. There was probably never a moment in my relationship with Lupita when I would have more liked to strangle her with my bare hands, but she enjoyed my fall thoroughly. The sight of a soaked Güero pulling himself out of the sand and surf gladdened her heart.

She didn't know how to stop and dismount, so stood over me on her pony and cackled. When we got back to the corral, dirty and soaked, she was already composing "Güero on his ass" stories. It was sheer joy for her. For an hour she was just a little girl enjoying Sunday at the beach.

I was still wet and had sand caked all over me when we reached the veranda in front of the Miramar Hotel. She ran in to fetch a towel and washcloth. When she came out, she wanted to play "mommy" and clean me off. I went along with it. She cleaned off my face like I was a little kid, mopped the sand off my shirt, dusted me off, and made me presentable again. As she said, just "like Gorda does for me twice a week."

I sat on a bench under the bougainvillea and let her clean me up. She enjoyed the switch in roles. I complimented her, then she confided that after Gorda had shown her what was proper, she cleaned up Juanito now and again when no one was around. When I asked why Juanito's mom didn't do that, she said "paralyzed" and jerked her thumb to her mouth, local sign language for "she drinks." It was Sunday, so I let it go.

Negro was stuck at the hotel, but Eva showed up in a taxi a few minutes later with two kids in tow, so we all packed into the Rambler and drove downtown to the ballpark. On the way Burro spotted me, honked, and pulled up, window-to-window. He was turning his taxi over to the afternoon man and wanted to know where we were going. "Ballpark," I answered.

"Wait for me, fifteen minutes," he begged. "No problem." We got there late—partway through the first game of a doubleheader. The ballpark consisted of a large, ordinary semicircle of wood and steel bleachers surrounding a dusty field. Food stalls lined the area near the front gate.

The Guaymas team (Los Marineros, "The Sailors") was good, and about five thousand people packed the park. There were kids everywhere, and fans shouting for the Guaymas home team. The local girls were wearing every color of the rainbow.

Some even wore shorts, still rare at the time. Eva, the hooker, thought it wasn't appropriate. Burro, to be polite, nodded in avid agreement with her, even though he had just leaned over and whispered to me to get the refreshments, because he had a huge boner *(parado)* over a very cute teenager in shorts a couple of rows down. I loved the ironies.

Since Burro was temporarily "indisposed," I went for Cokes and hot dogs. The local hot dogs came with a thick topping of coarse-diced tomatoes, sweet onions, cilantro, green chile, and cucumber, tossed with a mayonnaise-style sauce. Oh, my! I've never had better.

The hot-dog and beer vendors were everywhere. The ice-cream vendors' sing-song "*¡Heladitos! ¡Heladitos!*" filled the stadium. Vendors also sold corn on the cob. The Guaymas version was impaled on a stick, then garnished with hot oil, salt, and powdered red chile.

Mangos on a stick were another ballpark item. Our big, juicy mangos were drenched in lime and dusted with red chile powder. Lupita and I sampled everything. Between us we did some heavy-duty hot-dog, corn, and mango stuffing that afternoon.

Since Burro and I had been doing well on our fayuca, we sprang for tickets in the shade. In Mexico the price of tickets in arenas depends on whether the seats are in the sun *(sol)* or in the shade *(sombra)*. Shade costs. Sun is cheap.

No matter where they were seated, the enthusiasm of the Guaymas baseball fans was impressive. Especially given the searing heat. The crowd chanted, "¡Guaymas, Guaymas, Guaymas!" every time there was a *jonrón* (homerun). The Guaymas brass band also struck up on every score or unusually fine play.

Lupita enjoyed being with the other kids. I simply introduced her as my *ahijada* (goddaughter) to Eva's kids. Lupita was happy—she later asked if that was what having a family was like. I told her it was, only better, since real families often fight.

342

Eva's kids begged her to bring them again and for me to bring Lupita. She had been on stunningly good behavior—she never once used any "p" or "c/ch" words, just as I had requested. In Spanish these word categories included a surprising number of the most offensive among Lupita's daily favorites. But since she'd never seen a baseball game from inside the stadium before, she didn't want to risk excommunication.

The doubleheader was over about six. I dropped everyone off, but Lupita wasn't through with me yet. She had extracted a promise that I would take her to the movies. The ticket line at the cinema a few blocks from the Rubi was so long that it was already a sellout as we stepped up to take our place. It was an American flick with Spanish subtitles. I assumed from the huge male-dominated crowd that some blonde had to be the leading lady.

I hoped Lupita would give up, but she insisted I take her

to a theater on the outskirts of Empalme that she had heard the boleadores talk about. Instinct told me to pass, but her pleading and big eyes won. I agreed.

As we were deciding what to do about the sold-out movie, we stopped and had malted milks and ham and cheese sandwiches on the roof of the Copa de Leche, overlooking the harbor. Then we walked up to the Sitio Rubi and took a taxi to Empalme.

Actually it had been a good move to go in a taxi—I didn't even know where this "movie house" was located. Lupita was ecstatic when we arrived. They were having a cartoon festival for kids. To describe it merely as pandemonium would be a substantial understatement. It was bedlam incarnate, and the theater itself was extraordinary.

It was on a dusty street, blocks from Empalme's tiny plaza, in a big adobe building with double doors that looked somewhat like the doors to a church. A billboard outside announced the day's feature. To one side of the front door, and right on the sidewalk, a little newspaper kiosk had been converted into the ticket window. It cost only fifty centavos (four cents). I wondered why the movie was so cheap, until we stepped inside.

The theatre had no roof! The floor consisted of hard-packed dirt. What had once been a fine adobe building had been gutted by fire, and the roof and floor had burned. Afterward it had simply been replastered and the dirt floor leveled to convert it into a theatre.

An elevated platform projecting from the rear wall supported the old-fashioned movie projector. A ladder provided access. Seating consisted of about two hundred folding, wooden chairs, like the ones once used in stateside churches for Sunday School. The movie screen was attached directly to the front wall. Wooden latticework replaced the roof and supported reed mats, which several boys were rolling out to darken the interior as we stepped inside.

Once seated it was clear that several hundred kids were crammed in on parents' laps—all shrieking and squirming at once. Vendors went through the rows with sweets and shaved ices. All the poor kids in the district apparently came to these fifty-centavo shows.

As the projector began to flicker cartoons against the front wall the children screamed, jumping up and down in unison. A number chanted along with the dialogue. Obviously these kids had seen the same cartoons many times over. At one point an "evil" character tried to hurt one of the "good" ones. In response the kids hurled a wall of *palomitas* (popcorn) at the offender.

Until the *Rocky Horror Picture Show* came out in the States years later, I had never seen anything quite like it—cartoons, food, and "acting-out" all rolled into one event. Lupita was completely enthralled. "*¡Qué Domingo!* (What a Sunday!)" she proclaimed, on our ride back to Guaymas in another taxi.

Now that Lupita was emerging from her shell, she seemed hungry to experience everything, all at once. God! It had been an exhausting day. Is this what being a parent is like, I wondered? I almost fell asleep in the taxi.

By then it was deep twilight. We dropped her off at Gorda's, then I went to the hotel, showered off the last of the sand from my ill-fated pony ride, and changed. Next I went serdaneando, enjoying another Sunday evening in paradise.

Finished with my evening rounds on the street, I passed through the lobby and headed to my room. Ramón jerked his head almost imperceptibly, indicating that Marta had arrived. She had grown softer and gentler of late, touching me more and laughing easily. Unfortunately, that wasn't the Marta who awaited me at my door.

She had been drinking heavily—Castillo rum from the god-awful smell of her. She swayed back and forth as she ranted, her voice like the sound of tearing newspapers. It reminded me of the blues tune "Cross-Cut Saw."

As with Lupita it began with hysteria over the "blonde you took to Hermosillo." It ended with her accusation that I was screwing both the blonde (Sharyn) and the chamacona (Lupita). In between she had called me many ugly names, but the one that actually hurt most was *pinche gringo.* That ripped it—I cursed and ran her out. She took off, crying as she shot past El Huevón and ran into the street, still hysterical.

Ramón was at my door two minutes later, glassy-eyed, "¿La pegaste? (Did you beat her?)" I shook my head. "No." Visibly disappointed, he went away. I wrote in my journal, shaking, as I smoked a couple of cigarettes. The shaking wouldn't stop, so I made a tape of recent events—just as I'd done several times that summer when I'd had too much to drink.

An hour or so later, I slipped out to walk. A couple of the taxistas asked if I'd beaten Marta. I told them "no," but said I wished I had. That ended their enquiries.

As I walked up the Serdán on the seawall side, I spotted Lupita stationed at her lamppost, motionless and staring out across the harbor. As usual she didn't notice me, and I walked on. I shouldn't have.

According to my journal it was August 23. How could I have known that this would be the last Sunday I ever spent with her?

THE LAST SUNDAY

fourteen

THE TEMPESTS

On Wednesday my new life in Guaymas began to self-destruct in slow motion. I was in the Rubi bar drinking Orange Crushes and reading the newspaper when one of the deskmen hustled in to announce that I had visitors.

"Who?" I asked. He answered, "Una señora (A lady)" and shrugged. I was expecting no one, so walked up the long corridor past the big mahogany telephone booth and stepped into the lobby.

Dear Lord! It was Iliana's mom and little sister, Lisa. They had come to check on me. Obviously I had been spotted in Empalme with Lupita. They must have presumed Lupita to be the little sister of a new girlfriend. This was not merely an uncomfortable scene for me—it was a nightmare! Rather than talk to señora D. in the lobby with everyone watching, I hustled them back to my room.

We talked for about five minutes. Señora D. told me that

she had news for me from Iliana. Iliana wanted me to know she was "okay" and again asked me to wait for her to return until the fifteenth of September, as I had promised.

I had never been comfortable with Iliana's mom, and she certainly didn't help her cause by checking out every square inch of my room while little Lisa talked to me. I assumed she was looking for signs of a female on the premises.

But the señora struck out—Marta never left traces of her visits. She actually seemed disappointed to find a classic bachelor's room, fairly well kept.

The sad part was that Lisa started crying and clinging to me, just as she had when I first arrived from Ecuador. She was emotional, sobbing that I was suffering from living alone.

What could I say? "Look, Lisa, don't get too excited— I've got a lady friend who sleeps with me on Sunday nights, and I spend several nights a week partying out in the red-light district"?

Rule one—do not take adult failures out on a kid. Iliana had hurt me deeply, but I stuck to my rule, patted Lisa, and started maneuvering the pair back toward the lobby. As far as I was concerned, Mamá's reconnaissance was over.

Once in the front lobby, I gave senora D. taxi fare back to Empalme. But little Lisa didn't want to go. It turned into a heartbreaking tug-of-war—her mom trying to pull her away while she pleaded to stay with me. Finally Mamá threw her hands in the air and stomped out to get a taxi.

I tried to console Lisa. Reaching down, I put my arms around her and squeezed her to me with one arm. I held her head in my other hand. She was crying so hard, I felt bad for her. After all, she was the one I had missed the most.

The next nightmare was visited on me when I looked up.

There stood Lupita in the lobby doorway. She was motionless, her eyes wide with horror. Silently she watched me squeeze Lisa, as Iliana's mom babbled hysterically about getting us back together and marrying in a few weeks.

Poor Lupita! She looked so beaten. I peeled Lisa off, handed her back to Mom, and went after Lupita. She accelerated into a dead run, heading straight up the Serdán. There was no way I could catch her, so I yelled at El Burro to chase her in his taxi. He tried. But Lupita ran and ran—Burro couldn't catch her. He chased her until she spotted him and began to dart in and out of buildings and alleys. She was clever . . . and she was gone.

The poor thing must have imagined her world collapsing. Must have been convinced that I was going back to my fiancée with a built-in little sister, and that there would be no place for her. That scenario was utterly inconceivable. But how was she to know that?

I walked back toward the hotel, intent on a couple of stiff drinks at the bar. As I neared the Rubi I spotted Enrique on the sitio corner rocking back and forth, his cigarette behind him. When I reached him he interrupted his cigarette dance and immediately hurried me into the bar.

Both he and Jesse were concerned. Everyone had heard that the *suegra* (mother-in-law) had been there with little sister. Señora D. had made quite a noisy scene, so everyone was already talking about the visit. I had a couple of tequila-and-beers on the house, and tried to calm down. When I quit shaking, I thanked them and walked up to the Colmenar, hoping that I'd find Lupita. No sign of her. Shit! I wanted to explain.

I kept an eye out for her around town that afternoon. At the Colmenar I asked Juanito to look out for her and to tell the other boleadores to do the same. Then I went serdane-ando. I even stopped by the Almita around six.

I asked folks in the restaurant to keep an eye out for Lupita, and I left messages at several taxi stands to send her to me if any of the taxistas saw her. From her reaction I feared that she'd go underground for a day or two. She had done that several times before when she was really pissed off.

As I walked back down to the Rubi around seven, heavy storm clouds darkened the western sky. This was the first time that the clouds had really piled up. The heat had been build-ing for weeks on end, so the shade from the storm bank had reduced the early evening temperature—it was only 102° or 103°, instead of 110°, but the humidity was fierce.

As we played dice in the front bar, black, boiling clouds continued to roll in from the Sea of Cortés, forming an omi-nous horizon. Jesse and Enrique were convinced that a gen-uine storm was moving in and that we'd lose the electricity. So they chose not to open the back bar that night.

349

The public bar's huge glass windows faced toward the harbor, offering natural light. It would be much easier to work there with the electricity out, and there should be enough of a breeze through the double malecón doors to provide relief.

In preparation for a storm they stuffed candles into the necks of several beer bottles, set them out, and checked flash-lights. Jesse pulled a huge camp lantern next to him under the bar, in case he either had to turn off the electricity or ward off ghosts. Jesse did not like the dark.

It was simply amazing to see this leaden sky after months of intense, unbroken sunshine. Everything looked different outside—forbidding and surreal.

According to the radio, the city of La Paz, on the Baja peninsula, had just been hammered by a hurricane—the first of the season. That storm had swept across the Sea of Cortés, north of Mazatlan. In Guaymas we were about to get the northern edge of the storm front.

As we tossed dice, Jesse interrupted. "*¡Mira! ¡Viene!* (Look! Here it comes!)*"* An immense ash-gray cloud rolled in less than a hundred feet off the water and swallowed the malecón. The first sheets of rain rattled on the front window, then passed.

I stepped out to the sidewalk with Enrique and stood, looking up, into the weird half-dark that sometimes accompanies a storm. The smell of ozone enveloped us. For thirty seconds or so it was eerily still. My ears popped just as Enrique exclaimed "*¿Qué?*" (What?) and held his ears—a major air-pressure change. Then the skies opened up with a roar.

My God, I was surprised! I expected the drops to be warm. But a spray of freezing cold rain hit me in the face, then the wind howled, rattling the bar's front windows. Just five minutes out front left us freezing and soaked. The air temperature had dropped about forty degrees in ten minutes.

At first I had enjoyed the cold rain immensely. With it came the deepest breath of cool air I had felt in months. But Jesse hollered to get inside as lightning exploded all around us.

Soaked, I told Jesse that I was going to my room to change clothes. As I walked down the long hallway to the lobby, the whole building shuddered in the storm and the lights went out.

I passed into the front lobby just as a group of the taxistas hurried inside. I asked what they were doing. They told me the electric lines were coming down. I stuck my nose out the front door and looked to the right, toward the shrimp-packing plant. Blue sparks were dancing off of the nearest transformer. By the time I turned my head again, long tongues of flames were shooting back and forth across nearby light poles, like a disco light display.

I ducked, shook my head in amazement for the benefit of the taxistas huddled there, then walked back to my room in the dark. I had candles, so lit one and changed into dry clothes. Then I went back to the bar with my flashlight in one hand and a spare Gokey shirt for Enrique in the other.

Several of us sat in the bar watching the rain. It came down in amazingly dense sheets. Within half an hour from the first drops on the front window, the Serdán out front started to flood. At times the wind blew so hard everyone expected the glass to break.

The Chapúltepec pavilion jitter-bugged on its pontoons like a bizarre carnival ride, alternately tilting back and forth then bobbing up and down. Soon the foaming seawater from the harbor and the rain water running down the streets collided into one turgid sheet that surged crazily back and forth through the seawall's drain holes.

The patrón, Hector Morales, rushed in and told us to close up. The regulars departed during a temporary lull. Meanwhile the rest of us shuttered everything we could, then closed the entire south side of the hotel.

The only lights in the hotel came from candles or flashlights as employees passed, battening down the hatches. As the storm raged, the hotel actually seemed sinister—flickering candlelight and long, dark hallways, punctuated by pounding rain and howling winds. The hotel's massive walls shuddered and moaned as the storm peaked. Two- or three-foot-deep waves washed against the lobby doors. I helped caulk the cracks with rags, so the water was only a few inches deep inside.

Huge quantities of water rushed down the side street next to my room—runoff from the immense sandstone promontory that rose four blocks behind the Rubi. All the steep streets that ran down to the harbor from the rugged hills above had become huge, temporary drains. They carried enormous quantities of water, debris, clothing, even furniture—all from the hillside neighborhoods above us, which were getting pounded by the storm.

By 10 P.M. most of the remaining taxistas and employees, excluding several night men, used a second lull in the storm to head home. Even going home was complicated. Hector Morales hired a taxi for them, but the streets were now flooding on blocks above the waterfront.

The taxi drivers who couldn't drive home had all taken their cars uphill several blocks and parked them in the cross streets. I drove the Rambler two blocks uphill in water deep enough to leak under the door sills and parked it in a narrow side street below a huge stone wall.

When I got back down the hill, soaking wet, I discovered that Ramón, El Huevón, had not shown up for his shift, so a half dozen businessmen, Eva, and two deskmen kept me company.

Eva was still in the hotel—an ill-timed liaison with one of the businessmen had left her stranded. I changed clothes for a second time, dug out a heavy Gokey field shirt for her and a big rain slicker I'd taken to Ecuador.

I covered her and took her upstairs to the balcony and settled into several big rocking chairs that overlooked the harbor; the shrimp plant was right below us. We sat there, the rain pounding all around, and talked. Eva was always charming and warm-hearted, and I'm not romanticizing her!

She snuggled up, bummed a smoke, and wanted to talk to me about Marta. She wanted me to know that Marta was upset over the "American" girl, and drinking again.

I told her I already had a blow-up with Marta over "La Rubia," but that there was absolutely nothing to it—I had just helped this girl and her mom out and had only ever seen her for an hour or so in Burro's taxi. That surprised Eva—apparently Marta had been indulging in lurid fantasies.

We talked until about midnight, when Eva told me she thought I ought to break it off with Marta. That it wasn't going to work out after all. Surprised, I asked why. Eva said, "Two reasons. You are not *macho* enough for her—that is what she is accustomed to. And she believes you love Lupita—it drives her wild."

353

I retorted, "But Lupita is just a little girl!" "So is Marta, Davíd. So is Marta." I told Eva I thought it was over anyway. She just smiled. I walked Eva to the Rambler when the storm subsided and drove her home.

In the car she asked more about Lupita. I told her that Marta had accused me of sleeping with her and how much that accusation had hurt my feelings, because I had been thinking of adopting her. That Kiami was going to recommend a lawyer. Eva was quiet for a minute, then leaned over and kissed me very gently on the cheek.

She said, "Well, I should have known that it was like that. You told me that she ran away today." I said, "Yes, she saw me with the *suegra* and the little sister." She said, "Davíd, have you told her you want to adopt her?" I said, "No. I was afraid she'd say 'no,' and I didn't know what I'd do."

Eva nodded, "So that's it—well you can't have them both, you know. Neither one of them will stand for it. You will have to choose." I said, "Eva, right now I'd choose Lupita. I'm deeply attached to her." She said, "Well, you know, Davíd, if you adopt her, you'll never get yourself a nice, educated, well-off señorita from the *gente fina* (upper class) here. You will have to settle for one of the working-class girls."

I said I didn't think that would be so bad. She grinned and laughed. Before she stepped out into the rain-slickened mud street, she told me to find Lupita and tell her how I felt about her. I promised I would.

By early morning the storm had passed and Guaymas began to dry out, leaving sodden streets, leaking roofs, no electricity, and huge amounts of mud and debris all over el centro. The afternoon newspaper was late coming out but, while reading it, I realized just how bad the storm had been. Tragically, several people had drowned the night before, including an unidentified young girl. I panicked, convinced that it was Lupita.

354

I left my meal unfinished at the Colmenar and rushed back to the Sitio Rubi, where old Mateo drove me to the morgue. I had no clue where it was. I walked in alone, numb with fear. A young attendant ushered me to the corpse. As he pulled the sheet back, I began shaking uncontrollably, certain I would see Lupita's face.

Mercifully, I was wrong. What a relief when it turned out not to be Lupita! Relieved or not, by then I was so light-headed that I had to sit down. Tragically, it was one of the young girls who rode around with the sleazier taxi drivers to turn an occasional late-night trick. I doubt that she was more than fourteen or fifteen.

I'd seen her a few times in the taxis at night and been told she was in el ambiente (prostitution). Hopeful, the attendant asked if I wanted to claim the body—someone would have to take care of her funeral expenses. I shook my head. All I wanted was to get out of that place.

Mateo was waiting outside to take me back. He looked inquisitive as I stepped in. I shook my head, "no." He nodded and we pulled away.

That night was clear and cool, one of the prettier ones I remember in Guaymas. It felt almost like an early spring evening—a dark gunbarrel-blue sky, a cool breeze in the air, and the rich, spicy smells of a thousand meals being prepared.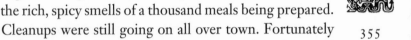

Cleanups were still going on all over town. Fortunately most of the damage had been superficial, even though several people had drowned in the cascading torrents of runoff from the rocky crags behind the town.

I asked everywhere to see if anyone had spotted Lupita. No sign of her. I hoped some of the boleadores and other street kids might have seen her, but they'd all vanished as the police, Red Cross, and uniformed navy men from the small base nearby descended on el centro to assist with the cleanup.

Upset that I couldn't find Lupita, I drove out to the Miramar to see Negro. Busy with cleanup at the hotel, he suggested I go up the beach and relax. Go fishing. Have a beer. I said goodbye and drove over to Playas Primaverales.

I hadn't spent as much time there in recent weeks, partly because of the heat and partly because my life in el centro had been keeping me busy. Manuel, our local "Zorba the Greek" wasn't around, so I talked to some of the other barmen, swapping accounts of the *tempestad* (tempest, storm).

It got late and I still had my hammock in the Rambler, so hung it in my palapa about ten. Swinging gently to the rhythm of the surf, I watched the stars. No good. I was simply too restless to sleep. And it seemed strange to be in my hammock at Primaverales once again. That belonged to a phase of my life now over.

Agitated, I gave up about one-thirty in the morning, rolled the hammock, tossed it into the Rambler again, and drove back to the Rubi. On a night like this I would ordinarily have put in an appearance at the Río Rita, then the Almita, but wasn't in the mood. So I retreated to my room and again tried to sleep, but couldn't. I chain-smoked Mexican Raleighs, wishing I had saved some of the smooth Pall Malls I had brought in as fayuca on my last trip. I'd sold them all.

Finally I pulled on my boots and tip-toed through the lobby where El Huevón was asleep on the couch, then walked quietly upstairs to the balcony. I rocked, paced, smoked, and worried about Lupita.

I didn't know it then, but was to discover in just a few days that Lupita could actually see me from her hideaway on the roof of the packing plant as I smoked and rocked on the balcony. I could have thrown a baseball to her had I known. But I didn't know.

On Friday night I decided to go out to the Río Rita, followed by a late dinner at the Almita. It was time to quit worrying and enjoy life. But it wasn't easy. Everywhere I asked, nobody had heard from Lupita. Not even Juanito, who gave me a shine at the Colmenar. He was panicky without her, but reminded me she had gone into hiding before when she was pissed off. After a shrimp dinner at the Colmenar, I worked my way back to the Rubi, serdaneando on the way. Time to spruce up for a Friday night floor show.

That night we reenacted our now classic Rubi bar-closing routine about eleven and went out to the Río Rita. Negro came in from the Miramar and Saldívar from the Ladies Bar. Enrique Velarde went with us for a change. We took both the old Rambler and Negro's turquoise and black Ford Crown Vic.

Chang greeted us at the door and installed us at a good table. Mariquita waved and smiled—I had taken her and a couple of the other girls to the beach a few days before. That had impressed the hell out of the taxistas, but I wasn't balling any of them, so it was fun and uncomplicated.

We took in the floor show and had a good time talking to the girls. Chang came over and went through several Coca Colas, chugging them compulsively while he caught up on Jesse's parrot jokes. Enrique was too much of a straight arrow to go to the zona often, but he certainly enjoyed the floor show.

He was a delight to watch when he saw a pretty girl. His eyebrows would go up and he would get a huge Cheshire-cat grin. He was so expressive—he'd roll his eyes, wiggle his mustache, and flick his cigarette compulsively while he blushed. Just like he did the day he helped me lift La Rubia into Burro's taxi for the trip to Hermosillo.

The evening ended with a late-night meal after a two-car race to the Almita through muddy streets. Ana María was her usual upbeat self and the milanesa was great. I was feeling good again. Everything would be okay. I tried to stick to my routine over the next few days, but street life just didn't seem the same without Lupita around to cook up conspiracies.

It was an unsettling week. A few afternoons later Jesse and

I were standing by the front window of the public bar when a flatbed truck carrying a *trapiche* (cane press) came roaring around the corner. There were a half-dozen men in there with the press, trying to open the huge rollers that had jammed shut on one fellow's arm. That poor man was screaming and trying to pull his arm out of the press.

Ten feet from the front windows of the hotel's public bar his coworkers struggled frantically to get the machine open. And they were having no success. After standing there riveted to the spot by the poor bastard's screams, we ran out with a large iron bar to help. We tried to wedge open the trapiche. Impossible.

There was blood and pulped arm everywhere. Two minutes later the driver waved us off and sped away, shouting for us to call the social security hospital. Jesse ran in and phoned.

I hate to paint such a distressing scene, but it was part and parcel of life in Guaymas. We read about the details several days later in the newspaper. The poor guy caught in the press was young, perhaps twenty-three or twenty-four. The surgeons had to amputate his arm right there in the truck bed to free him from that damn press. Fate left him with one arm, a pretty severe economic problem for a farmhand.

As I read about the young man who'd gotten his arm smashed, someone at the bar commented, "Dear Lord, where is he going to get a job now? What kind of work can he get with one arm?"

People worried about these things. They could happen to you. Mexico wasn't like the States, where bad stuff always happens to some other unlucky son of a bitch. These things happened to you, or to people you knew—and if not to them, to people you saw daily on the street.

In the States we expect, even demand, a perfect world. Healthy babies with ten fingers and toes. A pretty wife. An educated husband. A fair boss. A benign government. Excellent schools. Smooth roads. New cars. A free education. Nice house. TV. Our list is endless.

In the Guaymas of 1970, no one I knew on the street had a TV at home. People stood on the street in front of appliance stores every afternoon to watch the TV news from Hermosillo. For the taxistas, cantineros, waiters, and others I knew, a great day in paradise meant "I ate twice, got laid, have forty pesos in my pocket, two smokes left for bedtime, and some real friends." End of list.

That whole week I kept an eye out for Lupita. But I didn't see hide nor hair of her. So I went nightclubbing. I went out to Miramar a number of times. I even went fishing off the rocks, harkening back to my early days in Guaymas. Of course I wasn't going to run fayuca or a new movida without Lupita. I could have, but I didn't.

My journal from this period was erratic, but I think it may have been about the beginning of September when we got another big blow moving in. According to the radio there had been another hurricane across La Paz. Now it was our turn again.

The first tempest off the Sea of Cortés had been a doozy. Now it seemed like the rains came about every other night. As the latest storm rolled in I lay in my room with my hands behind my head, both windows wide open. It had begun raining while I was at the Río Rita, so I left early, about one-thirty in the morning. I didn't want to get the Rambler stuck in the red clay streets out near the zona.

Just as it had the week before, the rain quickly shorted out the transformer strapped to the electric pole above the Sitio Rubi, fifteen yards from my room. Then the side street flooded.

As a precaution I had already parked the Rambler behind the hotel near the corazón de la India tree under which Burro and I had first sold our fans. Then I curled up inside my room with a book, my net bag full of ice and Orange Crushes, and candles. As a child I had always loved the sounds, smells, and enveloping chaos of a storm.

When the lights went out I set my candle in the bathroom, lay in the dark, and listened to nature unfettered. By two in the morning I pretty much had the hotel to myself.

The usual coming and going of taxis outside my window had stopped, and there was none of the occasional ringing of the sitio's telephone. I was deeply engaged in the roar of the storm. No distractions. Every time lightning struck nearby, I breathed in the ozone and shivered, just as I had done since age five.

About three the storm began to blow itself out, the wind dropping quickly to below ten knots and the torrents settling down to a drizzle. Still daydreaming and trying to slip off to sleep, I listened to the lull, then thought I heard someone call my name, "¡Güero! ¡Güero!"

I chalked it up to my imagination, then thought I heard it again. So I got up, went to my north window, and looked out. This time I was certain someone called me—then sobbed. Oh, my God! Somewhere out there, probably on the roof of the shrimp-packing plant, Lupita was calling me.

I pulled on my boots and a shirt, then headed for the lobby. Fat Ramón was asleep, dead to the world, and had already locked the leaking front lobby doors. I panicked when I realized I couldn't go out that way, so returned to my room, unhitched the screen, and went out the window.

Man, it was wet out there! The wind had died down, but there was water everywhere, running down the street and covering the sidewalks. I looked around the corner at my car and saw that it was okay. Up to the hubs in water but no real damage. I waded across the street to the big wire gates at the rear of the packing plant. I opened them, slipped in, and called to Lupita.

She answered! On the roof there was the shell of a concrete room. She was in it. I shouted, "Lupita come down here! You can spend the night in the room with me."

Groaning and bawling, she called back that she couldn't. I asked what was the matter. She groaned back, "¡Estoy enferma! (I'm sick!)" "How?" I shouted. "I'm all bloody. I'm bleeding inside." I asked, "Can you move?" "No!" she bawled. So I asked, "Well, how the hell do I get up there?" She cried, "Climb the boxes!"

So I climbed a tall, treacherous stack of wooden palettes, slipping and cursing. I managed to reach the roof over the loading dock, climbed a concrete parapet above it, and worked my way toward Lupita.

She was inside her little concrete shelter. It was dark, and in my panic I'd forgotten a flashlight, so couldn't see much. I fumbled, then scooped her into my arms and pulled her to me. I cradled her and again asked what was wrong. She said she was all bloody.

When I had first grabbed her I thought she was just wet,

but after a minute or two I realized I was sticking to her. She was hemorrhaging somewhere. I asked if she had cut herself. She said, "No." She said she had started bleeding and having cramps earlier in the night.

She whined, "Oh, I prayed for you to come back from the zona. I crawled to the front with my head out so I could see your room. Finally I saw you standing in the doorway of your room and I knew you had come."

So I drug her out and started down the roof. She clutched me tight, telling me she was "sorry," over and over. I got a better look at her as we reached the edge of the roof. Light was coming from somewhere.

Dear God! She was a bloody mess. The bottom of her smock was soaked in blood. She had to have been bleeding a while, because it had already started to clot. I asked, "Where's the blood coming from? Did somebody stab you?" She said that she was bleeding like a señorita. I said, "You mean from the vagina?" She looked at me and said, "*Yo no sé que es* (I don't know what that is)." So I said, "From the *panocha?* (pussy?)" She said, "yes."

I told her we were going to the hospital and asked if she could hold on to my back as we went down. She said, "I'm going to bleed more like that." I said, "You've got to! I can't get you off this *pinche* (frigging) roof holding you in my arms."

She asked me to retrieve a little cardboard box for her. I grabbed it and held it open while she reached in and pulled something out, then asked me to look away. Apparently she plugged herself with it. Done, she wrapped her skinny arms around my neck and hung on for dear life. I told her if she got faint to tell me. Partway down she said she was starting to faint, so I stopped, balanced, and whipped off my dad's canvas and brass army belt and opened it all the way.

Then I slipped it under her butt and around my waist and cinched it so she had a seat to hang on to. I told her to lock her hands tight. It must have taken me fifteen minutes to get her down. Miraculously, I only slipped once or twice but didn't fall backward on her. By then it was raining harder again.

I got her into the courtyard and uncinched her. She had about had it—shaking like a leaf. So I carried her across the street. Wading through the torrents of water, I got her onto the Rambler's front seat, her legs up and against the front passenger window, her head next to me. She was still shaking. Shock! I jumped out, pulled an army blanket out of the trunk, wrapped her in it, wiped off my glasses, and prayed the Rambler would start.

It cranked right up. Thank God! Now I had to find a route to the hospital that wasn't flooded. The water was still coming down heavily in the side streets, running from the hills above town. So I drove uphill, then due north, crossing one block above the plaza on Avenida 16, then turned down at Calle 19, near the Sitio Medrano, turned right again, and pulled up behind Sánchez's clinic.

Relieved, I jumped out and pounded on the clinic door. Lupita had gotten quiet, which scared the hell out of me. I knew from my emergency-room work that the noisy ones often survive and the quiet ones are in real trouble. So I kept pounding.

After several minutes a watchman came to the door, pissed off—"The clinic is closed!" I snarled, "Well, for God's sake, can you get it open? Can you get Doctor Sánchez in here?" He said, "No, no! The doctor doesn't come in at night. He has no patients staying in the clinic. Closed!" I snarled again,

"Where's the pinche hospital?" He said, "Well, which one?" I said, "The closest!"

Just then Juanito, Lupita's little ward, emerged from the passage to the Colmenar, hollering, "Güero, Güero, I saw your car!" I yelled, "Juanito I've got Lupita with me! She is sick. We need to go to the hospital. Do you know where it is?" He answered, "Oh, yes."

"Which one's the closest?" He croaked, "El Municipal." I pleaded, "Well, *por Dios*, get in. Show me!"

He jumped in with his wooden box—too valuable to leave anywhere—and stood over the back of the seat. I slammed the door and took off again, telling him, "We need to find a route that isn't flooded." The street kids knew every inch of the downtown. He guided me to the old municipal hospital in seven or eight minutes.

On the way, he stood over the seat, sobbing, "*¿Vive, la Lupita?* (Is Lupita alive?)*" I told him she was. I'd checked the pulse in her neck. Thin. Reedy. Far too fast, but still beating. I asked Juanito why he was in the passage instead of at home. He told me his mother was mad at him because he hadn't brought as much money home since Lupita disappeared. This was the downside of paradise.

We parked at the base of a long set of steps up to the old city hospital. Juanito helped me pull Lupita out and guided me up. I couldn't see well, carrying her. I was winded when we reached the door, so Juanito started banging.

After several minutes of standing there in the rain, an older nun came to the door and asked what was the matter. I told them, carrying Lupita past her. She told me there was no doctor in the house that night, so I asked her to call one. She couldn't. She said the phones weren't working. Jesus!

I turned to Juanito and asked him to go to the social security hospital—swim if he had to—and get a doctor. I offered a hundred pesos, but he was already heading out the door. The other hospital was about a half-mile away. So Lupita's misshapen little ward hustled off into the raging storm, one leg dragging.

I told the nun, "We've got to get this kid a bed!" She took one look at Lupita and ushered me down a long corridor, into a gallery-style dormitory. It was basic. Old-fashioned iron cots lined up in a row. She asked, "Well, who will be responsible for her?" I said, "I'm her godfather and will pay for everything."

Lupita made weak gurgling and mewing noises, but that was all. They wanted me to leave, but I refused.

I could hear a generator going, so they had lights. I laid Lupita on a cot while the nun got pissed off over what a mess she was. They made me stand outside a screen while they looked her over, undressed her, and got a gown on her. I asked them to find several warm blankets for her. Lupita was in deep shock.

I also asked them to get a transfusion going. They said they had no way to type blood at that time of night and that the storm had knocked out the little refrigerator where they kept plasma. I said, "Well, for God's sake, can you get any saline solution?" They said they didn't know if they should do that without a doctor. "Check her vital signs! She'll die without treatment."

The older nun was defiant—wait for a doctor was her drill. But a younger one dressed in white went for a nurse, and they got an IV drip going. They hung a bottle of saline from a metal pole. I raised it as high as I could, straightened her little arm, and got a fairly good drip going into her by squeezing the bag very gently to keep it flowing. After a while Lupita started to come around. I was so relieved.

I asked for a chair and said I was going to stay. The young nun who had got the nurse said, "They're going to get angry." I said, "No matter. I am her only family and am going to stay with her. That's all there is to it." She didn't protest any further.

Then she asked what I knew about the case. I said, "Nothing." That she'd gone missing for a few days and I had worried about her. That's when she told me that the older nun thought Lupita was pregnant and miscarrying. I said, "You've got to be kidding! She's just a little girl—only ten years old." I found the older nun's "diagnosis" unbelievable. I was barely civil when the old harridan asked if I were the unborn child's father. She stayed away after that exchange. Perhaps it was my tone, or the look of cold rage in my eyes. I didn't care which.

366

By then the warm blankets and saline drip were really beginning to have an effect. I held my hand on Lupita's little wrist. Her pulse was down to about a hundred and a lot stronger. She was beginning to come around and to talk. The nurse and the young nun wanted information. The nurse was into the sex thing, too.

Lupita wouldn't talk, so they asked me to question her. "Lupita, have you been with a man?" Astonishing me, she said, "Yes. But I didn't want to." I said, "Are you sure you slept with a man? Do you know what that is?" She said, "Yes. *Me metí con un hombre*," explaining again that she didn't want to, that he had hurt her, then afterward paid her two hundred pesos.

She told us she was scared so didn't say anything. I was having a tough time with this. "Who?" I asked. "A sailor," she whispered. No wonder she didn't like sailors. I was sick.

I flashed on the night Jesse had refused to let her in the bar, "Don't bring her in here. One of these days when she starts talking that stuff about taking some guy out behind the corner, some sick SOB is going to take her seriously." Out loud I said, "Oh, my God!" Then, regaining my composure, I reassured her, "The doctor will be here. I sent for a doctor."

I asked, "Lupita, where's your mom? It's time you told me." She said she didn't know. She had left with a man and promised to come back. "She asked me to wait for her." "Recently?" I asked. She shook her head, "no."

I asked "Well, how old were you when your mother left?" She said, "Maybe five or six, I'm not sure." I pressed, "Well, how old are you now?" She said, "I think eleven, but I'm not sure," then began crying and twisting around.

367

I asked, "Are you in a lot of pain?" She said yes, that her *panzón* (stomach) was killing her. Persistent, I asked if she knew her full name. She shook her head. "No." "Do you have family?" was the next question. She murmured, "no." I said, "Well, you had to have been born somewhere. Did anyone ever say?" She didn't respond. "Lupita, were you born in an orphanage?" She whispered, "No, I think I was born in a place called the Club del Bosque."

Not thinking, I exclaimed, "But that is a *casa de viejas* (cat house) in Torreón!" Sobbing, she looked away, then answered, "Yes, my mother was a *puta* (whore)." . . . I sat speechless at the head of her bed, hating myself. I'd pushed too hard and made her yield up her most private secret in front of strangers. What a terrible thing to have done!

Lupita with her big eyes and shaggy mop of hair had apparently been born in a whorehouse in Torreón, across the Sierra in north-central Mexico. In fact the same damn place where La Blanca, one of the girls at the Río Rita, had once told me she had been born.

I looked down at my little mandadera, born in a whorehouse, abandoned on the street when she was five or six, and silenced for a lousy two hundred pesos (sixteen dollars) after some sailor forced himself on her. My head was swimming. I had come to see her not merely as my clever little mandadera, but as my child!

About five in the morning she again began to bleed heavily and slipped back into shock. I asked the young nun to get another bottle of saline solution and to find out what had happened with the doctor. She said she'd ask. Presently she came back and told me that a crippled boy had come to the door a while ago and that the older nun wouldn't let him in. But the boy had told them at the door that a doctor at the social security hospital had said he would come.

On around five fifteen or so in the morning, Lupita started going into convulsions. She was in agony and delirious, calling me *papi* (daddy). God, I felt bad.

Just before five-thirty, a young doctor came in. Nice-looking, clean-cut, Mexico City accent. He wasn't thrilled to be there, but examined her immediately. She woke up, screamed, and cried. The doctor pulled the stethoscope off, looked up and asked me in accented English, "Does she understand English?" I said, "No, none." So he said, "There is no baby, but it might be a ruptured tubal pregnancy.

"We're going to have to operate quickly if we are to save her. I'm going to ask them to get an operating room ready."

I asked, "Are you sure it has to be done that way?"

He said, "Yes. That's her only chance. She's in bad shape. She's too young. She's lost a lot of blood. I've sent down for some plasma. We've got to get some blood into her. Whoever got the saline going into her probably has saved her life so far." Momentarily that made me feel a bit better.

He returned after a few minutes and said, "Well, they're getting things ready. How is she doing?" I answered, "Poorly. She's cramping. I can see her belly heaving. She's bleeding again." He checked her vitals once more and began calling down the hall to see if things were ready—but they weren't.

That's when Lupita screamed for her mother, "*¡Mami, te esperé!* (Mommy, I waited for you!)" waking several nearby patients. One cursed her. More nightmare!

369

I stroked her hands. She grabbed my wrists, holding on for dear life as she writhed in pain. She had bit clean through her lower lip, and was bleeding all over her face faster than the sweet, young nun could wipe her off.

The doctor shouted again, "*¡Ándale! ¡Ándale!*" to get things moving in surgery. But it was too late. At about twenty to six in the morning, with her little hands wrapped around my wrists so tight I couldn't get away from her, she screamed, "*¡Güero! ¡Me muero!* (Güero, I'm dying!)"

She began breathing erratically and frothing at the mouth. The young doctor jumped up and pounded on her chest, but there was nothing to be done. She died just before six in the morning.

I knew when it happened because she lost her grip on my wrists as she died. Her little hands fell down. I was crying silently. It was the first time I had cried in years, tears just running down. There she lay, blood from her lip all over her face.

So frail. So little.

The young doctor apologized profusely. He was beyond speaking in English now, his Spanish flowing. He said, "I came too late. I came too late!"

Remembering rule two, "Don't blame the one who tried to help," I said, "No, what could be done? No phones. A stormy night. You came when you were called." Then I asked the young nun, "What now?" She said, "You'll have to leave." I said, "Okay, I'll leave. What's to be done next?" She said, "Well, I'll find out." I said, "Let me know, won't you? I'm señor Stuart and I'm at room 21 in the Hotel Rubi. She is my goddaughter and employee. I will take the responsibility."

So I walked out. By then it was dawn and, just like the previous storm, incongruously clear, a touch of coolness in the air. Numb, I walked down that long flight of steps. They seemed endless.

Juanito was asleep on the backseat of the Rambler. I got in, reached back, and tussled his hair. He stuck his head up, asking "¿La Lupita?" I said, "Oh, we'll talk about that later." He insisted, "¿La Lupita? I want to know how she is." So I told him, "She's gone. She's dead!"

"Did you love her, Güero?" he asked. I said, "Yes, like my daughter. Why do you ask?" He said, "Well, she had told us so. She told all of us in the street, *en la calle*, but I didn't know whether to believe it." I said, "Well, it was so. *Pues, así fue*. He sobbed softly in the backseat as I drove.

I dropped Juanito off in front of the Pasaje Marví on the Serdán, just as a crystal-clear day was breaking and the town was stirring. As he stepped out, clutching his shoeshine box, he confided, "I loved her, too!" Then, convulsed in grief, he shuffled away.

THE TEMPESTS

fifteen

DARKNESS IN PARADISE

I drove back to the Rubi. By then the lobby doors were open. As I entered, El Huevón, who had finally awakened, asked me where I had found a place to be whoring around until morning on such a stormy night. The man was a delight. For one moment I considered whipping out my Buck knife and sticking him in the guts. But I resisted the impulse and said nothing.

Lupita had become MY business. Guaymas had not taken care of her. What happened now was MY job. If I made a fuss about her, there would be talk on the street. She would be remembered only as a little puta, like her mom. No way!

Even though I was exploding inside, Alonzo Chang's "Rule of Silence" was the way to go. I owed it to Lupita. So I went back to my room, closed the door quietly, turned on my fan, and lay down. Later, when Marisol came to clean, I let her pound.

About three in the afternoon, the deskman knocked, shouting through the transom that I had an important visitor. So I pulled on my boots and went out front. The little nun had come. We went upstairs to talk on the balcony.

The doctor wanted to know if I wanted a postmortem to determine the cause of death. Incredulous, I asked if I were allowed to decide. She nodded. The gringo in me wanted answers. But El Güero wanted Lupita, his mandadera, whole. Just as she had wanted her trophy fish. I shook my head, "no."

She told me the body would be ready to claim by evening. I told her I would meet her later at the hospital and would appreciate any advice that she could give me. She said, "Surely," and left. Depressed and exhausted, I returned to my room, locked myself in again, and slept until evening.

That evening I got up, made a brief appearance at the bar, then drove to the municipal hospital, where the young nun in white was waiting for me, accompanied by a different older nun in black habit. Lupita's body had already been taken to a nearby mortuary.

I asked what I needed to do next, how to claim the body and make funeral arrangements. The young nun offered to go with me, looking to the older one for permission. She smiled, nodding, and pushed the young one toward me.

Following her directions we arrived at a modest funeral parlor. The little nun asked if this place was "satisfactory." I nodded. We stepped inside. I braced myself.

She told me they had gotten a small burial plot assigned in the municipal graveyard—where Lupita and I had met señor X. She said that Lupita should be buried quickly. "Tomorrow?" I asked. She nodded, then reminded me that there would be *gastos* (expenses). I said, "No problem. I brought money to settle arrangements." Then she whispered ever so softly, "It is time."

I nodded and swallowed. The funeral attendant who had been standing silently nearby ushered us into a small side room, off the old-fashioned parlor where we had entered. My little mandadera was laid out, awaiting me.

She looked small and pale. Peaceful except for her tiny hands curled defiantly, as if she were still clutching my wrists. I looked down at the red and purple bruise starting to encircle my right wrist, created when she had clung to me just thirteen hours before. For a moment I simply wanted to lie down beside her, cuddle her, and rest. I was so very tired.

The nun touched me on the arm, drawing me away. It was time to make arrangements. I asked the funeral director for a small casket. He said that his workers had already started a small, plain wooden one for her. I said, "That is fine. Can you paint it blue?" He looked surprised, but said, "Of course."

373

I asked them to find her a bright blue dress and shoes to match. He nodded. In Mexico a child like this would almost always be buried in pure white. But I was a gringo—so he went with it. No telling what he actually thought.

"Flowers?" he asked. "Red *buganvilla—tres ramitas* (three sprigs)." He hesitated. Red is the color of passion, not innocence. This had begun with bougainvillea. I intended to end it with the same. I repeated, "*Tres Ramitas. Buganvilla—SU favorita* (Three sprigs of Bougainvillea—HER favorite)." He nodded, "Of course."

"Anything else?" he asked. "A padre and a six-piece brass band—one of the *cofradías*, perhaps—and a few more to help with the casket and a proper procession." He nodded. "The hearse?" "A pickup truck. Can that be arranged?" "Her favorite?" he asked. I nodded. "Of course," he answered. "One o'clock tomorrow," I suggested.

Finished, he estimated the bill, telling me I'd pay the cofradía separately. I paid cash—less then three hundred dollars. I wanted Lupita to have the funeral she had admired at the graveyard in July.

As we walked out I asked the little nun if she would attend. She seemed surprised, "Is there no one else?" "Two, perhaps, but no relatives." She said she'd be there, but looked very sad. I dropped her off at the convent of Sagrado Corazón (Sacred Heart) near the hospital and told her I'd come for her the next day.

I stopped by the Colmenar and sipped from my bowl of soup. Mercifully, Juanito appeared. I asked quietly if he'd like to be with me the next day. He shook his head, "no." I asked again, even more softly, as he finished my boots. "*No me aguanto* (I can't handle it)," he sniveled. He was terrified without Lupita. It was a huge loss for him.

That evening I spent a little time in the bar, listening distractedly to Jesse's parrot jokes and watching Enrique rock back and forth on his heels, laughing, cigarette behind him. At one point Jesse came over. "Why so quiet, Davíd?" I shrugged. "¿La Flaca (Marta)?" he suggested. I nodded. End of story. Truth be told, I was in the numb stage of grief.

That night I walked for hours. The first time I passed by Lupita's streetlight my heart pounded. I wanted her to be there. Then came the sick ache in my gut. She wasn't coming back. Our adventures were over.

About 3 A.M. I tried to sleep. As I lay on my bed, I looked over to the roof of the packing plant, remembering Lupita's "nest" up there. I slipped out a side door behind the lobby and climbed to her hiding hole, my net bag stuffed in my pants.

When I reached her secret place, I discovered I could see my room in one direction and her favorite lamppost in the other. The lamppost had to have been where her mother once left her. Lupita's whole world had apparently revolved around it.

It took me only five minutes to retrieve her possessions. I stuffed everything in the bag, climbed down, and waved at the taxistas in passing. I ducked into my room, lit a smoke, and went through her stuff.

It was a tragic assortment of odds and ends. The torn Gokey shirt I had loaned her at the motel on our first trip to "the other side." Some notes—several that I had written her to take to people and others in a handwriting I didn't recognize. A change and a half of clothes. Some rags, including the dress she had worn daily when I first met her. One of my business cards from Ecuador—she had obviously nicked it from my room at some point. Several matchbooks—one from the hotel in Tucson, another from Denny's in Nogales, and the Guerrero matchbox featuring Hernán Cortés.

375

The most poignant items were an empty pack of my Pall Mall reds, carefully flattened; a lock of my distinctive wavy brown-black hair, which she had probably scooped up from the hotel's barbershop floor; and several folded "notes" on wide-lined grade-school paper where she had attempted to write my name.

I sat on the bed, the pathetic remains of her life arranged around me like a miniature altar. I cried, silently. Tears flooded down my cheeks. I was full of remorse. She should not have had to die to get the blue dress she so badly wanted!

I went into the shower and soaked, as if my sorrow could be washed away. When I came out, I separated her things into a memento pile, which went into my dad's footlocker, and a "give to Gorda" pile. The small amount of cash she had left up there went into my rear pocket for Juanito. Since she was his patrona, I reckoned he was her beneficiary.

The next day I got up late, ran down to the bar for my Orange Crushes, then went back to the room to dress for her funeral. First I laid out my good clothes, then I remembered that she preferred me "dressed as El Güero." So I put on my best tan field shirt, pressed Wranglers, Red Wings, and the Panama hat I'd brought from Ecuador.

I walked out and cranked up the Rambler, stopping at Gorda's. I told her about Lupita and asked if she wanted to go with me. She sagged and said she couldn't . . . "not since I buried my husband. No more funerals." I told her I understood, gave her the odd bag of clothes, and walked back toward the car. She was in her corner window, sobbing, as I closed the car door and pulled away.

The little nun was waiting for me as promised. We went to the funeral home and I got one last look at Lupita before they closed her little, blue casket. The blue dress helped. They had combed her hair nicely, her blue barrettes holding back her shaggy mop.

I leaned to her, kissed her forehead, called her "hijita," and finally told her I loved her. Then I put my Timex in her hand and told her that her mom would meet her by the lamppost *en un ratito* (in a little while), and that both of them would be in Heaven within two hours, "gringo time."

The little nun was crying softly when I straightened up and put the sprigs of bougainvillea into her other hand. She gave Lupita a little rosary. I leaned over once more and removed her blue butterfly barrettes, putting them in my buttoned shirt pocket.

Then I motioned us out. We walked away quickly. I didn't want to hear them drive the nails into her coffin.

At the cemetery we waited for the pickup. It arrived in a few minutes, casket, band, and extras crammed in the bed. Black, old, beat-up, and round-top, it was perfect. The driver, funeral director, and one extra were in the cab.

The maestro of the band looked amazed when he stepped out and saw me. I wasn't what he expected. His eyes went immediately from my face down to the boots that folks talked about on the street.

He figured it out, nodding knowingly, but said nothing. He turned smartly and pulled his group into formation for the procession I had requested. Mended white guayaberas, black pants. Pickup truck, brass band, the nun and I, then the mourners—hats in hand. The band struck up the same slow-cadenced march Lupita and I had first heard in July.

377

The old pickup truck groaned and rattled up the hill, until it could go no further. Then four of us grabbed the rope handles of Lupita's little casket and carried her the final yards up the hill, the young nun walking in front of us. God, it was hot. And every second seemed like an hour.

The young padre awaited us by the grave. He gave a short service. But I don't remember much about it. When they were ready to lower her into the grave, I asked for another Sousa march. That's when I noticed a small spray of yellow flowers on the casket. I looked around, surprised.

Burro's taxi was on the hill above. He stood there, just an outline in his plaid shirt a hundred yards away, a woman next to him. It was too far away to see who she was, so I just nodded.

As the padre pronounced the benediction I could hear children playing in the barrio where Lupita and I had once eaten tacos. Then they lowered my mandadera into her grave, and the little nun threw in the first handful of dirt. I couldn't.

More silent tears streaming down my face, we walked down the hill in procession, the band playing a final funeral dirge. The nun waited for me at the door of the truck while I paid the band's maestro and thanked them all. We stood and watched the battered truck pull away. It was over.

I turned back to the nun and told her, "I feel so bad. I never told Lupita I loved her when she was alive." She consoled me, "Well at least she had someone to cry for her. So many of them don't, you know."

378

Lupita gone, I simply tried to go back to my routine. To that point my whole life had been a search for somewhere I fit in, some place I could belong—a place where darkness came only in the night. Guaymas had given me a taste of that.

I didn't want to lose it on top of losing Lupita. I needed the warmth of my friends, my place on the street, hearing my name called as I did my rounds. And I wanted the blue skies, bright colors, food I could taste. All of these Guaymas things were intoxicating.

I thought it would be easy to put Lupita out of my mind and hold onto the rest. But it wasn't. Since childhood I had dealt with bad things by detaching from the events around me. I was good at it. Or so I thought.

As I sat in the Rubi bar after Lupita's funeral I simply

could not erase her face from my mind. In my imagination I leaned over to call her "hijita" again and again, hoping that she would open her eyes, come to attention, and rise from her casket—if only I did it perfectly. But, try as I might, Lupita would neither open her eyes for me, nor go away. Losing mental control I began to panic, so went serdaneando.

Once on the street I felt better. I hadn't been able to breathe inside the bar—it had become suffocating. I took deep breathes and walked. Yes, good. I was in control again . . . until I passed her lamppost.

Then she came back, walking along with me, insisting we go to the border to fill more orders for fans. I kept telling her I loved her, but she couldn't hear me. So I shouted at her. Still no response. My God, it was yet another nightmare!

Thankfully one of the boleadores with his shoeshine box tugged at me, wanting a shine. That snapped me out of my twisted daydream. I shook my head and took more deep breaths.

379

I thought he'd ask about Lupita, but he didn't. In fact almost no one had. It was amazing how quickly and quietly she disappeared from daily life. It was as if you had pulled your hand out of a bucket of water to observe the space your hand had just occupied close over—as if it had never been there. My silence on the matter was a big factor, but I expected the street kids to notice the loss of one of their own. Apart from Juanito, they seemed oblivious. That rattled me.

I walked on up to the Colmenar and chatted with Mercedes. She was bubbly and pleasant, as always. I had a café con leche and sat outside by the fan to read the paper. No news in it of Lupita. Thank God for small favors.

Soon Juanito came by, calling me "patrón"—he needed

another protector. I remembered Lupita's stash of pesos in my rear pocket and gave them to him, "*herencia de la patrona* (Lupita's bequest to him)." He sobbed and choked on one of the massive gobs of snot that were one of his medical trademarks. Man, he was dirty and smelly. Then I remembered that Lupita had been caring for him until she went to ground. Poor thing.

Time to visit La Gorda. After coffee I walked him along Avenida 15, which zigzagged past several old plazas a block behind the Serdán. At Gorda's, she ushered us into her corner room—the first time I had been in it.

380

It was big and the tall, barred windows made it seem even bigger. A bed in one corner, a small dining table and two chairs, two *roperos* ("his" and "hers" wardrobes, I guessed), a wooden bench, and a big rocker made up the furniture. A two-burner propane stove and a small cast-concrete sink served as the kitchen. Her beans were simmering. The smell of cilantro, fabulous. No telling where the toilet was.

On one wall her tin Virgin of Guadalupe was graced with two lit candles. As I looked at it, she nodded, "La Lupita." "*¿Y su marido?* (and your husband?)" I asked. She nodded again. "*Era buen hombre. Muy trabajador* (He was a good man—a hard worker)." Then we got down to business.

I explained Juanito's relationship to Lupita. This wasn't entirely news to Gorda, but she didn't interrupt. We arranged for beans, rice, tortillas, and an egg every other day, along with two trips a week to "the shower" and his clothes cleaned. Juanito appeared uncertain of the prospect, until Gorda said he could take Lupita's place at her table—it was still set for the meals she had never come back to eat.

"*¿De veras?* (Really?)" croaked Juanito, smiling as best he could. "Yes," she nodded. Still staring expectantly at Lupita's empty place, Juanito said he didn't have a change of clothes to leave so that his could be washed. I pressed a hundred pesos into Gorda's hand for the month's food and another forty for Juanito's second-hand change of clothes. She was ushering him to Lupita's place at the table as I walked out.

When I passed her window she was already mothering Juanito, asking him if he liked his beans rolled in his tortilla, burrito-style, or preferred to dip his tortilla in them. I rattled the grate and waved.

She hollered, "*Gracias*, Güero. *¿No puede usted comer con nosotros el domingo que viene?* (Thanks, Güero. Can you eat with us on Sunday?)" "*¡Hecho! Gracias* (Done! Thanks)," I replied, asking the hour.

Then I walked the Serdán, stopping at the Ladies Bar for a tequila and a beer. Chasing away the ghosts, you know. That night I rocked on the balcony of the Rubi after an evening at the Río Rita and a half-eaten meal at the Almita. As I rocked I watched the roof of the packing plant, wondering what really happened to a person once they died.

I tried to think through the situation, taking long pulls from the liter of tequila I had carried to the roof. I had promised Iliana I would stay till September fifteenth. Subsequently I had decided on staying forever, but the Guaymas sky already seemed grayer and more somber since Lupita's passing. It had begun to feel just like my childhood, where the darkness of the days and of the nights all blended together into one endless shade of gray. I had worked hard to escape that shadow world, but it now began to clutch at me again.

Each day I tried anew to convince myself that I could put Lupita's death behind me, wall it off, and recapture the joy of daily life in Guaymas. At first the tequila helped. But several nights after she died, a lifetime of my smothered emotions erupted like a volcano.

I drove out to the graveyard in the dark. Flashlight in hand, I climbed the muddy hill to her grave, stared at her little wooden cross, and came undone. It had rained again, the red clay sodden and puddled. I lay down on her grave and sobbed noisily—the first time I had done that since I was ten. Then I got angry. I wanted her back. I pounded my fists into the wet clay, cursing and shouting. Then I begged her to forgive me for asking about her mother at the hospital.

Lupita hadn't been just some kid I liked. She had never had a fair chance to be just a child. At times she was detached, frightened, sleeping where no one could get at her. Trying desperately to please an adult. Defiant. Full of bullshit bravado. Yearning for closeness, yet afraid of it from the many fires that had scorched the fingers of her soul when she dared reach out to another. And she had "secrets." Poor thing.

My problems as a kid had been less dramatic than hers, but I understood them. We were merely at different points on the same spectrum. She once told me I was the first reliable adult she had ever known. That amazed me, and I took it seriously. As a consequence I had worked to become even more predictable and reliable for her.

It was far too late to save my childhood, but it hadn't been too late to save hers. Her death cheated us both of that, and I wanted her back to finish the job—to make things right for her.

Perhaps these were only my own childish rescue fantasies. But wounded kids basically have two choices. They can try to become the person who hurt them, acting out the defects again and again, like the physically abused child who later becomes a bully. Or they can try to become the person they'd have given anything for the ones who actually hurt them to have been like.

Lupita had been capable of affection—she cared deeply for Juanito. And she cared for me. Someone had once instilled the flame of "love" in her as a child. It may not have been perfect, or burned brightly, but it had flickered within her all those lonely years since the lamppost, awaiting the fuel to nurture it. She might never have become "normal," but she was no Chingón. Of course none of this was going through my head that night at her grave. I simply wanted her back.

As I lay on Lupita's grave, I thought I was making an idiot of myself. Out of control. And I despised "out of control." I didn't realize it then, but I had already taken the first few steps toward my own redemption. At the time I was genuinely astonished and panicked that I was not able to cut off the pain of Lupita's death and emotionally walk away from the trouble.

The "time to go" strategy of my life had finally failed me. I simply didn't realize that Guaymas and its people had already begun to transform me.

As I slipped and slid down the hill from Lupita's grave, I felt a little better. Jesse's "you've got to do things for people" was running through my head like an endless tape. When I reached the Rubi, I passed El Huevón, dead asleep, and walked back to my room.

Marta was inside, waiting. She was distressed at the sight of me. I was covered in red mud, soaking wet, and emotional. This was not the Güero she knew. I wasn't happy to see her— she was a complicated, angry thing, and I didn't need that. But she surprised me.

She hustled me into the shower, laid out clean clothes for me, turned on the fan, and cuddled me when I came out. She had a long talk with me about Lupita. Her jealousy. How badly she had wanted me to choose her instead of Lupita. I tried to tell her it had never been a choice. She disagreed, but let it go.

Then she asked about Lupita's name, pressing to find out if I had tried to find Lupita's full, given name. I assured her I had tried, without luck, asking her why it mattered. "God can't find you without your baptized name," she confided, telling me that someday she would tell me her real name.

"You mean it isn't Marta?" "No, none of the *viejas* use their baptized names." That was probably why Lupita didn't really know her mom's name. She asked me to write my full name down for her and put it in her purse, assuring me that should I die in Guaymas, she would make certain the padre knew my Christian names.

For the first time she slept with me long into the night. I got up again later and took a long, slow shower, trying to calm down. When I came out, I heard a rhythmic sucking sound. I walked quietly over to the bed. Marta, illuminated by the soft outdoor light, lay on her side in a near-fetal position, sucking her thumb. Exactly as Lupita had done at the motel in Tucson. No wonder the two were in competition. They were both damaged kids. One merely older than the other.

I had been unable to acknowledge any of the woman in Lupita. Or the child in Marta. A wave of uncontrollable nausea overcame me. I ran to the bathroom and vomited. Our sexual relationship was over—I was never able to get it up for her again.

The next days passed slowly. My rounds on the Serdán grew longer. The taxistas and my other friends were kind. In Mexico when shit happens, your friends gather round, supportive, even if they don't refer directly to your troubles. In the States it's the other way around—if you get snake-bit by life, your friends flee and scatter, lest they catch your bad luck.

Burro was particularly kind, squeezing me on the shoulder, always buying an extra taco so he could hand me one and make certain I ate. We went to the ballpark again with Eva and her kids, who had obviously been told not to mention Lupita. Burro drove. Eva hugged me a lot as we sat in the bleachers.

One afternoon at the Colmenar a few days later, sweet Mercedes told me she was carrying a baby and asked if I would be her compadre (coparent) and baptize her child. I was delighted. It's a great honor, and the thought of holding a baby in my arms really picked me up. She told me she expected the child in November or December. I accepted.

When Kiami came by I told him the news. He told me he thought that was propitious, and asked directly how I was doing. I told him it was a difficult time, then asked him to fill me in on a godfather's responsibilities. Always happy to explain Mexican culture to his favorite pilgrim, he gave me the rundown. Bottom line, I would raise the kid if Mom died and would participate in the events of its life—baptism, confirmation, marriage, etc.

But thinking about Mercedes's baby panicked me after Kiami left. What if Iliana did return on the fifteenth? And with a new babe in arms? Oh, my God! I wasn't up to dealing with that. I told myself I would keep my word about staying in Guaymas, but didn't know really what to do if she did show.

During that period there were other kindnesses, as well. One night in September, as I sat at the end of the bar in the Río Rita, my friend Alonzo Chang commented to me, "Davíd, you look preoccupied. September is passing slowly for you, is it not?" I said, "Yes, Chino. It is a long month." "Drink your Coca Cola—on the house," he said. It was then about the tenth of September, a Friday night. I halfheartedly watched the floor show, still wondering if Iliana would return, but not very well tuned in to my immediate surroundings.

I was becoming more detached. The tastes and smells of Guaymas were fading. Each day seemed a bit darker than the one before it. The sky a little less blue. I worried constantly about Iliana's return.

A while later Chang came back and asked, "Another Coca Cola?" I nodded. He must have had psychic powers, because he brought it up. "Davíd, listen to me. This month of September . . ." I said, "Yes." He asked, "Are you still waiting for her, for your fiancée?" I said, "Yes, but how did you know of it?"

He answered, "This is a small town, and you have many friends here. You cannot wait forever. She may not return, you know?" I said, "Perhaps so, but I gave her my word." He looked at me and smiled, "So very like you. . . . Listen (*oye*), you need a party, that is what you need. Sunday, a compadre and I are having a fiesta, a *quinceañera* (fifteenth birthday party) for several of the girls in our family. Would you come, please, as my guest?" I was flattered and accepted the invitation.

It was a wonderful interlude. But when it was over the darkness returned. My routine simply wasn't going to overcome Lupita's loss, so I decided to go back to the States after the fifteenth of September, when I had fulfilled my promise to Iliana. The old urges, including the sense of "time to go," were swallowing me again.

I made several calls to Albuquerque from the big mahogany booth in the Rubi's hallway. First I arranged for my graduate assistantship, then called a classmate to help me find a place to stay.

I let people know I would be going over to "the other side" for a few months and began settling my affairs in Guaymas. I went again to see Gorda and asked how it was going with Juanito. Smiling, she pointed to a tiny canvas cot near the window, "Very well. When his mother is angry he sleeps here. He is a sweet child. But one of the boleadores keeps stealing his money."

387

I told her I'd check with Juanito on that and gave her a thousand pesos to take care of him until I returned in May. Juanito confirmed it was Chingón stealing from him. I asked Kiami for help with this. He liked Juanito, so went along with the request.

We summoned Chingón to our table in front of the Colmenar. I explained that I had work for him. He was to protect Juanito and his territory—take no *mordida* (bite) from him, and that if Juanito was fine in the spring when I returned from business on "the other side," señor Kiami would pay him five hundred pesos.

I handed the Cuauhtémoc to Jimmy Kiami, who smiled while I explained the flip side. "If Juanito tells señor Kiami that you continue to steal from him or let him be hurt, you will lose your place on the street and be sent away forever. Kiami is now Juanito's patrón." Chingón had enough *cojones* (balls) to heckle taxistas, but Kiami was major-league baseball in Guaymas. Not wanting to vanish completely, the overgrown feral rat understood us perfectly.

Juanito taken care of, I relaxed a bit. As Lupita's patrón, I had acted for her and seen to it that the little guy was taken care of. Lupita's chain of patronage was intact through Gorda and Kiami. Sacred is sacred!

When I told Mercedes I was going, she was disappointed that I wouldn't be there for the birth of her child. But I gave her my solemn word that I'd return in late May for the baptism. She accepted that, graciously. I never asked about her husband, since she never mentioned it—Chang's Rule, you know.

I went out to the Río Rita on the Sunday before I left and had a farewell *comida* (lunch) with about twenty of the girls. As I departed the goodbye comida at the club, Francisca again asked me to her private room across the street.

One last time she told me to find a nice girl, marry, and settle down. She actually made me laugh. Then she became serious, asking if I'd ever return. I promised I would, but told her I "had business" that winter "on the other side." "Graduate school," I explained. "*¡Mierda!* (Bullshit!)" she replied, then hugged me tight, saying, "Thank you" several times. I was baffled.

"For what?" I asked. "That you did not *desconocer La Mandadera al fin* (ignore Lupita at the end)." I asked, "How do you know of it?" She told me all the girls knew. I broke down. She rocked me. I told her I was sorry I had been able to do nothing for Lupita. She retorted that I had "done everything" for her and that it mattered to the girls at the club, "because Lupita was like so many of them."

Several of her tears fell on my cheek as she rocked me— the gift of absolution from a whore. And it had been poor, crippled Juanito who went out into the storm to save Lupita, his beloved patrona. Say of them what you will, but God does not err when he chooses his own mandaderos.

389

epilogue

Iliana didn't return. Relieved, I had a lovely casual lunch at the Colmenar with Max, Negro, Jesse, and Kiami on the fifteenth of September. Juanito polished my Red Wings one last time, then I spent nearly four hours serdaneando.

I said goodbye to Marta that evening. She gave me her baptized name to keep with me in case anything happened to her. We had farewell cabrito tacos and Orange Crushes in the Rubi's public bar on the evening of the sixteenth. Still no Iliana. Jesse gave me the bar's dice set as a memento.

About eight-thirty that evening I packed the Rambler, said goodbye to room 21, and passed by the Colmenar to pick up one last bag of burritos de machaca. Then headed up the Serdán.

I was fine until I reached Imuris, where I beeped at the riflemen manning the army checkpoint. They waved, the Rambler now a familiar sight. A few minutes later, overcome,

I pulled over and cried again for my Mandadera, and for Guaymas. I considered turning around, then remembered Lupita crying as we left Kino after her dinner. Sometimes it really is best to move on.

I arrived in Albuquerque about 6 P.M. the next day, met by my friend and former graduate-school roommate, John Bröster. He had a little apartment picked out for us four blocks from campus. On Saturday I went out and bought another Timex. I was on gringo time again.

The watchband covered the last of the fading yellow bruises from the night of Lupita's death. I said nothing about her for another fifteen years.

David E. Stuart is Associate Provost and Professor of Anthropology at the University of New Mexico. His most recent book, *Anasazi America*, is also available from UNM Press. Visit him at www.anasaziamerica.com